Tie-break!

Tie-break!

Justine Henin-Hardenne,
Tragedy & Triumph

Mark Ryan

 ROBSON BOOKS

This edition first published in Great Britain in 2004 by Robson Books, The Chrysalis Building, Bramley Road, London, W10 6SP.

An imprint of Chrysalis Books Group plc

British Library Cataloguing in Publication Data
A catalogue record for this title is available from the British Library.

ISBN 1 86105 752 0

Typeset by SX Composing DTP, Rayleigh, Essex
Printed in Great Britain by Creative Print & Design (Wales), Ebbw Vale

Dedicated to the Henin family. It was sometimes harrowing just to listen to your experiences. For you to have lived through them is almost unimaginable. I hope this book does justice to your strength and that you ultimately achieve your reconciliation.

In memory of Marie and Julienne Henin, Florence and Françoise Henin, Georges and Berthe Rosière.

With thanks to the *Mail on Sunday*, the *Sunday Times* and the *Observer Sport Monthly* for the use of archive material. The views expressed in this book are not necessarily shared by those organisations.

Thanks should also go to Jeremy Robson of Robson Books for his faith in the project, and to senior editor Jane Donovan, copy-editor Lesley Levene, art director Richard Mason, picture librarian Zoe Holtermann, proofreader Libby Willis and publicist Sharon Benjamin for their extraordinary patience and professionalism.

Photographs supplied courtesy of the Henin family (p1, p2, p3, p4, p5, p6, p8 and p10).

Contents

CHAPTER 1

Seeing it Out

'Out!' she cried, waving her finger at the umpire's chair. 'Out!' Her eyes were insistent now. 'Out! It's out!' There was no let-up in the verbal volley, no room for contradiction.

It was the final of the 2004 Australian Open in the Rod Laver Arena, Melbourne Park. Four times in three seconds, Justine Henin-Hardenne had bombarded umpire Sandra de Jenken with a claim that subsequently seemed breathtaking in its audacity, given the evidence beamed around the world by television.

Perhaps Justine was so anxious to win her third Grand Slam title that she genuinely thought she had seen a drive volley from Kim Clijsters land long. With all the authority of a world number one, she wagged her finger in protest and made the call for the umpire. Players were not supposed to do it, particularly if their judgement turned out to be questionable. But the stakes were high, and Justine was no ordinary player.

* * *

Back in Belgium, José Henin, the father Justine had ignored for so long, stared at his television screen, quietly absorbing the fresh controversy. He thought back to Roland Garros the previous year and the unsavoury scenes during the French Open semi-final against Serena Williams. There, Justine had raised a hand during a vital Serena serve, thereby indicating she wasn't ready. Distracted, the American had faulted, and it was only natural that she had asked the umpire for two more chances. But Jorge Dias hadn't spotted Henin-Hardenne's original gesture and Justine stayed quiet during Serena's remonstrations. Instead, she attacked the second serve and seized her opportunity. It had been the turning point.

Perhaps this was different. Her father reserved judgement until he could see a slow-motion replay of the latest drama from down under. Coverage on his favourite BBC strongly suggested that the ball had struck the baseline. These images were greeted uncomfortably back home.

For Kim Clijsters, such evidence came too late. Sandra de Jenken had overruled her baseline judge, who had remained silent all along. Instead of deuce, it was game over. Clijsters had effectively been denied her right to sustain a remarkable comeback, one that had already seen her reduce a 0–4 deficit to 3–4. Instead of being granted the chance for parity in the third set of that memorable final, she was told she trailed 3–5.

Whether or not Justine's swift intervention had influenced de Jenken on a subconscious level, it was hard to say. But the umpire's decision had now left Henin-Hardenne only one game from glory.

Justine's father knew there would be an inquest later in the media. 'Not good,' said José Henin. 'And not the first time.' But he acknowledged that nothing Justine had done contravened any law of the game and after all, she didn't make the final decisions.

Henin-Hardenne's eldest brother, David, plump and friendly like his father, was also watching the match live in the early hours back in Europe. 'Is this fair play?' he asked himself.

They loved Justine as much as anyone did; and, despite the fact that she had shunned them for years, they genuinely wanted her to achieve her Grand Slam hat-trick. But even her family didn't like to see her gain the upper hand with such a questionable overrule. Still, this was the cut throat world of professional tennis and you had to scrap for what you could get. If you didn't scrap, you didn't get it.

'Did you see that out?' was all a helpless Kim could ask the umpire.

De Jenken assured her that she had. The French official apparently believed that she had seen the ball better from up in her chair than the judge deployed by the baseline for that very task. De Jenken had convinced herself – with unwavering support from Justine – that she had witnessed something now being contradicted by the evidence of the television replays. On such a big point, it was excruciating.

As the crowd in Melbourne Park booed loudly, Clijsters shook her head and accepted the apparent injustice of it all. Given that 15,000 fans were ready to back her, she didn't argue her case with sufficient vehemence. Preferring to maintain a sporting dignity, Kim simply got on with the match. It was typical Clijsters, and many would say it was the nice thing to do. But few had ever beaten a woman as single-minded as Henin-Hardenne by being nice.

The whistling and howling of those disgruntled spectators didn't seem to trouble the player who stood just one game from the fulfilment of yet another dream. The Australian Open had so far eluded Justine. She wanted a full set of Grand Slams. She wanted this one and she wanted Wimbledon. She wanted it all.

* * *

Of all her relatives, alive or dead, Justine most resembled Jeanne Henin, her grandmother. It was a reality that Justine seemed to push to the back of her mind as she strove to become the best tennis player on the planet. At the time of writing, Justine hadn't contacted her grandmother, or indeed seen most of her family, for years. Right or wrong, that decision caused a lot of pain.

Noble and emotional, Jeanne was in her late seventies in early 2004. She found it hard not to cry when she talked about her famous granddaughter. But the tears weren't just provoked by the pride she might have felt over Justine's stunning achievements; they were also born of despair and frustration. And she was not alone in her suffering, because Justine's grandfather Alphonse and her father, José were sometimes similarly affected.

Her brothers Thomas and David, her uncles Jean-Paul and Jean-Marie, her cousin Maud – many had been hurt by the superstar's chosen course. But Jeanne's facial features made her stand out from the rest, for to look at Jeanne is to imagine Justine fifty or sixty years down the line. And there was something particularly poignant about the way Jeanne gave voice to the sense of rejection the majority of her family had experienced. Could Justine have continued to play such superb tennis if she had really known what some of her closest relations were going through?

'Justine doesn't understand the pain,' Jeanne said, fighting back the tears. 'If she really knew the pain we have had to bear, she wouldn't have done what she has. I remember the last proper chat we had – I think it was in 2001. When she left the house, she turned back and waved. She said, "Je vous adore" – "I love you." And I don't think we have seen her since. But even now, our door is always open to her. The family home should never be closed to a child.'

More emotional words soon tumbled out, though to appreciate them it is better to hear Justine's whole story first. And for Henin-Hardenne, that story was always predominantly about tennis.

* * *

John McEnroe had called her single-handed backhand 'the best shot in the game – women's or men's'. As she tried for a Grand Slam hat-trick at the 2004 Australian Open, she knew from the start that she would need all the heavy weaponry at her disposal. As the new world number one, Justine was under immense pressure, though at first she tried to tell herself otherwise.

As the tournament progressed, it was impossible not to admire her indomitable fighting spirit, her stubborn refusal to succumb under blanket fire. If necessary, she could call upon another element to her tennis – for the 21-year-old Henin-Hardenne seemed to have learned, during her meteoric rise, the value of legitimate mind games when it really mattered. Physically and mentally, she had it all, and from 2003 to early 2004 she got her act together like no other player on the planet. Justine's father, José, said: 'What sets her aside from the rest of her contemporaries is that when she has a problem on court, she usually finds a solution.' Beyond Melbourne, there loomed the return to Grand Slam action of the previously injured Williams sisters. Even so, Justine looked determined to stay at the top, capable perhaps of going on to become the next Martina Navratilova – a true sporting legend.

But for those who knew something of Justine's background, an uncomfortable question hung over her Melbourne campaign: had any other world-beater ever shut out so many members of her close family with such determination? You wondered how on earth Justine managed to reconcile the professional and personal sides of her life. How could she have become the best while such misery lingered in her family's home? There was no doubting the results on or off court. The tough personal choices that Justine made certainly led to a clear professional vision, one that had brought her the number one crown she craved. Few, if any, of her rivals could match her focus. But could that dominance have been achieved in another way?

Her uncle Jean-Marie thought so. 'Why does she say she had to separate from her family in order to succeed in her tennis career?' he asked, clearly exasperated. 'That's crazy! The Williams sisters had their father and mother around them, and they did pretty well!'

Jean-Marie's face is tough and worldly as well as kind. It wasn't just his love for his brother José talking when he added, 'Justine was playing great tennis when she had her family around her, too. She was best in the world at various teenage levels, it didn't just suddenly happen. Of course she is doing even better now. She is bigger and stronger, and it is normal to progress as you move into your prime.'

* * *

Perhaps no blame for what happened between late 1999 and early 2004 should be apportioned; Justine had her reasons for doing what she did. Some of them are examined later. And a source in her camp, someone she would consider very close but who didn't want to be named, assured me, 'She didn't take those decisions easily or lightly. It has been hard for her, just as it has been hard for everyone else in the family.'

Feminists may prefer to applaud the way Justine broke free from a male-dominated adolescence in order to pursue her own professional ambitions to the full. And not even her biggest critics would try to claim that she always had it easy in life. Sadly, death was never far away during some of her character-forming years. Untimely tragedy almost became the norm in a family still haunted today by the horrors of the past. Yet Justine absorbed blows that might have thrown others off their chosen path. She focused on her present and future. Some may see her story as a triumph of life over death. She has even founded a charity for children with cancer (Les Vingt Coeurs), so that she can make her own positive contribution to the battle to beat a disease that runs in her genes.

Of course, Justine isn't the first sporting great to have tackled adversity head on. Others have known dreadful trauma, and managed to emerge and thrive. Yet her story remains unique. For although many stars have lost family members under tragic circumstances, few world-beaters have then gone on to 'lose' so many more as a matter of choice. Fathers have been shunned before, on and off the tennis court, but to sever normal relations with most of her surviving family? That was a little different and, even among the most ambitious of her sporting peers, might have seemed just a touch excessive.

But Justine didn't seem to think so. She was prepared to condemn her father, brothers, uncles and paternal grandparents to a world of conflicting emotions, where they followed her push for stardom almost as though watching a stranger. The family bond was all but broken; and yet it remained, leaving many likable people in a kind of limbo, with no solution in sight. Tie-breaks are common enough in tennis; but away from the game, Justine had appeared to engineer a tie-break like no other.

On court, ironically, the required ruthlessness came and went. Often, she struggled to find her best form and had to return from the dead to steal glory. Or else she earned herself a winning position and suddenly switched off, throwing her advantage away. Was it the threat of defeat that sometimes caused the unwritten rulebook on etiquette to be overlooked? Whatever the means by which she fought her way out of trouble, it always made for the most spellbinding drama.

Off court, Justine's steely will was applied with much greater consistency, as she chose who was to play a part in her life and who wasn't. Sparks flew at first; tears were shed for longer. But this was no soap opera – these were real people with real feelings. Yet Henin-Hardenne seemed to decide quite consciously that she needed to clear her head of unwanted emotions more effectively than a complicated compromise. But then Justine never had been one to follow the crowd. What she seemed to lack in regard for some close relatives, she made up for in devotion to her husband, Pierre-Yves Hardenne, and her coach, Carlos Rodriguez, who masterminded her push for independence and her subsequent, stunning charge up the tennis rankings.

Tennis players are often plagued by an inability to forgive their own errors and missed opportunities. They don't get over such moments sufficiently quickly to realise that they could have won the match anyway, if only they had let themselves move on. Justine seemed to forgive herself very readily most of the time, both on and off court. Unfortunately, she found it harder to forgive others – at least, that was how most of her family saw it by early 2004.

Those she had left behind, several of whom had helped set her on the road to stardom, were severely punished for their imperfections. They seemed no longer to matter, except in so far as their elimination from the equation spurred her on to greater feats of mental endurance. Their absence from her life seemed to lighten her load immeasurably. Justine answered to no one now.

You can go a long way in tennis just by watching your opponent beat herself up over some chance mistake. Justine sought to free herself from any lingering threat of neurosis or self-doubt, the sort of anxiety that sometimes comes when a player feels she has to fulfil her family's dreams as well as her own. The tennis circuit is pressurised enough without the additional weight of expectations. As Henin-Hardenne tried to reduce her vulnerability, she seemed to cast off members of her family almost like old clothes. Soon she was dressed in a new reality – her reality.

* * *

Perhaps, during the Melbourne final of 2004, Justine's view of reality became blurred once she reached that controversial eighth game in the third set. Rather like the previous year, when Roland Garros was reduced to near anarchy and Serena Williams to tears, Henin-Hardenne focused primarily on the fulfilment of her own ambition.

Justine wanted the Australian Open. And even if she won that, she still wouldn't want to rest for long. There was the French crown to defend, and then there was a more elusive crown to fight for – Wimbledon.

CHAPTER 2

The Price of Success

First Roland Garros, now Flushing Meadows. Justine Henin-Hardenne would never forget the summer of 2003. Two Grand Slam titles in a matter of months, domestic bliss with her husband, Pierre-Yves – what could be better? Justine's world was like a fairytale, or at least it seemed that way until you looked more closely.

What didn't appear to belong in that fairytale was the bittersweet atmosphere in the Henin family's modest apartment, tucked away down a side street in the Belgian town of Marche-en-Famenne. When her closest relatives thought of Justine, a conflict arose within them, only accentuated by her triumphs in the world of tennis.

The night she won the US Open, her father, José, and her sister, Sarah, were left at home on the other side of the Atlantic. Deep down, they knew that her wonderful victory should also have represented one of the greatest moments in their lives. But then they remembered there would be no phone call home from the uncrowned queen of tennis. In fact, José suspected that, in his own case at least, there would be no more contact at all – ever.

For her own reasons, Justine had seen fit to disown her father several years earlier. She claimed that he had made too many emotional demands on her and she needed to escape. Perhaps she was right. But the gossip wasn't pretty. It centred on the most scandalous rumour that he had once made an incestuous approach towards her, and José hadn't heard Justine say anything to dispel the growing sound of malicious whispers.

He insisted it was laughable. Perhaps Justine hadn't heard the gossip or thought it unnecessary to dignify such allegations with a response of her own but José was convinced that a simple denial from his daughter would have put the rumourmongers in their place. Instead, José was left to defend his reputation and protest his innocence. Sarah, a bright, pretty teenager with longer, darker hair than Justine, stood by their father and deplored her big sister's attitude towards him. For her own reasons, Justine had turned her back on most of her family. Now she had become some kind of sporting superwoman. No one begrudged her those tennis triumphs. But how were her closest family meant to feel, having been left to watch her dreams come true from such a geographical and emotional distance? They were detached from Justine's glory.

Henin-Hardenne had just won the US Open, her second Grand Slam, having already achieved a life-long ambition to win the French Open at the start of the summer. The victories in both finals – against arch-rival, compatriot and world number one Kim Clijsters – were impressive enough. But it was the way Justine had dug so deep to reach those finals that stuck most in the mind of her loyal supporters. She had simply refused to be beaten. Twice she had stared defeat in the face at the semi-final stage, but against the odds Justine had won through to defy the giants of the sport.

This latest success would raise Justine's profile in the USA and turn her into a superstar. For her family back in Belgium, this should have sparked a night of wild celebration. Instead, they sat in silence, trying to come to terms with the usual sense of confusion.

This sporting backwater, a world away from the glamour of Flushing Meadows, New York, had spawned an unlikely world-beater. In towns like Marche, Rochefort or Han-sur-Lesse, the tennis clubs were tucked away discreetly, a sideshow to the main attraction. Most of the action in this corner of Europe centred on the tourist trade. Outsiders arrived in their droves to check out the spectacular local caves, a hidden world beneath the gentle wooded hills that formed the gateway to the Ardennes. Once the needs of the visitors were catered for, the residents liked to take comfort in a quiet existence centred on their families. To many here, family was still important.

Sarah Henin, sixteen and sensitive, stared at the tough, happy face still dominating the television screen. She turned to her father and said, 'It feels like she's not even my sister any more. It's like watching someone else.'

José couldn't help but smile. This was exactly what he had been thinking, although he hadn't wanted to hurt Sarah by saying so. Now it didn't matter. 'Don't worry. It feels like she's not my daughter any more either,' he replied sadly.

They had just watched someone they had once known so well and loved so dearly climb to the very summit of world tennis. She was the best in the world now – even if the official rankings still placed her at number two. She had beaten Clijsters, the only girl above her, not once but twice where it really mattered – in Grand Slam finals. The statisticians could say what they liked. In most people's eyes, those victories made Justine the new queen of the courts.

* * *

A Belgian television crew had filmed José and Sarah at home as they watched the great Belgian battle over in New York, studying their reaction to Justine's gutsy fulfilment of her American dream. José had allowed them in, though he didn't know why; perhaps it was to counter that terrible feeling of exclusion that haunted him during the big occasions these days.

He had kept his reactions positive in front of the cameras, and he didn't need to pretend. Part of him really was pleased for his daughter, even though she had effectively disowned him three years earlier. Now that José and Sarah were alone, however, a wider reality took over. In the privacy of their modest family home, they could voice other, more complex feelings.

* * *

The family feud didn't appear so complicated to Justine's elder brother, Thomas, as he drove me to his father's apartment a week later. It was only a short ride from the bank where they both worked in Marche, which was just as well, because Thomas didn't have that much to say about Justine's latest glorious achievement.

A good-looking man who sometimes seemed to hide his emotions behind his thin beard, Thomas had once interrupted his own career path to accompany his little sister to the tennis academy in Mons. He had acted as her confidant and protector during some of the most difficult years of her life. By September 2003, all that seemed a very long time ago.

I asked Thomas what he thought about the unfounded insinuations coming from certain compatriots at the time. Their innuendo had suggested – quite wrongly – that Justine had taken something to boost her physique in the build-up to her stunning summer of success. As she landed back in Belgium after her US Open triumph, an astonished Justine had been forced to protest her innocence at Brussels airport, and although her critics had quickly retracted their wild claims and ill-advised words, a rapturous homecoming had been partially tarnished.

'Her physique has changed,' was all Thomas would say.

That much was true. She had been working on her body strength with a respected physical trainer, Pat Etcheberry, in Florida prior to the US Open. And Justine's increased power had been achieved legitimately, even if Thomas seemed in no hurry to point that out. Though not accusatory, his words hardly sounded like a robust defence of his sister, and as we got out of the car I told him so.

Thomas turned round, fixed me with a stare and said, 'Justine is not my sister. Sarah is my sister.'

* * *

How had it come to this? Tensions between siblings were one thing, but Thomas's last comment showed just how far family relations had deteriorated behind the glittering scenes of Justine's sporting success. If this was the price you paid for glory, one had to wonder whether it was worth it. Likable people, Justine's own flesh and blood, had become embittered as the queen of tennis focused on her game, her husband, and the future.

If Thomas sounded harsh, it was perhaps understandable. Like his brother, David, he hadn't heard from Justine for years. And when the big star occasionally spoke to her little sister Sarah, a few kind words seemed to be less than adequate.

Sarah is normally one of the nicest people anyone could wish to meet. Yet by the autumn of 2003, it was more than three years since she had been able to enjoy the sort of relationship she would have liked with her sister. That's why Sarah's voice fell uncharacteristically flat when she confirmed, 'Once I saw Justine at the tennis club in Han-sur-Lesse, but we only exchanged a few words. We're not really friends these days.'

It was hard for Sarah to show much of her natural warmth to a sister who didn't even invite her to her wedding in November 2002. Personal touches mean so much more than money. Yet on another occasion, Justine and Pierre-Yves had apparently tried to assure Sarah that she stood to benefit financially from her big sister's growing wealth. The younger Henin sister was reluctant to welcome such overtures, especially when Justine had so far refused to help their father escape from crippling debt.

But then Justine and José had both felt aggrieved over money at one stage or other in their troubled relationship, and this seemed to be a significant contributory factor in the tension between them. Justine's camp pointed to the way in which she left home, without a penny in her pocket. José didn't dispute this version although he insisted that his daughter wasn't short of resources upon which she could draw if the need arose and initially only left to stay with her aunt Geneviève, around the corner in Han-sur-Lesse.

And José, a former post office manager, claimed, 'Sometimes, as she was growing up, I put Justine first financially, and in every other way, at the expense of my other children. Everything was geared towards her success and my other children sometimes had to make sacrifices as a result. They know that and yet they have forgiven me. But they have found it harder to forgive Justine for the way she has sometimes behaved since. Tell me, if I was such a terrible father, why are they still so close to me? Can anyone explain that?'

For her part, Sarah refused to become intoxicated by Justine's outstanding triumphs in 2003. She didn't want to bask in the reflected riches of sporting glory, she wanted a loving sister back – the one she had had before.

Sarah's attitude was simple: 'If you want to help me, help our father.'

After all, while her multi-millionaire tennis star sister splashed out thousands on lavish presents for those around her, José was trying to combat serious financial problems. While Pierre-Yves and Justine had already enjoyed and exchanged a Porsche, Sarah's father was helpless to prevent the repossession of his Volvo. While Justine and Pierre-Yves moved into a luxury home on the banks of the beautiful River Meuse in Wepion, Namur, José and his younger daughter had moved from a good-sized house in the pretty village of Hamerenne into smaller, rented accommodation in the town of Marche.

Such contrasts made it easy to understand why José harboured mixed feelings about his daughter's incredible success in Paris and

New York during 2003. The double Grand Slam triumph meant that the poison of celebrity would sink deep into the local consciousness. José had become another local attraction, even among those who lived in the area.

He explained, 'You know what I just can't stand any more? People who come up to me in the street and congratulate me. "Congratulations on Justine's victory! It's wonderful. Allez, Ju-Ju [Justine's nickname]. Congratulations!" I can't bear it. They know we don't talk any more, but they still feel they have to come up and say it. I don't feel part of this any more, but I still can't help watching her big matches on television.'

* * *

José had found himself caught in a recurring nightmare. Sometimes he drank, and his weight had ballooned to dangerous levels, especially for a man with a heart condition. He said he didn't care. He made dark remarks about not having long to live. He insisted that he wouldn't kill himself, because he didn't need to; he just wanted to put his affairs in order and then let nature take its course. Nature, food and drink, he clearly believed, would do the job for him soon enough. He talked like an old man, even though he was only 54. He wondered if he was clinically depressed. He didn't know what you called it; he just wanted the pain to go away.

His sons provided whatever support they could. Thomas enjoyed an influential position at a local bank and was able to arrange a minor administrative role there for José. It wasn't the answer to all his financial problems, but it kept the wolf from the door and meant that Sarah was able to continue to enjoy a relatively stable upbringing.

Always the perfect gentleman, David also treated José like a friend, inviting him for meals or morale-boosting drinks whenever an occasion arose. The sons' loyalty was unwavering, even touching.

As for Sarah, she seemed to enjoy as warm and loving a relationship with her father as any daughter could hope for under such difficult circumstances. It made a mockery of what some malicious tongues had insinuated when they whispered about José and Justine. During 2003 Sarah felt comfortable enough to bring home her steady boyfriend whenever she wanted, knowing that he would be made to feel welcome. José clearly liked the young man and trusted his intentions. He created a relaxed atmosphere, of the kind that would promote his younger daughter's happiness as she moved from adolescence to adulthood.

And he wasn't scared to tackle the gossip head on, with the contempt he insisted it deserved. He said at the time, 'The rumour is that I touched Justine sexually. I don't know who started saying it but some people here in this part of Belgium like to explain our falling out with this sick story.

'It's not true that I touched Justine sexually and there has been nothing in my behaviour that could possibly have been interpreted like that. Why do people say I was so dangerous for Justine and that she had to leave because of that? Why do they say that, and never raise the issue of my other daughter, Sarah?

'If what they say were true, they would have had to take Sarah away from me, wouldn't they? But Sarah is happy, so I repeat the question. Why do these malicious tongues never pose the question about Sarah if they think I did that to Justine? My parents asked my sisters, Geneviève and Françoise, that very question not long ago. My sisters had no answer.'

* * *

Justine's paternal grandparents, Alphonse and Jeanne, continued to support their son as the family feud raged on. Their reluctance to take Justine's side against her father appeared to exasperate the tennis star.

José's sisters, the younger but seemingly more dominant Françoise, 42, and Geneviève, 45, seemed to side with Justine in the swiftly escalating conflict. José's parents listened and stood firm; they refused to condemn him, they only wanted an end to the family feud. Their reward was to be treated as though they were no longer worth their granddaughter's notice.

To some observers, Justine's actions would look like revenge for her grandparents' chosen course, even though a diplomatic middle road was virtually the only one available to Alphonse and Jeanne. It was as though their decision to say or do nothing that might be construed as a betrayal of their son had deeply offended Justine. She didn't seem prepared to understand. She was a big name now, with equally big ambitions, and she didn't have to compromise with anybody any more. When you are fast becoming the most famous sportswoman in the world, it's possible suddenly to adopt tunnel vision.

Family complications aren't compatible with the world of a winner. Her coach, Carlos Rodriguez, had told her to embrace life before it overwhelmed her. The man of Justine's dreams, Pierre-Yves Hardenne, was hardly likely to disagree with that philosophy. Justine had felt overwhelmed by some of her close relatives before, and he had fought for her freedom. Unwanted family did not have to be embraced or even acknowledged – even on a showpiece family occasion like Justine's wedding day. Especially on Justine's wedding day.

CHAPTER 3

The Wedding

On 16 November 2002, Justine Henin married her sweetheart of four years, Pierre-Yves Hardenne, in twin ceremonies at the town hall of Marche-en-Famenne and the church of St Isidore, just a few hundred metres up the street from their first home in Marloie. Pierre-Yves had announced their engagement the previous year without even bothering to inform Justine's father first, let alone asking him for his daughter's hand in marriage.

When José had to read about it in a newspaper, he began to suspect what turned out to be the painful truth: he wasn't going to be invited to his own daughter's wedding. However, that November day was to be far more humiliating for José than even he had come to expect.

From the Henin family, only José's sisters, Geneviève and Françoise, were exempted from this harsh treatment. They were invited to the ceremonies and subsequent reception at a fifteenth-century château called Lavaux-Sainte-Anne.

Not only was José to be denied the right to lead his daughter down the aisle, those close to him were going to suffer as well. Justine didn't invite her sister, Sarah, to her wedding, or her brothers, Thomas and David. Neither of her paternal uncles, Jean-Marie and Jean-Paul, received an invitation. Even her grandparents, Alphonse and Jeanne, were deemed unworthy of inclusion in the celebrations.

To make their pain bearable on the big day, José and the rest of his family congregated for a consolation meal in the Taverne du Centre, his brother Jean-Paul's friendly restaurant in the centre of Han-sur-Lesse. As José explained, 'We wanted to be together at this time. It would have been even worse to be alone as we contemplated what was to happen without us that day.'

A major complication lay in the fact that Justine Henin was only a short distance away from those she had cut off. She had chosen Geneviève's house for her wedding preparations. It was almost as though she were oblivious to the added pain this would cause her closest relations.

As a result of Justine's decision, the police force from the nearby town of Rochefort had become involved. Officers blocked one end of the street where, in the privacy of Geneviève's home, Justine had by now slipped into her stylish ivory wedding dress. Another two policemen were positioned at the other end of the same street to keep out any undesirables.

José noted the police presence and wondered whether such measures were really necessary, since he couldn't see a single fan – obsessive or otherwise – loitering in the village to offer their best wishes to his daughter on her special day. As it turned out, big crowds had gathered in Rochefort, through which the procession was due to pass later on. But from where José was sitting, the show of force in gentle Han-sur-Lesse looked a little over the top, to say the least.

Before the day was very old, José became aware of a strange sensation. He explained later, 'I had this funny feeling that I was being watched or followed. I told my sons, Thomas and David. They laughed and told me I was really starting to lose it if I was getting that paranoid.'

Trying to shrug off this bizarre state of mind, José asked David to drive him down the rue de Grottes, the main shopping street in the village. Alphonse and Jeanne were waiting to be picked up from the quiet residential area at the end of that road so they could participate in the day's events as best they could. Son and grandson picked up the elderly couple and began the short journey back to the restaurant.

At precisely this moment, Sarah Henin was walking along the same street on her way to the restaurant for the family gathering. Suddenly, she heard the crackle of a walkie-talkie as one policeman tried to communicate with another. She distinctly heard the words, 'The car is on its way back towards the centre of the village.' She listened as he confirmed a number plate. It was her brother David's – she recognised it immediately. As soon as she was reunited with David and her father, she told them about her strange experience. Horrified but trying to stay calm, David confronted one of the policemen, a man he knew socially.

'Are we under surveillance?' he asked the officer-acquaintance.

'No,' came the embarrassed reply.

But David, a shrewd and friendly character, was in no mood to let the matter rest. 'My sister has just heard you give out our number plate on your radio.'

That revelation made it difficult for the policeman to persist with his denials. He admitted that the authorities were keeping an eye on the uninvited section of the Henin family, just to make sure there was no possibility of an incident.

Hearing this, José confronted the police officer in charge of the increasingly bizarre operation in Han-sur-Lesse, asking, 'Do you really think this is necessary?'

The police officer replied, 'We're just trying to make sure there isn't any trouble.'

'What kind of trouble?' José demanded.

The policeman looked him in the eye. 'We all know what happened to Monica Seles in Germany, don't we?'

José could scarcely believe what he was hearing. He recalled later, 'That was just a ridiculous thing to say. Seles was stabbed in the back by a crazy fan during a match against Steffi Graf. What did that have to do with my daughter's wedding?'

So he met the policeman's gaze and asked him straight out, 'Are you saying that you think I am capable of stabbing my daughter on her wedding day? Because if you are, you are the one who is crazy.'

When he got no response, José turned away in disgust and joined the rest of his loyal family in the restaurant, wondering who could have put the police up to their strange day's work.

A few minutes later, Justine's white limousine drove down the road on its way to the town hall in Marche, where the first part of the ceremony, the signing of the paperwork, would take place in the presence of the mayor.

Meanwhile, Jeanne, Justine's grandmother, had set her sights on reaching the venue for the service itself, the church of St Isidore in Marloie. The setting didn't exactly ooze romance. The church was a modern building, along with most of those in the village. A British aircraft had swooped in 1944 and knocked out a German munitions dump at the nearby station. When the munitions exploded, ten Nazis, 40 locals and half the village buildings were taken with it. Scores of local people were mutilated and hundreds were injured. So modern Marloie was hardly the most beautiful place for a star bride to tie the knot with her young husband. Not that Jeanne could be deterred from going there for Justine's big day.

She told me, 'I wanted to see her get married. I wanted at least to have that image to treasure in my head later. I didn't want to miss it.'

Her son Jean-Paul took up the story: 'My mother hadn't received an invitation to the church but she wanted me to take her there anyway. I explained that there was a fair chance we would be turned away, but still she insisted that we give it a try. My father, Alphonse, hadn't been feeling too well, so it was just the two of us.'

Alphonse admitted to me later, 'I didn't want to cause a scandal.'

Jean-Paul continued, 'When we got to about 300 metres from the church, we came up against a police roadblock. I thought that might be it, but they let us through, even though they must have had details of the number plates of cars belonging to those members of the Henin family who hadn't been invited.

'So we arrived at the church, to astonished expressions on the faces of some of those who hadn't been expecting us. But I knew some of the security staff there, and they knew better than to turn away a 77-year-old woman, particularly when she was the grandmother of the bride.

'We sat down in the church and my mother was so happy because she had a seat right by the aisle. It was towards the back, but from there she would still be able to see everything. The main thing was that Justine would pass right by on her way out with her new husband, and at the very least my mother would enjoy some eye contact with her granddaughter and perhaps they would be able to give each other a nod or a smile.'

Justine entered in a beautiful ivory dress, a perfect blend of classic and modern styles. She was led to the altar by another uncle, Hugues Bastin, the husband of her aunt Françoise. Bastin wasn't even her flesh and blood, and Jean-Paul knew it should have been his brother up there, giving away his daughter in the traditional manner. What made this choice even more painful for the absent José was that

Bastin had been the family doctor when Justine's mother had been diagnosed with cancer. (Unfortunately, the cancer had done its dreadful initial work without leaving any obvious clues, and had therefore not been detected early enough to give her any chance of survival.)

To rub further salt into José's wounds, Carlos Rodriguez, Justine's coach, sat in a place of honour among her guests.

The ceremony went smoothly, Justine holding a huge bouquet of white roses and Pierre-Yves looking dapper in tailed jacket, waistcoat and striped trousers. It was not long before the time had come for the newly wedded couple to kiss and make their way back down the aisle, returning the smiles of their loved ones as they went.

Jean-Paul recalled, 'Justine came up the aisle towards us with Pierre-Yves. Now she was right next to her grandmother, whose white hair is unmistakable, even in photographs of the day taken from behind the altar. My mother smiled at Justine and tried to get some eye contact with her.'

Jeanne's sense of disbelief was still evident when she took up the story: 'We were only about 50 centimetres apart, and she knew full well I was there. She knew I was looking at her. I felt it. And she just walked straight past.'

Jean-Paul added, 'There was no eye contact at all. My mother had come to the church because she wanted her own personal, visual memory of her granddaughter's wedding. But she was very disappointed to be ignored like that.'

She wasn't the only one. Justine's limousine drove through the crowd of well-wishers in Rochefort that day without stopping to allow them a good look at the famous bride.

The mayor of Rochefort, François Belot, who helped conduct the civil ceremony with his colleague in Marche, later leaped to Justine's defence: 'Details of the arrangements for the wedding day had been printed in the local newspapers and people were informed that they could see her in Marche.'

But one Rochefort citizen, who didn't want to be named, told me, 'People weren't prepared to go all the way to Marche, they wanted to greet her in her own hometown, and they were disappointed when they didn't get the chance.'

* * *

Back in Han-sur-Lesse, where most of Justine's family had stayed together to absorb the pain of their collective exclusion, José could scarcely take in the way events had unfolded. He decided to make it his mission to find out exactly who had set the police on him. Was it conceivable that his own daughter had subjected him to such humiliation on the very day when, according to tradition, he should have been leading her down the aisle?

Commissaire Claude Gregoire, Rochefort's police commander, later admitted that Justine's manager at the time, Vincent Stavaux, had called him shortly before the wedding day. Gregoire, a relaxed and unpretentious man, revealed, 'Stavaux contacted me to organise the security measures for the wedding and explained that there were some concerns because there was tension between the Henin family and Justine. I'm not saying I specifically ordered surveillance on José Henin or anyone else. We just kept an eye on the situation in general. I can't speak for the private security guards and what they did, but we were just there to make sure everything went calmly.

'Rochefort is small and the police know all the cars, so there was no need for any specific briefing on individual vehicles. Obviously, my officers were given instructions before they went out, but they were more general than you are suggesting. We just wanted to prevent an incident because someone could have thrown something. That was one of the reasons why we erected the barriers at the end of the road.

'There was always a risk of some incident, whether that might have involved the family or the general public. José Henin complained about his treatment and I explained to him that my officer wasn't suggesting he was going to stab his own daughter. The officer was giving an example of how someone could potentially hurt Justine in the way Seles was hurt.'

As for how much Justine knew about the surveillance operation herself, or might have feared for her safety, Gregoire wasn't prepared to speculate. Neither was Stavaux willing to say. But he did reveal this: 'We used private security as well, because you never know what can happen and we didn't want anything to damage the image of the day. When you look at what happened to Seles, if she had had more security around her at that time, it could never have happened. You have to have your own security. There are some strange people in the world.'

When it came to the big day itself, Justine probably cared more about her own starring role than she did about any potential for unsavoury sideshows. Others had effectively protected her from an imaginary threat from her family. She didn't seem to stop and consider how perfectly absurd her situation had become. For Justine, the wedding day had been a stunning success. For Stavaux, it had been a triumph, too, although Jeanne Henin's sudden arrival at the church, with her son Jean-Paul, had probably caused a few anxious moments on this carefully planned occasion.

Stavaux didn't want to talk about that, but he concluded, 'It was a lovely day, it went well. But for me it was a crazy day, too, with a lot of stress.'

CHAPTER 4

Florence

Justine Henin-Hardenne is José Henin's elder daughter, but not his first. Florence Henin will always be Justine's big sister, even though she didn't reach much of an age. What happened to Florence, more than thirty years ago, started a chain of emotional reactions that may have led to the current state of chaos in the Henin family. As she happily conquered the world of tennis, perhaps even Justine didn't know the full story, or appreciate the long-term consequences of a tragedy that took place long before she was born.

At two and a half, Florence was already desperate to be older. It was as though she wanted to reach the next stage of her childhood as fast as she could. José, her proud father, often took her on walks down the rue de Grottes – in their home village of Han-sur-Lesse. He recalled, 'Florence used to love watching the other children, some as young as three, on their way to the nursery school behind the village church. She used to look up at me through her blonde hair and say, "Papa, I want to go, too! Let me go to school with the other children."

'I'd smile down at her and reply, "Not long now, darling, just a few months more and you'll be old enough." It wasn't just the other children she loved. Florence adored old people and used to spend much of her time with her great-grandmothers, who both lived near the stream and the famous caves at the bottom of the village.'

One great-grandmother was called Julienne, and she lived in a house right opposite José's parents, Alphonse and Jeanne. The other great-grandmother, Marie, was bedridden, so Alphonse and Jeanne gave her a room in their home. That way, she, too, could be close to her loved ones.

What made life still particularly special for Marie was how much Florence adored her. It wasn't unusual for the little girl to visit her ten or twelve times a day, to tell her what she had been doing and ask the frail old woman how she was feeling.

Florence was also very close to her maternal grandfather, Georges Rosière, and they would often be seen walking through the village together.

Feeling secure under this protective family umbrella, Florence became the friendliest child imaginable. José remembered, 'She was hardly ever any trouble and seemed to cry a lot less than the other children we knew.'

She seemed to sleep less, too. Her grandmother Jeanne recalled, 'It was as though she knew time was short and wanted to make the most of every waking hour.'

Alphonse chipped in, 'And how she could talk! At just two years old, she spoke like a lawyer. I've never heard anything like it, before or since.'

José's wife, Françoise, fell pregnant again towards the end of January 1973; both parents were delighted with their timing. José explained, 'Apart from anything, we were thrilled for Florence, because we thought she would soon have a little brother or sister for company. We knew she had all the qualities to fulfil the role of big sister to perfection, since she had already developed this caring, considerate side to her nature. It seemed to come from somewhere well beyond her years.'

But no child is perfect, and Florence wasn't old enough to have worked out why it might not always be a good idea to burst into her parents' bedroom early in the morning and climb into bed between them. When she bounced on to the parental pillows painfully early one Saturday morning in May 1973, two factors prompted her mother to reproach her. First, she was four months pregnant by now and valued her sleep. Second, José was due to play in one of the most important football matches of his life that afternoon, and his wife knew that he, too, would appreciate a lie-in before his big challenge.

So Françoise frowned at her daughter and said, 'Florence, this is the last time we will let you do this. Mummy and Daddy need to be peaceful together sometimes.'

José recalled, 'She gave us such a smile that we let her stay in bed with us anyway. But she knew it would be the last time.'

By now his mind had already turned to football. It was a game he had always loved and taken seriously. Standard Liège, one of the most famous clubs in Europe at the time, had shown an interest in José's progress when he was younger. But somehow he had never wanted to make the many sacrifices necessary to follow the path into professional football. He was still a very useful striker, though, and played for his local team, Han-sur-Lesse.

The end-of-season play-off against nearby Neffe was only hours away. The prize for the winner would be promotion to Division Two of the Namur District League. It might not have been a sporting contest of national importance, but you couldn't tell that to anyone in the villages above the caves. To them, it was a matter of life and death.

José shouldn't really have played, since he had broken his wrist only two weeks earlier. But he hated the idea of missing the big match, especially when 700 local people were expected to cheer on their heroes. Call it ego or a keen sense of responsibility to the team, but José decided to take off his plaster early and play his part.

This was very much a family affair. José was a striker and one of his younger brothers, Jean-Marie, operated just behind the front two. The other, Jean-Paul, acted as the team's sweeper and hatchet man in defence. If any opposition player dared to foul one of his brothers with a degree of violent intent, Jean-Paul would walk up to that player quite casually and say, 'You have less than five minutes left on this pitch.' More often than not, Jean-Paul found a way to keep his word with a bone-crunching revenge tackle, one that soon forced his target to limp off in agony – if indeed he didn't need to be carried.

That May, the three Henin brothers were already the toast of the village because they had enjoyed such an exceptional season. However, each man knew that his good work throughout the winter would count for nothing if the team didn't win on that final, fateful day.

After a light lunch, José said goodbye to Françoise and Florence. Both were fragile in different ways, one pregnant and the other tiny, so mother and daughter had decided to avoid the chaos at the football club and settle instead for the peace of the village playground. There, Florence would bump into more children of her own age and enjoy the sort of company she was denied on schooldays.

Most villagers were already heading in another direction, towards the outskirts of their community. The Han-sur-Lesse football ground boasted an impressive modern stand running along one side of the pitch. And when they were needed, there was even a set of working floodlights at the club's disposal. You could hardly call it a glamorous stadium, though. The village cemetery sat on a gentle slope above one touchline, as if to remind the team's stars to keep their feet on the ground.

On this particular day, however, the humble arena could have been Barcelona's Nou Camp or Milan's San Siro, such was the sense of anticipation and excitement. The adrenaline pumped through the Henin blood as each brother changed into his familiar white strip and prepared for battle.

With hundreds of screaming supporters turning up the heat, the players were so nervous that they felt considerable relief when the match finally kicked off. Under such extreme pressure, Han-sur-Lesse didn't achieve the domination they had expected. Even the starring trio of Henin brothers struggled to find their best form on the day. After 85 minutes, the scores were locked at one-all and the home side was lucky to be on level terms. That's when a player called Michel Delculée, who had only just joined the Han-sur-Lesse team, innocently set in motion a chain of events that led to disaster. Timing his run to perfection, he met a cross with incredible force and his header flew into the top corner of the net from outside the area.

The crowd erupted, there was pandemonium all around the pitch and the shell-shocked Neffe team didn't have time to hit back. The final whistle blew, Han-sur-Lesse was promoted and wild celebrations began in earnest. With horns sounding and pedestrians dancing, a spontaneous procession passed through the centre of the village and headed down the rue de Grottes, towards the house where the Henin brothers' parents lived. One wag had decided that their mother, Jeanne, should be presented with flowers, since she, above all, could be considered responsible for the team's promotion. Jeanne had brought three of the best Han-sur-Lesse players into the world, and therefore was the true heroine of the hour.

Her sons were thrust to the head of the procession and witnessed the touching presentation of a bouquet to their blushing, speechless mother. Out of the corner of his eye, José noticed that Françoise and their daughter were already back from the park. Usually Florence would have played there late into the evening, laughing and skipping with her friends as they enjoyed the lingering light of early summer.

José remembered, 'My wife simply told me she had decided to bring Florence home early, she didn't know why. Perhaps they wanted to hear how the match had been won.'

Florence stood beside the gate to the small front garden at her grandparents' home. Her great-grandmother Julienne was right next to her as the procession of cars ground to a halt. Since Alphonse and Jeanne lived in one of the last houses on the rue de Grottes and a stream made the street a dead end there, the cars began to execute three-point turns. Still hooting and waving, most of the drivers achieved their aim with ease. There was one exception.

José recalls, 'I stood in conversation with a friend, soaking up the glory, just a few metres from my daughter and grandmother. Suddenly, a yellow Toyota jolted and flew at the gate with a terrible roar. Before she even had time to scream, Florence was dragged under the car. Julienne was also hit and thrown high into the air. She crashed against the wall of the house before landing in a heap outside the front door.

'For a second I froze in horror as the car, with Florence trapped below, shuddered to a violent halt in the garden. In that moment, friends dived beneath the Toyota and pulled Florence out. She wasn't moving and we carried her into the house to try and revive her. Others tended to Julienne, who was conscious and in terrible pain.

'I looked at my daughter, who was lifeless but strangely unscathed. It seemed so bizarre that there wasn't a mark on her body. How could she be dead when she still looked so beautiful? I couldn't face this awful sight for a moment longer and staggered into the back garden in a deep state of shock.

'Perhaps I should have tended to my wife, Françoise, who was distraught, but I just couldn't. I was numb and shaking, beside myself with grief. I just stood there alone, trying to take in the horror of what had happened.'

José knew the young man who had caused the tragedy. Later, it emerged that the offender had been drinking and didn't own a driving licence. The culprit was the younger brother of another player in the Han-sur-Lesse football team. José didn't know what he was going to do to make him pay for what he had done. But any thoughts of retribution were suddenly disturbed by the sound of shouting from inside the house.

'José, she's alive! Florence has woken up! She seems to be OK!'

Scarcely daring to believe his ears, José ran back into the house and saw his daughter looking up at him, fully conscious but a little bemused. 'I'm thirsty,' is all she said. 'I'm very thirsty.'

Her father felt that he had witnessed a miracle, and there were tears of relief when the doctor-on-call arrived to confirm what José and Françoise had prayed for. It seemed they had been spared every parent's worst nightmare. 'I can't see any signs of lasting damage,' the doctor said, adding, almost as an afterthought, 'Better get her to hospital, though, just to make sure.'

Although the ambulance had already been called, it took half an hour to arrive. José and Françoise climbed in to accompany their daughter on the twenty-minute journey to the nearest hospital in Marche. There, the doctors studied Florence's eyes more carefully, and saw something that seemed to cause them deep concern.

'She will have to go to hospital in Liège,' they announced quickly. 'There's no time to waste.'

Within ten minutes the confused child, who had complained only of excessive thirst, was dispatched to the big city with more sirens wailing, her anxious parents still by her side. Their only comfort lay in the fact that Florence showed precious few signs of distress, and they knew she would soon have the very best experts and equipment to help her.

José took up the story: 'On that hour-long journey, she quietly began to slip away. We still didn't understand, because she had survived the impact without a scratch. We thought the worst was over. We saw her close her eyes and thought perhaps she was just sleepy now. But the frantic reactions of the medical staff soon told us a different story. By the time we reached the hospital in Liège, Florence was dead.'

The crushing impact of the car had ruptured her liver, which had then burst inside her body. There had been massive internal bleeding and the autopsy showed that no one on earth could have saved her. She was still only two and a half.

José recalled the moment when all hope was taken away: 'When we were told in Liège that Florence was gone for ever, we didn't know what to believe or how to react. She had been taken from us, given back in one piece as if by a miracle, then taken away again – all in the space of two hours. It seemed too ridiculous to be true – some kind of grotesque joke.

'Three hours earlier, I'd been worried about the result of a football match, which had seemed to me then like a matter of life and death. Now we knew what it really was to face such a moment – and it wouldn't be the last time.'

Julienne had somehow survived the impact of car and wall. The elderly woman had sustained shattered hips and gone into severe shock. She spent four months in hospital, but she pulled through to return home fully recovered.

Florence's other great-grandmother, bedridden throughout the commotion on that dreadful Saturday, didn't fare so well. Marie waited in vain for further visits from Florence, whose body was released after two days and brought back to the very same house. As family and friends paid their respects downstairs, no one dared tell Marie what had happened. She never asked about her great-granddaughter and perhaps she didn't need to. The expressions on the faces of those who visited her room probably told the story better than words ever could. She didn't know that Florence had died on 6 May. However, already a frail woman, Marie died on 23 May. Some of the Henin family think she wanted to go and look after her favourite little girl.

Still four months pregnant, Françoise tried to force herself to look to the future. At fourteen, she had faced the devastation of losing her mother, Berthe, to cancer. Now she had lost her daughter. It was more than any pregnant woman could be expected to take. Overnight, much of her mousy-brown hair turned grey. But somehow she struggled on, to protect the baby inside her. It is a tribute to her selfless determination that she also decided to visit Julienne in hospital just a week after the tragedy.

The lingering shock and extra weight that Françoise now carried combined to make her legs unsteady. As she climbed the hospital steps to see Julienne that day, she slipped and broke her foot. Bereaved and prematurely grey, Françoise now had a new problem – how to cope with pregnancy on crutches. Undaunted, however, she eventually gave birth to a son, David.

José recalled, 'It came as no surprise to us when he showed initial signs of having a nervous nature as a toddler. They say any trauma that a pregnant woman suffers, her baby also feels in her womb. Personally, I can well believe it.'

José also believed that Florence's death, and what happened in the days that followed, might have planted more than just a temporary sense of despair in the body of his wife. He speculated, 'Some experts say that cancer can lie dormant for decades. If stress really can cause it, then perhaps my wife's eventual destiny was also decided that month.'

José fought his own inner battle that summer – to conquer his demons. Some might have snapped and gone looking for the driver in order to exact swift revenge. He decided to put his faith in the Belgian legal system and let justice take its course. His reward was to see the culprit released from prison after little more than a month.

José revealed, 'When the driver showed his face around the village in the following months, I ignored him and he ignored me. I don't think he really knew what he could say. "Sorry" wasn't going to bring Florence back, after all.

'I tried to leave my anger behind, before it got me. Eventually, I succeeded, because I knew the boy didn't mean to kill my daughter. Yes, he had been drinking and he didn't have a licence. But he didn't set out that day to ruin my family. It was an accident. I don't even want to make him suffer by naming him here.'

The Henin brothers might even have continued to play for the Han-sur-Lesse football team in the higher league the following year, alongside the drunk-driver's brother, were it not for a stunning piece of thoughtlessness only days after Florence was killed. An evening of celebration, planned by the club before the tragedy in order to mark its much-anticipated promotion to Namur District League Division Two, went ahead as though nothing had happened.

José was disgusted. He explained, 'The people who attended were in full control of their actions, unlike the drunk-driver, and they knew what an insult that celebration would be to my daughter's memory. Her remains had only just been laid to rest in the cemetery near the football club.'

The Henin brothers had the last laugh, albeit a bitter one. All three promptly joined a rival football club called Eprave, which was promoted to Division Two the following season – the very same year that Han-sur-Lesse slipped back to Division Three. In the long run, their hometown club's celebrations had been as futile as they had been insensitive.

* * *

Justine Henin-Hardenne knows some of what happened in that terrible month of May more than thirty years ago. Enough, you might think, to know that sporting success in itself is not the key to life. She has certainly learnt, through this and other family tragedies, just how fragile that life can be. The need to seize the day – in fact, everything life has to offer – is ingrained in her character.

As she grew up, the memory of her sister was never very far away, whether she liked it or not. José explained, 'Justine was brought up to remember her big sister's loving character and how cruelly her life was cut short. We tried to make it so that she knew Florence almost as a living person. I have passed on the same knowledge to her brothers, David and Thomas, and her little sister, Sarah.

'My wife, Françoise, and I decided that it was right to preserve the memory of Florence so vividly for them. But I have never tried to set her memory above my love and respect for my other children in any way whatsoever. I have merely offered them some intimate knowledge of a wonderful sister, a little girl they were sadly unable to meet personally.

'Not a day goes by when I don't think of Florence. It may be for five seconds or ten minutes, but I remember her. I also feel happy that the brothers and sisters who came into the world after her may also think about her and even love her if they wish to do so in their own private way.'

Florence's short life and cruel death may well have had a psychological impact on Justine. It may not be exaggerating the case to suggest that she has been competing against a ghost all her life, the perfect image of an elder sister long departed. The middle Henin daughter lives her own life with a fierce intensity. Perhaps she lives it for Florence, too. Her late sister never had the opportunity to realise her own modest ambition, to join those other children in the nursery school in Han-sur-Lesse. Against that sort of background, nothing in Justine's life could ever be taken for granted. She exploits her own abilities and opportunities to the full. But she also steers clear of family ties that, if maintained, would one day inevitably result in more bereavement, more pain. Perhaps somewhere deep down she has decided that there is only so much family tragedy one person can take.

Above all, it was the impact of Florence's death on José that seems to have had significant repercussions for the young tennis star. How it changed José as a parent may well have sown the seeds for an ongoing family feud. Even José was honest enough to admit that Florence's death may have impaired his ability to remain an entirely healthy father figure for his second daughter.

He said, 'I certainly don't offer what happened to Florence as some kind of excuse for any errors of judgement of which I may have been guilty when it came to Justine. But sometimes I wonder if my overanxious behaviour had its root in the fear of losing another daughter.

'It was years before Françoise and I felt ready to have another baby girl. We were relieved when our next two children were sons. By the time Justine came along, we thought we were ready for another daughter and we were delighted. But perhaps there was still an underlying fear of losing her. Maybe that fear caused the sort of suffocating love that Justine talks about, the kind she claims drove her away. Perhaps I was overprotective or interfering at times. I was certainly not a perfect father. I have made errors of judgement like any normal person and I am sorry for those. But Justine is unforgiving.'

* * *

As José looked back on Florence's death, he was clearly still tormented by what might have been. He explained, 'Regrets can last a lifetime. They play on your mind. My decision to take off that wrist plaster back in 1973 and play the match . . . That ridiculous header, the one that won us the game so undeservedly and sparked the celebration in my village . . . And my wife, how do you think she felt? When she told Florence off that Saturday morning, she didn't know it would be the last time our daughter would ever be able to get into bed with us. When they came back from the park earlier than usual that afternoon, how were they to know what would happen? We all had to live with the consequences of our actions, and we tried to forgive others and ourselves. What happened caused all sorts of regrets and stayed in the marriage for a long time afterwards.'

Justine must have wondered how her father and mother coped with the long-term legacy of Florence's tragic death. Despite her family's sad history, however, the tennis player seems unable to have a normal relationship with her sole surviving parent. For whatever reason, José Henin was effectively disconnected from his daughter's life.

Regrets can last a lifetime, her father said. At the time of writing, however, Justine has shown little outward sign of regret over her chosen course.

CHAPTER 5

Françoise

After two baby boys, David and Thomas, Justine Henin arrived on 1 June 1982. She was born in Liège, where Florence had succumbed to her injuries just over nine years earlier.

Although Florence was never far from her parents' thoughts during Justine's early years, Françoise and José quickly saw that their latest daughter was a bubbly individual in her own right, unique and distinct from the little girl they had lost. Perhaps she was less tactile, maybe she was more of a tomboy, but she was still a sheer delight. Like Florence, she seemed to have an extraordinary force of personality for someone so young.

As she passed the age at which Florence had been so cruelly taken away, Françoise and José realised that their small and robust second daughter was starting to show an appetite for sport. By the time her little sister, Sarah, came into the world, Justine was five and was already mixing it with the local boys on the football field. She wore her hair short and straight like the opposition.

José recalled, 'Not only did she hold her own, she was usually top scorer. She carried on playing football right through to the age of twelve – and continued to score more goals than anyone else.'

At five, however, another passion emerged – one that would soon eclipse her love for football or anything else. José explained, 'I played a tennis match at a small tournament in Nassogne, not far from home. Justine had picked up the scoring system and she was shouting the points for the crowd. "It's 4–2 and 15–0," she would tell everyone. People didn't mind, because she was right. Even if my wife, Françoise, went off for a drink, she knew Justine would update her correctly when she got back.'

'After the match, Justine said, "Papa! I want to play!" So there she was, aged five, and she had hold of this huge racket. We started to play and people were amazed. She played so well! She saw the ball beautifully. She attacked it when she needed to and stepped back at the right time to make space, too. A member of the Nassogne club took me aside and told me, "I think you need to get her a good teacher. She can be big." I smiled.'

Before José and Françoise took that step, they waited to see whether Justine would develop an appetite for tennis comparable to her love of football. Sure enough, every time José played, Justine would step on to the court for five minutes afterwards, slowly developing her skills.

Her parents were shocked by what happened next, although it meant Françoise would have plenty of time to look after her toddler, Sarah, without needing to worry too much about occupying Justine.

José recalled, 'That Christmas, 1987, we bought Justine a little tennis racket. She was five but through that winter she played thousands of volleys against the kitchen wall.'

Justine couldn't wait for the warmer weather to arrive and, when it did, she wasn't slow to take advantage. José continued, 'We took Justine down to the local tennis club in Rochefort. She played all day. She would start at 9 a.m. and only break off for lunch at midday. By 1.30 p.m., she was back on the tennis courts. And that is where she would stay, until 7 or 8 p.m. if she could. Françoise and I would go down and watch her, and eventually in the evening we would take her home. The only question was whether she had played six, seven or eight hours of tennis on any given day.'

Justine told anyone who would listen that one day she would be the best in the world. Her mother heard this boast more often than most, and José still remembered her reaction fondly in 2004: 'My wife would smile and tell Justine she was right. She would be the best in the world. Not everyone she told was so sure, and it is incredible to think that it all came true.'

If she failed, others might have thought, it certainly wouldn't be for want of trying. If this was how she approached the game at five or six, what would she be like later?

In fact, her punishing routine was already causing logistical problems at the club. José explained, 'After a while, the director of the

Rochefort club delicately pointed out that Justine's new passion had given rise to a minor problem: other members couldn't get on court! But Justine was certainly in demand among the other youngsters. All the kids, even up to ten and eleven, came calling for Justine at home if she wasn't at the club. They wanted to face the incredible six-year-old and see if they could learn anything!'

When the local kids could no longer provide stiff enough opposition to give Justine a proper game, she began to test her skills against her family. 'She was playing a lot of tennis against me and Thomas by now,' José recalled. But he correctly realised that his daughter should go back to basics and get the foundations of her game absolutely right before her desire to progress to higher levels began to outstrip her technique.

'We chose a trainer through the Belgian Tennis Federation. They had adopted a new type of tennis for youngsters called mini-tennis. So by the time she was six and a half, Justine was practising in a more professional tennis club called Saint Gilles, in Ciney, under a coach called Patrick Sacre.

'This was when Justine really discovered that fantastic backhand action, using only one hand. She didn't need two hands because the shot flowed so naturally with one. In fact, she played much stronger single-handed backhands than older girls could manage with two!'

So the shot was born, Justine's most ferocious weapon, her devastating trademark, the one that later led the tennis legend John McEnroe to remark, 'Justine has the best backhand in the game – women's or men's!'

Mini-tennis couldn't contain the shot, or the girl, for more than a year or two. According to José, 'At the age of seven, Justine won every mini-tennis tournament she played.'

But it wasn't all tennis. There were fabulous family holidays, in Canada, for example, where Françoise had relatives, and the little girl had far more opportunities to enjoy the beauty of the wider world than many children her age.

* * *

Much as she enjoyed breaks like these, however, Justine usually couldn't wait to return to the familiar, thrilling swing of her racket as she developed her skills on the courts of Belgium, and between the ages of eight and nine she received additional tennis tuition at her local Rochefort club from Luc Bodart, a coach who shared everyone's astonishment at her precocious talent.

But it wasn't just Belgian tennis coaches who realised they were in the presence of someone special during those formative years. The most famous developer of young tennis talent in the world, Nick Bollettieri, landed in Brussels one day to run a clinic. The children didn't have too much time to impress the USA's foremost sporting guru at these clinics, because hundreds of hopefuls attended them and they all needed to be looked at. As each kid took a shot or two, Bollettieri, the man who had discovered Andre Agassi, would chip in with a nugget of perceptive advice and then perhaps move on.

When it was Justine's turn to step up, the ball came to the nine-year-old on the backhand. She flashed a perfect bullet of a single-handed return straight back over the net for a winner.

'What was that?' an astonished Bollettieri asked as hundreds gasped in admiration. 'I've never seen anyone hit a backhand like that before.'

He sought out José, and didn't waste words. 'I want to work with her,' he said simply. 'I want her with me now, in Florida.'

José and Françoise knew they had to give Justine her big chance. Her father recalled, 'We were over there soon enough. But when we arrived at Nick's academy in Bradenton, it turned out he was already committed to spending time with another player, so it was left to one of his coaches to film Justine with a video camera.'

Without knowing the result of this audition, the Henin family eventually left the academy, trying to hide their disappointment. But they had learnt one thing: if she were let loose at this level, Justine would be a small fish in a very big pond. Perhaps it wasn't fair to have such big dreams for a daughter who was still so young.

Ten days later, however, Bollettieri was in touch. 'Come back as soon as you can,' he pleaded.

For the second time, the Henin family flew to Florida. And this time, José remembered, Bollettieri was ready to greet them in person when they reached Bradenton. 'He was there waiting for us at nine in the morning, and he only needed to play tennis with Justine for about fifteen minutes. Then he came up and said, "When she's old enough, I'd like to keep her here for a year." '

Justine's feelings about this exciting offer were of paramount importance. And three times in all between 1991 and 1992 she was allowed to spend a fortnight at Bollettieri's academy, getting a feel for a professional life overseas. A deal was signed with IMG, Mark McCormack's sports management company, which helped to finance those stays and supplied the latest tennis wear, too.

After a heart-to-heart, however, it gradually became clear to her parents that Justine simply wasn't ready to contemplate living so far away from home on a long-term basis, not even at some point in the future. They were grateful to Bollettieri for his extraordinary faith in their daughter's talent and IMG remained on board, but for the moment the prospect of school in Florida was put on hold.

* * *

Back in Belgium, there would be other opportunities for Justine, with coaching available through Belgium's Tennis Federation, for example. She was still so young and her talent would shine through again sooner or later. But it was going to cost money to give her the best possible chance – more money than her parents had. Justine's father therefore put together a consortium of family and friends to help finance her training.

So the family stayed together, despite the suspicion that one day Justine's search for glory and excellence would take her overseas for much longer periods. For now, family seemed most important of all, and, in the light of the tragedy just around the corner, this was not a decision Justine would ever regret.

Soon she was back on the children's tennis circuit in her native Belgium, with one major sporting adventure already under her belt and IMG watching her progress. In a little country like hers, Justine should have been undisputed queen of the castle. But almost unbelievably, there was another Belgian girl, a year younger and from the Dutch-speaking north, who was said to be just as good.

Kim Clijsters was her name, and the two girls first met in the semi-final of a respected tournament held each summer in Ostend. It was known as the Memorial Vandewiele, and the most junior branch of that tournament was called the Preminiemen.

José cast his mind back: 'I think Justine was only nine, so Kim would have been eight, even though the category was 10–12 years old. The sets they played went to four games instead of six. Otherwise it was normal tennis, because Justine was well beyond the mini-tennis stage by then.'

'This match drew a big crowd because there were a lot of Flemish people following Kim, whom we hadn't even heard of, since it was her first time at the tournament. Clijsters was the great new hope for the Flemish, who stood on their side of the court. On our side there were lots of French-speaking people, because Justine had already built a reputation for herself as a very good player.

'So this match became quite an occasion, especially when you consider how young the girls were, with Flemish on one side and Walloons [French-speaking Belgians] on the other. But Justine didn't mind the pressure, because she took the first set 4–0. Then, do you know what happened? Kim claimed she was injured, and that was it. Maybe she did feel a strain, but I think she'd also had enough of being played off the court and she didn't want to lose. Justine didn't need to play the second set. She had won. But the strange thing was, Kim was suddenly fit enough to play in a doubles match an hour later.'

Clijsters may have spared herself further punishment at Henin's hands that day. But neither girl was prepared to accept that it would always be so one-sided. Justine knew that Kim was a year younger and suspected that she would become a constant threat as they grew older. José later claimed, 'Justine was worried from the start about Kim's talent, and I had to reassure her that it would be something she could learn to deal with.'

The arrival of Clijsters on the scene didn't stop Justine from winning tournaments, though. And in 1992 she took an under-10s title in Brussels. The prize was a dream for any up-and-coming tennis player: two tickets to Roland Garros, to see her favourite player, Steffi Graf, take on the hottest new talent in the game, Monica Seles, in the French Open final.

For French-speaking tennis lovers, Roland Garros was bigger than Wimbledon, a sacred venue where fans and young players could worship the current greats of the game. Justine was thrilled with this chance of a lifetime, and looked forward to being taken to the big occasion by her father. Then a resourceful José found two extra tickets for a different part of the arena. It was therefore decided that Justine would sit with her mother, Françoise, in the excellent seats she had won, near the umpire's chair and close to the soft, sacred clay of the court itself. Meanwhile, José would take his younger son, Thomas, also an ardent tennis fan, to sit among the German supporters up at the back of the stands.

And so, on Saturday 6 June, just before 2 p.m., four members of the Henin family took their seats in two different parts of the Court Central. Justine, who had just celebrated her tenth birthday, couldn't believe the ferocity and determination of Seles and Graf, particularly in an epic of a final set. She knew from having seen them on television what great players they were. But to see Graf and Seles close up was to feel their passion and fire. Justine soaked up the atmosphere and let the fighting spirit of the players sink deep into her soul. Although Seles ultimately beat Justine's favourite 6–2, 3–6, 10–8, and the little girl was disappointed by the result, it had, in José's opinion, been 'the match of the century'.

As they all met up again afterwards, José noticed that Françoise was positively beaming. 'Do you know what she said to me?' Justine's mother whispered to her husband. 'She looked over to where members of the Graf and Seles families were sitting in the Tribune des Joueurs – the players' seats. Then she told me, "One day you'll sit there – you and Papa." And she pointed at the players and said, "I'll be out there." '

That's how José told the story, and he recalled just how much he and his wife admired their daughter's cheeky confidence. Justine later claimed that she had made an even bolder prediction to her mother that day. She said, 'I remember sitting on centre court and telling her, "I will play here one day and I will win." She probably thought, "This child is dreaming," and I was.'

Although Justine's vision made her parents smile, they also knew she was showing enough promise to suggest that such a scenario wasn't entirely beyond the realms of possibility. If she continued to show such determination and self-assurance, and if her physical strength developed to complement her technique, perhaps little Justine really could challenge the true greats one day.

Françoise and José might even have allowed themselves to picture the scene as their daughter held aloft the trophy and they led the applause from their place of honour in the stands. But neither could have imagined what cruel tricks time and fate would play on them. Years later, when Justine had the chance to win Roland Garros, neither of the parents she loved so much as a ten-year-old would be sitting in those favoured seats in the Tribune des Joueurs.

But no one could see that far into the future, and in 1993 it was hard enough just to determine what Justine's next move should be. Once again, the offer came from Nick Bollettieri for Justine to go full-time at the academy in Bradenton. And now there was a greater sense of immediacy, for Justine was reaching the sort of age at which talented children seriously consider making that longer-term move across the Atlantic. The issue needed to be addressed, and Justine's thoughts on the matter were sensitively sought. In the final analysis, she just didn't want to be uprooted from her family to live so far away from home. And it wasn't long before she wanted to be closer to her mother than ever.

* * *

In 1994, Françoise began to feel unwell, not a natural state of affairs for the strong and charismatic teacher of French, history and Spanish. The woman with such a forceful personality had often seemed so indestructible. Now she was losing weight and finding it hard to digest her food.

The willpower she had shown to keep her unborn baby when Florence was crushed under the car had been truly remarkable. Not even a broken foot could shake her resolve or end her pregnancy. Her eldest son, David, owed his life to such determination. So the idea that any physical ailment was getting the better of her seemed foreign somehow. She was so strong, so indomitable and so tough. In fact, her husband sometimes wished she were a little softer with him. But this was Françoise, and above all she was a wonderful mother. The patient side to her nature expressed itself best in her relationship with her children. And she wasn't about to change her priorities for anyone.

José explained, 'Sometimes teachers find it hard to leave their professional persona in the classroom and she would be bossy at home, too. We had already been through a lot, trying to get over the death of Florence, and at times the strain had almost split us up. But we came through together and had more good times than bad. We had great moments. The bossy side was part of her and I loved her just the same. She was a wonderful mother, even though it didn't always leave enough time for us. She realised that later.'

Knowing what had happened to her own mother, behind her strong exterior Françoise must have experienced more than the usual apprehension any normal person would feel when she went to see her doctor, Hugues Bastin, about her mystery ailment. Bastin was married to José's sister, also called Françoise, and therefore knew this particular patient better as a close relative. One can only imagine his feelings as he sent her to hospital for urgent exploratory tests. The verdict would be swift.

A phone call came through from the laboratory later that same day to warn that something was seriously wrong. They would know more soon and call back with the details. When the news was confirmed, it was devastating for everybody involved. Françoise had been diagnosed with cancer of the colon. How could this be happening again? Her mother, Berthe, had died in her early forties. Now her daughters and sons would be forced to endure the same pain that she had as a teenager, and there was nothing she could do about it. The illness hadn't been detected in time to do very much for Françoise. This in itself was not out of the ordinary, since cancer can often attack the colon without a victim experiencing any clearly identifiable symptoms in the early stages.

José and his wife tried to absorb the awful reality behind the news they had just been given. After all they had been through, why this? Their marriage had already had such indescribable peaks and troughs. They had lost their first child in the cruellest way. Together they had somehow learnt to live with that pain and bring four wonderful children into the world.

In their own relationship, there had already been issues to confront. José admitted, 'I made some mistakes and we had the same sort of problems as many couples do. But we loved each other and we loved our children. Perhaps Françoise and I loved being parents so much that we forgot to be a couple. But I loved her and I still do. I'm always thinking about her, even now.

'As for my wife, do you think that someone as strong as Françoise, an independent-minded woman with her own career, would have stayed with me for so long if she hadn't wanted to? We had been married for almost 24 years by the time we heard the worst news about her illness.'

An operation in April 1994 showed how quickly the disease had spread. The doctors didn't hold out much hope. She might have a year, maybe even less. At the end of that time, Justine and the rest of the children would be without a mother.

The sense of devastation was unfathomable. It would be even more difficult to put on a brave face in order to keep their awful secret from the children. That didn't stop Françoise and José from wanting to try. David, Thomas, Justine and Sarah would be better off not knowing the truth, at least for now, they believed. The couple were in complete agreement. Justine and the others should be protected from the finality of their mother's illness until the last possible moment. The alternative – to make the children live with such dreadful knowledge for a year or more – seemed even worse.

By doing it their way, at least José and Françoise could give their children a chance over the coming months to adapt to the idea that their mother was unwell. Françoise herself would also need time to come to terms with the reality of her terminal condition. For now, they would all carry on as normally as her health would allow. They would enjoy what time was left to them as a family, and try to be just like any other. Then, in the final few weeks, nature would take over.

To carry out such a bold plan required Françoise to show an enormous amount of personal courage. The immediacy and beauty of every moment with her children would sustain her through the living nightmare, although Justine, her brothers and little sister would only later be able to appreciate the significance of that precious time. But Françoise's strength wasn't just a façade. Her fighting spirit, her bravery and her consideration for others never wavered. Justine and her siblings would never forget the courage she showed.

Even so, José and Françoise couldn't protect their children entirely from what was about to change their lives. He later acknowledged, 'They knew she was ill. We didn't tell the children she had cancer, though, not in so many words. But they knew something serious was happening to their mother. Justine knew like the rest, but she avoided the specifics. She was still young and she didn't ask too many questions.'

Afraid perhaps of the answers she might receive, Justine preferred to express herself, as usual, through her tennis. She had long since broken through the constraints of mini-tennis, though her technique had undoubtedly been improved by the experience. At eleven, she had already begun to take Belgium by storm. By twelve, she was starting to compete on equal terms with the finest youngsters in Europe, even those with an extra year of competition under their belts.

In January 1995, as Françoise felt her strength finally starting to ebb away, Justine began to take out her frustration on her opponents on the junior tennis circuit. José took her to a big under-14s tournament, the Petits As, an indoor event at Tarbes in the Pyrenees. Her age didn't seem to matter to a girl desperate to give her mother something to smile about. Sure enough, a delighted Justine was soon able to phone home to tell her mother that she had reached the quarter-finals.

José recalled, 'She asked my wife to come down to watch her play the big match. Françoise had to tell Justine that she would find a way to come down if she reached the semi-final. After the call, I phoned back to reassure my sick wife that it was highly unlikely that Justine would win her quarter-final. She was just a twelve-year-old, up against a Spanish girl who was older and much bigger. I mean, come on, it wasn't likely.'

Perhaps subconsciously, however, Justine had realised that her mother was not going to be around to watch her play tennis for very much longer. The dream of winning the French Open while her mother cheered from the stands somehow seemed beyond them now. Still, there was Tarbes, and the incentive of a mother-and-child reunion at the semi-final. Maybe Justine sensed that this could be her last chance ever to have her mother watch her play tennis live, in the flesh. But first she would have to cause an upset in the quarter-final against the fancied Spaniard, Eva Trujillo.

José took up the story. 'Justine went out and won 6–0, 6–0. It was incredible. Nothing was going to stop her. And nothing was going to stop Françoise either. She got in the car and drove 1,200 kilometres to be with her daughter, even though she was only months away from death. She drove all through the night to be there for that semi-final. You have to realise, Françoise was in the advanced stages of a terminal illness. But she wasn't going to let her daughter down, and Justine wasn't going to let her mother down. She caused an even bigger upset to win that semi-final, too.'

And, typically, she did it in dramatic style. Françoise watched her beat a Hungarian called Zsofia Gubacsi 6–4, 2–6, 7–6. The last time Justine won a big match in front of her mother, she did it on a tie-break. She had rewarded Françoise for her nightmare journey, and doubtless there were some extraordinary scenes of joy afterwards. Both had proved their point and demonstrated a bond of almost superhuman strength. Amazing forces of will had been at work.

Now, however, reality took over, and not even Justine could overturn the odds to win a final against an opponent who was far more physically developed and well on the way to the five feet eleven and three-quarters she would eventually reach. The technique of twelve-year-old Mirjana Lucic was simply too sound to allow yet another giant-killing and the Croatian won the final 6–3, 6–2. Two and a half years later, when Justine was still finding her way in the juniors, Lucic reached the fourth round of the US Open. By then she was already ranked 52 in the world. Only later did Justine reach her full potential, as Lucic fell down a slippery slope towards sporting oblivion.

Somehow the outcome of the final didn't seem to matter, because of the incredible feats that had already been achieved. Justine had done her mother proud, and Françoise, her biggest fan, had returned the compliment. In tennis terms, it was a fitting farewell. Or at least that is how some would describe what happened in Tarbes. Not Justine, however. When her French Open dream finally came true, she stated with complete confidence that her mother had witnessed everything from above. As far as she was concerned, Tarbes had simply been the last time when others could see that her mother was watching. In the player's mind, the bond between mother and daughter remained unbreakable, a secret weapon that gave Justine the edge over her opponent – the strength of two women.

Back in Tarbes, however, Françoise had precious little strength left, and José still faced the logistical nightmare of how to get her all the way home. He remembered, 'Twenty-four hours later, Françoise had to do the journey all the way back again. I offered her my air ticket but she insisted she wanted to return in the car. I drove so that she could sleep.'

Time was running out, although the gravity of her condition was still unspoken. José added, 'We still didn't tell the children just how ill their mother was. They might have sensed it, but they never asked directly. The issue was avoided.'

Justine's mother knew, though, and José later claimed, 'A few months before her death she told me, "The most important thing is to keep the family united after I'm gone." ' It was a promise that he was ultimately unable to keep, though in these harrowing days the family grew closer than ever, each member doing what he or she could to make the unspoken, inevitable process more bearable for all concerned.

In March, José and Françoise knew her condition couldn't be ignored for much longer. And it was decided that Françoise would see out her last days in the house of José's parents, Alphonse and Jeanne, at the end of the rue de Grottes.

Jeanne recalled, 'We told them to come to us and we prepared her bed. I still remember doing Françoise some eggs two days before she died. The next time I asked her what I could get her, she just said, "Nothing more." '

But even now, José believed, his wife was thinking of others: 'She managed to stay fully conscious until Thomas and David arrived home from college, so that they would be able to say goodbye.'

First, José attempted to prepare his children for their mother's death by leading them out on to the tree-lined track that winds its way towards Han-sur-Lesse's famous caves. He said, 'I took the children out for a walk and gently told them that their mum was about to leave us and join Florence in heaven.'

Jeanne and Alphonse watched anxiously from their bedroom window to see how the children would take the news. Almost nine years later, Jeanne remembered the scene. She recalled, 'Suddenly we saw the boys take their sisters up in their arms, and we knew then that José had broken the news.'

One by one, her children went up to say goodbye, and Françoise told each what a joy they had been in her life. But no one saw Justine go. Alphonse, Jeanne and José all tell it the same way. 'I think she was very scared and that's why she didn't go,' her grandfather suggested. 'And that is quite understandable.'

Eventually, Françoise slipped into a coma. José recalled, 'I climbed on to the bed then, and lay with her, holding her. She died in my arms the following morning. It was two months before our twenty-fifth wedding anniversary.'

Françoise passed away on 26 March 1995. She was 48 years old.

* * *

Justine didn't react to her mother's death in the way her father had anticipated. There are no rules to mourning, of course. Some fall apart, or behave irrationally; others don't react at all. People cope with the pain of bereavement in different ways, although medically it is widely accepted that it is better for those left behind to cry and let out some of their grief, rather than to keep it trapped inside.

José didn't see his twelve-year-old daughter shed any tears, not even at her mother's funeral. He remembered this quite clearly, since it eventually became an issue of mild medical concern. He explained, 'After Françoise died, Justine didn't cry – at least I never saw her. At the funeral, instead of tears, she found another way to express her grief. She limped. I believe it was psychosomatic because I don't believe she was carrying any injury at the time.

'Her lack of tears, in public at least, caused concern because the family doctor mentioned it to me, a month or two later. He told me that it was important for Justine to cry, to let it all out. But as far as I know, she never did.'

As sometimes happens after a bereavement, Justine found it easier to talk to an outsider, although Jean-Denis Lejeune was also a family friend. As time went on, he became like an uncle to her, someone to whom she could express her innermost feelings, away from the suffocating grief in the family home.

In his mid-thirties, Lejeune was younger than Justine's father, and, not one of the family, less damaged by the loss of Justine's mother. He became a source of strength and helped Justine through the most troubled of times. Within two years, however, Lejeune was also to be struck by the most horrifying family tragedy. His eight-year-old daughter, Julie, fell victim to a serial killer called Marc Dutroux, who became known as the Beast of Belgium. She is buried in Liège, where Florence died and Justine was born.

For Justine and those around her, there simply seemed to be no escape from the tragedy of untimely death. The word 'curse' is a strong one, but Justine could be forgiven for thinking that strange powers were at work in a world where no earthly love seemed safe for more than a short while.

CHAPTER 6

Carlos and Pierre-Yves

When Françoise Henin died, her daughter's motivation seemed to die with her. First and foremost, Justine had always played for her mother. Although Françoise had never been the greatest fan of tennis for its own sake, she had delighted in her daughter's achievements and inspired her on towards even greater things.

Justine, in turn, had wanted to repay the complete faith Françoise had shown in her tennis ability. She said later, 'My mother was convinced I would succeed. She was just great.' Now she wondered whether there was any point in playing at all. Her father loved her and he loved tennis; but it just wasn't the same without her mother there to please. She became disillusioned by the whole idea.

Justine told the *Observer Sport Monthly*, 'When my mum died, I thought tennis was over. I wasn't finding any more reason to play . . . Then I thought that my mum wouldn't want to see me like this.'

Gradually, over the next year, Justine realised she had good reason to play on and stay true to the pledge she had made to her mother three years earlier at Roland Garros. Françoise would never take her rightful place in the special seats set aside for a player's closest friends and family, but that didn't mean she wouldn't be there in spirit. The dream, like the bond between mother and daughter, was still alive in Justine. Perhaps it was more intense than ever.

With a new motivation, one that challenged even death, Justine would be tougher than ever to beat. It was time for the world's best players to watch out. Life hadn't been very fair to this particular youngster, but she would use that adversity now and crush her rivals with her grit and her power. And eventually, she would be the greatest. Nothing, no one, was going to stand in her way. Somewhere deep in her soul, Justine Henin had always known she was destined for the very top. Now, her mother's tragic death somehow gave her an extra edge.

* * *

Over the next eighteen months, José Henin struggled to come to terms with his grief. Nevertheless, he did everything he could to help keep his daughter's tennis dream alive. Although he would occasionally offer his insights into various technical aspects of her game, his main contribution was logistical.

He explained, 'Contrary to what has been written, I was never really Justine's coach. It was more like I was her driver, and I carried on in that role year after year. I drove between 50,000 and 60,000 kilometres per year to take her to tournaments. Sometimes, when I should have spread my time equally among my children, I gave the majority of my energies to Justine. I regret to say that my actions meant that my other children often paid the price for this dedication to Justine's tennis.

'I am not proud to say that I was also pushy in my attitude towards Justine and her tennis. I was not perfect in my behaviour by any means. But I believe it is also true to say that, had I not been so pushy, she might never have made it to the top five in the world.'

Although José admitted that he wasn't the ideal parent, his ambition for his daughter coincided with her own determined push towards the top of the junior game. And 1996 was a remarkable breakthrough year. But there was an added factor, beyond the creative tension between father and daughter. An Argentinian coach called Carlos Rodriguez, who had won worldwide respect by helping the lower-ranked Dick Norman beat Stefan Edberg at Wimbledon the previous year, arrived on the scene and would soon become a permanent fixture in Justine's career. With his rugged good looks, the swarthy South American wasn't short of charm. And, not for the last time, José was instrumental in delivering his daughter into the hands of someone who would later play a key role in shutting him out of her life.

Rodriguez was working for the Association Francophone de Tennis, the French-speaking branch of the Belgian Tennis Federation, and his growing reputation had caught José's eye. When José met the coach in person, it served only to confirm his positive impressions. Later, he was almost kicking himself when he admitted, 'I gave Justine to Carlos – he was my choice. We had some conversations, Carlos and I. And I enjoyed his views on tennis. I liked his ideas for training and practice. He was interesting.'

Therefore José called the AFT's technical director, Eduardo Masso (whose father-in-law was the world-famous Tour de France winner Eddie Merckx and a friend of José), with a proposal. Justine would work under the federation at the Centre of Excellence in Mons, as long as Carlos Rodriguez, of whom she, too, had heard great things, would help coach her.

For the Argentinian, it wasn't difficult to agree to the proposal once he had met Justine. In 2001, he told the *Sunday Times* what first struck him: 'More than her talent to start with, it was her attitude, this desire always to do the best she could, this incredibly professional way of doing things, that made me want to work with her.'

First, Rodriguez had to free himself of his commitment to another Belgian star, and by this stage Justine's obvious talent had become a key factor. He explained, 'I was working with Dominique Van Roost when I first met Justine. Dominique was also very focused and was doing very well, but Justine had more potential and, as I told Dominique, the youngster needed me more.'

The man who would one day partially take on José's role and become a father figure for Justine had entered the picture. His impact on her game was almost immediate. Together they all travelled to Florida for the Orange Bowl, effectively the world under-14s tennis championships, in Miami. Justine didn't just compete with her customary ferocity – she won it.

A delighted Justine, now a spotty, tomboyish teenager, sent an unflattering photograph of herself to her uncle and aunt soon afterwards. It wasn't so much the picture that had stuck in their mind when they were shunned a few years later, as the message she wrote on the back:

> *Aunt Clelia and Uncle Jean-Paul, I offer you this photo, taken just after the Orange Bowl, as a little souvenir of my victory. I won't write an essay, I just want to thank you for everything that you do for me. I know that I can count on you, and that you will always be there for me. I'm very lucky to have uncles and aunts like you. Thanks for everything, Big Kisses, Justine.*

* * *

Strongly supported by the family she later partially discarded, Henin went from strength to strength in 1996. She won the European under-14s title in San Remo, Italy, to confirm her class. She also represented Belgium at under-14s level, too, often sharing hotel rooms with Kim Clijsters, the rival who was by now also a friend.

Behind such success lay more than the sporting wisdom of her new coach, Rodriguez. Her brother Thomas had also provided the moral support she needed during tricky times. He had unselfishly put his own plans on hold to help make his sister's dreams come true. He had delayed the studies so essential for a career in banking in order to live alongside Justine at the tennis academy in Mons. Thomas worked with all the children, but above all he was there to make life easier for Justine, who was the only girl in the entire line-up of hopefuls.

Without international room-mate Clijsters and not wanting to be alone, Justine used to creep into Thomas's room at night and sleep in one of the extra beds there. Thomas confirmed, 'Justine wanted to sleep in my room and that caused problems later. She was the only girl in the school and there was only me for company. We were brother and sister but we were also best friends. I think she became too attached.'

A thoughtful blend of professional and familial care soon brought even more spectacular results on the tennis court. Justine acquired a taste for glory with a stunning tournament victory at Le Touquet, France. Her confidence boosted, she went on to play Junior Roland Garros in that early summer of 1997 and faced Nathalie Dechy in a tough semi-final. Henin saved four match points with audacious shots that just clipped the line before winning 5–7, 7–6, 6–1. It seemed as though someone was smiling down on her at this special venue. In the final she beat Cara Black 4–6, 6–4, 6–4 to become the talk of the French-speaking tennis world. Her grandparents Alphonse and Jeanne were there to share her glory and couldn't have been prouder.

Justine later recalled, 'When I won the French Open Juniors, I knew it was going to be my job.'

* * *

Suddenly, there was media attention to deal with, and endless autographs to sign, and Justine must have sensed that she was on the verge of the big time. How delighted her mother would have been.

Privately, Justine could have been forgiven for suspecting that Françoise had even lent a helping hand somewhere along the line.

José knew that he had made a positive contribution. He said later, 'Justine once claimed that when she cut me out of her life, her fear of failure had been removed, and that meant she had been able to win big tournaments. Well, this so-called fear of failure didn't seem to stop her winning all the big junior tournaments while I was still very much part of her life.'

And it wasn't just the junior tournaments any more. When Justine won the Belgian national title that same year, aged just fifteen, she beat Dominique Van Roost, now a highly respected player who was ranked in the world's top 40.

* * *

At home, away from the novelty of microphones and television cameras, the Henin family was still adapting to life without a matriarch. In an interview with the *Sunday Times*, Justine later complained that she had been asked to fill the role in certain ways:

> *After my mother died it was never the same. It is wrong to say I became the mother of the family, because I didn't cook or anything like that. But I was mature very early and they all used to come to me with their problems, my two older brothers and my young sister. But it became difficult. I lead a very special life – I have to. But they didn't understand and then there were money problems and jealousy. It was impossible.*

Such a description doesn't tally with what Thomas remembers of his sister's early and mid-teens. After all, at Mons it was she who was coming to Thomas with her problems, day and night.

Her father told a different story, too. 'Mature? Her little sister, Sarah, was much more mature. Justine was the princess, the demanding one. Everything in the family was geared to her success and I have already explained that the others suffered as a result. They don't complain now, only Justine. I don't try to claim I was a perfect father. I was depressed and I drank sometimes and I put on weight, around twenty kilos. But I did the best I could when faced with difficult circumstances, and the other children understood what was happening to me. And through all this, I always put Justine's career first. Everyone knows that.'

* * *

The rift between family and coach, José and the Belgian Tennis Federation, had begun to appear in 1997 and widened through 1998, as Justine's promising career became threatened by one injury after another.

José argued that her physical problems were being mishandled. He recalled, 'She had a foot injury in 1997, which lingered for weeks. The doctor diagnosed tendonitis, so she was given cortisone injections for the inflammation. But in fact the foot was broken; and you can't use cortisone in such a case, because there is a risk of decalcification.

'When the federation finally realised their mistake, they sent her to Brussels and she was given a leg support to walk with, but two months had already gone by. Eventually, my friend Eddie Merckx, the famous cyclist and Tour de France winner, sent her to a specialist he knew. After three months' work with a physiotherapist, she was finally fit again.'

However, Justine's problems weren't over. José explained, 'In 1998 Justine developed digestive problems just as she was about to make her first appearance for Belgium in Bratislava, in the Federation Cup. I asked a doctor about the problem and he said she could go on the trip, even though she looked very pale and drawn. But he warned that if she needed a hospital out there, then the military hospitals were the best option – hardly reassuring.

'Justine left on the Monday and I joined her out there on the Thursday, as part of the federation officials and supporters' trip. She was very tired, and medical tests before she returned home revealed the presence of harmful microbes in her intestines. She went home that Saturday, but had to have three months' lay-off as she recovered from a course of antibiotics. I wasn't the only one to voice the opinion that it was a mistake that she had been cleared for the trip in the first place. The federation should have known something was wrong and she shouldn't have gone. It wasn't good for her and it wasn't good for the team.'

Given that his wife had suffered from problems in a similar area, it was easy to see why José might have been so outspoken, his anger fuelled by his desire to protect his daughter. After what they had all been through, Justine's health had to come before anything else.

José revealed, 'If I was getting nervous, it was because she was always injured or sick. I began to think that maybe she wasn't right for the sport after all. I lost confidence in the doctors, in the federation and in Carlos Rodriguez.'

But the more José complained, the more he played into the hands of the professionals who wanted to take control of Justine's career. Caught in the middle, Justine suffered a further but very necessary blow to what inner security she had as Thomas began to question the hold she had over him. He had come to realise that he couldn't be expected to live his entire life for his sister, especially now that he had interests beyond the family.

In April 1998, he had met Vanessa, the love of his life. The sleeping arrangements in Mons were suddenly looking unsustainable: 'When Vanessa came to sleep with me, Justine wanted to come into the room to be with us. She was always too attached. Our relationship was too strong.'

The claims of Justine's coach, Carlos Rodriguez, that the family wanted to 'own' her were too simplistic. And if there was any dependency at this stage, it seems to have been Justine who felt it.

Then a young man arrived on the scene, someone who came to represent something of a challenge for several Henin family members and their relationships with Justine. Before very long, Henin men appeared to become nothing more to Justine than symbols of a painful, unwanted past. It would be almost as though the arrival of Justine's 'knight in shining armour' had reduced these loving relatives to little more than ghosts. It seemed their efforts on her behalf over so many years were to be forgotten in the space of months.

In August 1998, Justine was due to hand out the winner's prize at an amateur tennis tournament in the family's home village of Han-sur-Lesse. José had officiated there in years gone by, and it was only natural that his increasingly famous daughter should be asked to award the prize. Pierre-Yves Hardenne, a local lad and a relative newcomer to the game, entered the tournament. 'It was the first I had ever played,' he told me later.

Amazingly, he won it. When Justine stepped up to congratulate the victor, who was more than a year older than she was, there was something about him that caused her to return his broad smile with interest. As their eyes met, they both spotted a sparkle in the other that they wanted to explore further. Pierre-Yves, who had no trouble remembering precisely what month it had been almost six years later, confirmed to me in 2004 that it had been love at first sight for both of them.

Their lives would never be the same; and José Henin was about to enter a new nightmare. Once again, tennis had played a major part in leading Justine to a man whose presence would gradually push her father out of her life completely.

Justine blamed her family for not making Pierre-Yves feel more welcome and claimed later, 'It was not Pierre-Yves my family didn't like. It was the thought of there being *anyone* in my life. But when I met Pierre-Yves, I thought, "At last, you can be happy."'

Thomas disputed this version. 'I wasn't jealous of Pierre-Yves at all. I had been with Vanessa for a while by the time Justine met him. We had our own projects to think about and Justine was nothing more than a sister. The problem was that I didn't think he was the right man for her.'

José also denied his daughter's sweeping claim: 'It is not true to say that we rejected Pierre-Yves straight off – it was quite the reverse. He was in my house all the time.'

Perhaps subconsciously José and Thomas remembered the great sacrifices they had made over the years in order to give Justine her big chance in the world of tennis. It was one thing to doubt whether such a physically and mentally demanding career would be right for Justine in the long run, especially if it appeared that her health was going to suffer. After all, they knew that no career was worth such a price, whatever sacrifices had been made by the family. But it was quite another matter to see everyone's hard work thrown away for the sake of some crazy teenage love affair. If they harboured such concerns, it would have been only natural. With the benefit of hindsight, José recognised later that he could have been subtler in his handling of the new passion in his daughter's life.

Not that Justine was particularly subtle in her reaction to the news Thomas broke that December. It wasn't easy for him to explain. He loved his sister and he had spent almost three years forgetting his own needs in order to look after her. She had progressed steadily in tennis terms, moving from an unranked position to 226 in the world. The previous month, she had enjoyed a highly successful trip to Israel, where she had won an International Tennis Federation (ITF) 'challenger' event called the Ramat Hashiro. She had teamed up with Clijsters to win the doubles, too, and they were pictured in high spirits on a Tel Aviv beach. She was on a roll and he hated to burst her bubble. But now that she was sixteen and a half, she needed to develop on a personal level, too, and Thomas had to move on. He had realised that he had to have a life of his own and wanted Justine to set him free. But he claimed she was reluctant to do so.

He said, 'When I met Vanessa, Justine was alone. The situation was complicated. I worked with Justine but I wanted my life back. I had been working with Justine for three years and we were very close. But I told her in December that I wanted to work for me now. And she was very angry because I didn't want to work with her. But my position was this: life with her wasn't a job for me. I wanted to work in a bank and I did so. My life now was with Vanessa.'

So Justine turned professional at the start of 1999 without Thomas as her escort, and José took time out from life at the post office to accompany her on the senior tour. The player's father therefore filled the void in her life created by Thomas's decision to follow his own path. One way or another, the family was still looking after its most demanding member, catering for her every need.

Everyone was trying their best to help Justine's tennis career, sustaining that 'special life' she later claimed they didn't understand. Trips abroad to play in 'challenger' tournaments weren't cheap; neither were they always free of trauma.

José recalled, 'We went to play a USTA challenger tournament about 40 or 50 kilometres outside Chicago in Rockford, Illinois. The total prize money on offer was $25,000. We had talked a lot about this trip beforehand, laughing about the city's violent reputation, with its gangster history.

'When we came out of Chicago's O'Hare International airport, Carlos, Justine and I were all feeling pretty relaxed, though – until the first thing we saw was a dead body. A policeman had just shot this black man. I don't know why. But he was lying there, face down in a pool of blood, stone dead. The officer who had killed him still had his gun out of the holster and various cops were moving around the body.

'Justine stayed pretty quiet, but then she reacted to most situations like that. She certainly didn't cry, and I think, of the three of us, Carlos was the most shocked. We didn't hang around, we just got out of there as quickly as we could and tried to put what we had seen behind us.

'After all, Justine had the tournament to play. She did all right, too, reaching the quarter-finals, where she lost to Miroslava Vavrinec in a third-set tie-break. We remembered the incident outside the airport more than anything, and we couldn't help talking about it for days afterwards. Can you imagine it? Chicago, historically the city of gangsters, and the first thing we saw was the aftermath of a gunfight!'

* * *

The intrepid trio faced the dangers that lurked in the wider world with courage and humour, even when that humour had to be black to cope with what life threw their way. Beneath the surface, however, tensions were mounting between coach and father, as both sought to get the best out of Justine in their different ways. Already there had been times when José had wanted Justine to use the wild-card entries that IMG-connected players could sometimes gain to the notable tournaments. Rodriguez, meanwhile, had appeared to favour a more gradual progression for Justine, under his own, closer control.

IMG was a powerful organisation, with an array of coaching talent at its disposal. It would not have been hard to understand if, during Justine's early teens, Rodriguez had wanted to cement his own relationship with his player before letting her loose in the worldwide circuit, where coaches with even greater reputations might have been attracted by his budding starlet's progress. On the other hand, perhaps he had just wanted to build up her confidence as carefully as he could, rather than throw her in at the deep end. Whatever their respective reasons, a conflict between the two men escorting Justine on the circuit had been looking inevitable for some time.

It is easy from the outside to imagine how José might have placed too much pressure on his daughter as she sought a major breakthrough in professional tennis. But then it is equally easy to forget that Justine wanted much the same thing for herself in life. Other factors contributed to a mounting tension. Subconsciously, José might have demanded too much from his daughter emotionally, as he continued to grieve for his wife. The tragic loss of his first daughter might also have engendered a more anxious, possessive approach towards the upbringing of the second. Such factors wouldn't have made any increased pressure on Justine right or healthy; but they did make any mistakes José made as a parent more understandable than they would otherwise have been.

If there was a problem, as Rodriguez claimed, it clearly needed to be addressed sensitively, in order to achieve a new, happier paternal balance. However, Rodriguez appears to have been more anxious to challenge the occasionally oppressive nature of José's influence over the rising star than to wait for the family to readjust under its own steam. Perhaps he hadn't suffered in life quite like Justine's father, or indeed the rest of his family. Therefore, during these tense moments between father and daughter, Rodriguez may have felt it appropriate to lay the blame at José's door, perhaps without seeking to understand fully the reasons for any difficulty.

Rodriguez was once quoted as describing himself like this: 'I am a polite, pleasant man, but I can also be a "son of a bitch" if I feel it's necessary to provoke, in order to take [Justine] to the objective she herself has chosen.'

He was speaking at the time about the techniques he used in ridding Justine of the complex she seemed to develop at one stage of her career with regard to arch-rival Kim Clijsters, and his light-hearted self-portrait shouldn't be taken out of context. But how tough was Rodriguez in his approach to the delicate question of Justine's relationship with her father?

If Rodriguez ever did try to use careful diplomacy to influence the family dynamic for the good of all concerned, those efforts didn't seem to last long. His own recollections suggest that any sympathy he might have had for José's traumatic past took a back seat as their personality clash escalated.

He later claimed, 'I don't know how to say it in English but he, the father, and the whole family, wanted to appropriate her. They did not respect her needs. I saw what they were doing to her and I spoke up very quickly. We had many arguments, the father and I.'

The stakes were high. Justine had turned professional and she looked capable of breaking into the elite group at the top end of the senior rankings one day. For years, most of the family income had been directed towards taking her where she wanted to be. Now, as she began to win good money, José saw the chance to recover some of that outlay for those who had financed her development in the first place. IMG had been on the scene for some time, taking care of many aspects of Justine's career. But with José now escorting his daughter on the senior tour, he saw that if the Henin family stuck together, those who had made the sacrifices for Justine, such as his brothers, could enjoy some rewards. José's other children could benefit, not least the twelve-year-old Sarah, who had behaved so graciously as Justine's lifestyle on the junior circuit demanded the lion's share of their father's attention during her formative years. As far as José was concerned, this wasn't 'appropriation', simply the restoration of balance.

But now the arrival of Pierre-Yves on the scene had put that process in doubt. What would this love affair do to José's chances of achieving some security for his long-suffering family at last? Just as important, would Pierre-Yves really be good for Justine and her own dreams? These were crucial questions, at a crucial stage in Justine's personal development, and they needed to be handled carefully. A mother's touch was sorely missed now. José loved his daughter and wanted what was best for her, as well as the rest of the family. But that didn't mean he always chose the right course of action, or the best words.

As Justine's uncle Jean-Paul observed later, 'Françoise would have handled things differently. José will admit that he didn't deal with all aspects of the situation in the most subtle way, although it was difficult for him at times.'

Both José and Thomas insist it was Pierre-Yves' alleged intolerance, not theirs, that was to cause the beginnings of what turned into a deeply damaging rift. At first, they all lived with the sudden changes in Justine's life, and watched to see how they would impact upon her tennis. Although 1999 was a transitional year in Justine's tennis career, there were some notable milestones, and key figures within the game began to recognise her seemingly unlimited ability.

Selected for Belgium's Federation Cup team, Justine won both her matches to help her country defeat Holland 3–2. She also became only the fifth player to win a debut WTA Tour title. She gained a wild-card entry to the Antwerp tournament and surprised everyone by thrashing Sarah Pitkowski, who had a world ranking of 35, in the final. Henin's 6–1, 6–2 demolition of such a respected opponent gave a tantalising taste of what was to come.

Meanwhile, Justine showed enough promise at the French Open to catch the eye of the most famous name in tennis. She may have lost in the second round, having only gained entry as a qualifier, but not before scaring the life out of the big-name American Lindsay Davenport. Henin lost the first set 3–6 on the Court Central, but hit back to take the second 6–2. John McEnroe couldn't believe what he was seeing. 'It was incredible how she hit the ball,' he recalled. Justine wasn't done, and served for the match at 5–4 in the third. She blew her big chance and lost 5–7 to a very relieved American favourite. While Justine was kicking herself, McEnroe knew he had seen something special. 'Few people are born with such potential,' he said simply.

Before long, he had become Henin's number one celebrity fan, and that wonderful comment wasn't far from his lips: 'She's the player I most like to watch. Justine has the best backhand in the game – women's or men's.'

Justine's fantastic showing against a player as huge as Davenport prompted a double celebration when she came home, since 1 June was also her seventeenth birthday. There was a party in a restaurant near the Han-sur-Lesse tennis club. It was perhaps one of the first times that Pierre-Yves and Justine's wider families really got a good look at one another in a social setting. And the Henin family claimed that it was Pierre-Yves who wasn't prepared to compromise, even as they sought to accommodate him in their lives.

Far from being jealous of Pierre-Yves, Thomas insisted that all the signs pointed to the reverse being true. 'I was dancing with Justine that night and my girlfriend, Vanessa, was having a cigarette, off to the side. Pierre-Yves went up to her and pointed at us dancing. He asked her what she thought about it. She didn't know what he was talking about. But Pierre-Yves said that Justine was too close to me, and that the situation couldn't continue, he didn't like it. That's when our problems began.'

Thomas had already begun to create a healthier distance between himself and Justine, so the last thing he felt he needed was some outsider telling him how to behave on his sister's birthday. But José alleged that Pierre-Yves didn't stop there: 'Pierre-Yves came right out with it at some dinner and told my daughter, "I think it would be better if you lived away from your family home so that you are self-sufficient." '

* * *

To Carlos Rodriguez, the idea wouldn't have seemed so strange. He had left home back in Argentina at seventeen, and therefore he would have done little to discourage such ambitions in his protégée. Justine mulled over her options that summer before taking a shot at the US Open. However, the sort of impact she had made against Davenport in Paris was not to be repeated so soon. She was drawn against the powerfully built Amélie Mauresmo and was knocked out in the first round.

José claimed, 'After that, I told Justine that it was time for me to create some space between us. I was nervous, I didn't even think it had been a good idea for her to play that tournament. I told her that Sarah needed me. She was only thirteen.'

Privately, Justine might already have been close to arriving at some fundamental decisions regarding her future. Although she wasn't quite ready to make the final break from her father, she did play a big tournament towards the end of 1999 – the Advanta Championships in Philadelphia – while José stayed at home. This was no small step for Justine, not after what they had been through in Chicago earlier in the year. She passed with flying colours and claimed her first big scalp, a glamorous one at that. Anna Kournikova was a top ten player and big news at the time; but Justine attacked the net, fed off Kournikova's nerves, and proved she was better than at least one of the so-called superstars of the sport. She won a tie-break to take the first set and closed out the second 6–4.

Years later, José recalled what it meant to her: 'She phoned to tell me what she'd done. I was so happy. I said, "That's great! You see! You can do it without me. Go it alone from here." She said, "I prefer it when you are there with me." '

José remembered the moment with pride, not just because it was one of Justine's first great moments on the professional circuit. He also believed that the exchange proved something else: that he was not always the pushy father that so many later tried to portray; rather, he was a man who had made mistakes, like any other parent, and tried to put them right as he went along.

He explained later, 'I'm not stupid, I know that it isn't always good for a player to have their father watching over their shoulder while they are on court. I pushed her too hard sometimes, but I was the first to see that. We needed some distance between us because effectively we had been on the tennis circuit together for ten years already. But that didn't justify what she eventually did.'

For José, his relationship with his daughter was never the black-and-white story of heroine and villain portrayed since. And the call from Philadelphia suggested that, despite frayed nerves on both sides, part of Justine was also reluctant to cut the ties with her father.

In reality, however, the process had already begun. If part of her still preferred to have her father by her side on the circuit, that inner conflict wouldn't last long. Pierre-Yves Hardenne would soon be the only important man in her life – apart from her coach, Carlos Rodriguez. José didn't know it, but he was about to be pushed into the shadows indefinitely.

CHAPTER 7

Tie-break!

Pierre-Yves Hardenne and Justine Henin knew they had more than a mutual physical attraction and a love of tennis to keep them together. The young man soon sensed Justine's need for increased independence – an identity separate from the emotional cauldron that bubbled away in her family.

But Thomas still harboured protective feelings towards his sister; and he was reluctant to be pushed aside entirely by a newcomer he didn't like. He hadn't spent years in Mons, helping cater for Justine's every need, so that some young upstart could – or so it seemed to him – waltz in and try to suggest that his role in his sister's life was effectively over. David, too – the eldest of José's children – was bound to support his brother in the face of the disrespect Pierre-Yves allegedly showed.

Justine simply wished they could all get on, and blamed her family for not making Pierre-Yves feel accepted. But José, Thomas and David claimed they would have found it easier to accept Pierre-Yves had he shown more purpose in his own studies and marked out an identifiable career path. Their natural fear, though ultimately this proved unfounded, was that a young man without a steady job or direction in life might turn out to be nothing more than a golddigger. That judgement, however erroneous, only sharpened the edge in what was slowly developing into a family feud.

José admitted, 'It was Thomas who first fell out with Justine over Pierre-Yves, and what was I supposed to do, support the boyfriend against my own son? No, of course not. But I wasn't very far behind in clashing with Pierre-Yves myself. We were eating dinner one night and I told him that I thought it was important for him to think about a career for himself, and work out what he wanted to do in life. I said he should be his own man. He didn't like being given that advice one bit, and it was the start of the tension between us. Yes, I was also annoyed that Justine wasn't giving much time to the family any more. And I may have feared that Pierre-Yves's increasing influence was going to undermine Justine's professionalism towards her tennis; but I was thinking of him, too, when I said those things.'

Like many teenagers, Pierre-Yves refused to be told how to run his life. And José admitted later, 'Look, if I'm absolutely honest, I might have reacted in exactly the same way had I been in his shoes. That's what you do when you're young.'

At the time, Hardenne didn't want to listen, and he soon realised that he didn't need to. For, apart from the obvious strength of his burgeoning romance with Justine, Pierre-Yves slowly gained a crucial advantage in the long-running battle for Justine's favour. Unlike José, he never challenged the authority of Carlos Rodriguez. In return, the coach was gradually won over to the new influence in Justine's life. When she explained how much Pierre-Yves was starting to mean to her, Rodriguez accepted it, no doubt seeing further potential in Hardenne as a new ally. After all, Rodriguez hadn't seen eye to eye with José for some time.

José suggested later that his daughter had contributed to the strain between father and coach. He explained, 'She used to come to me complaining about things and I told her to go to Carlos and ask for certain things herself, because if I did it there would be a war. Justine then went straight to Carlos and told him what I'd said. It showed he already had a big say in what went on inside her head.'

Her coach's acceptance of Pierre-Yves meant everything to Justine. Although there was always a possibility that her tennis might suffer initially, while she adjusted to her new emotional landscape, Rodriguez might also have felt that she would become a more rounded character if she had a loving partner. Therefore, it followed, she might be more able to handle the pressure in the really big matches. In time, Hardenne could help remove what Rodriguez saw as the problematic family influence over her career, and slowly start to erase the fear of failure that haunted her while she remained under the watchful eye of her father.

If this was the effect José had on his daughter, it wasn't necessarily his fault. Many fathers don't even realise when they are being pushy.

The tragedies in José's life had made him what he was. Although he was often fun, he could also be intense. But even Justine's father couldn't be as obsessive about her tennis career as the player was herself. And again, Rodriguez had the advantage of an untroubled perspective.

He was able to remain more objective emotionally. He was untouched by the deaths that had scarred and complicated the Henin family. He could find a way through Justine's past to present her with a clear vision of a brighter future. But he managed to feed her obsession for tennis excellence without appearing too pushy himself. Therefore he was able to engineer an increasingly powerful position in Justine's life, alongside Pierre-Yves. The men seemed to have an unspoken understanding. Hardenne kept out of tennis issues and Rodriguez stayed out of personal ones, unless, of course, Justine came to him for advice.

* * *

Even without the support of Carlos, Pierre-Yves would probably still have enjoyed the upper hand over José and Thomas. Any teenage girl striking out on her own is going to rebel against a father who fails to accept her boyfriend. If that father also takes the side of a disapproving son and brother against that boyfriend, he risks further alienation. And the more the family condemns the new boyfriend, the more determined daughter and boyfriend become to defy their detractors and go it alone to make a success of their relationship.

Not that the Henin family accepts that it was ever as hostile to Pierre-Yves as has been suggested by Justine. Her uncle, Jean-Marie, claimed, 'I met Pierre-Yves in the street once and said, "All right?" He answered, "Why?" I didn't think that was very polite or mature.'

The incident suggested that Pierre-Yves didn't care what Justine's family thought about him. It was what *she* felt that mattered – and for Pierre-Yves, that was plenty. The closer Justine and Pierre-Yves grew, the more exasperated José and Thomas became. The Henin family wasn't unique in any of this. It is a scene played out in families all over the world as teenage girls prepare to fly the nest. Parents or elder brothers lose their influence, they worry about the relative they love, and the loss of control can be a frightening feeling.

But such loss of control can be especially traumatic in a family to whom fate has been so cruel. In such a family, control over any aspect of their lives becomes a precious commodity. Letting go, when you have already lost so much, is no straightforward matter; especially when the girl in question is on the verge of breaking into the tennis big time. Would Justine put her tennis at risk? And how could this boy suddenly be more important than all those people who had loved her since the day she was born?

José claimed that Justine's attitude to her game suffered at this time. Love tests most people's professionalism in the early, dizzy stages of a relationship. José later acknowledged that he probably overreacted when her attentions turned elsewhere. But with so much riding on his daughter's tennis dreams, it was hard not to feel protective, perhaps even aggressive, when an outsider suddenly appeared to threaten her destiny.

If her father had known then what a positive influence Pierre-Yves was to have on his daughter's long-term career, perhaps he would have reacted differently. Hindsight, as they say, is a wonderful thing, and recent tennis history has made his attitude to Justine's future husband appear even more mistaken. But at the time, it seemed to José that Pierre-Yves represented a threat – nothing more, nothing less.

Yet José noticed that Justine still expected her father to put himself out for her when it suited her, and when Pierre-Yves couldn't be there. He recalled, 'Justine and I had a big fight before we left for Australia at the start of 2000. I was reluctant to accompany her by then.'

The tennis started well enough, with a quarter-final appearance at the warm-up tournament in Hobart, Tasmania. But by the time they reached the Australian Open, tensions between father and daughter were almost unbearable.

José claimed, 'Her heart didn't seem to be in it. She was always calling Pierre-Yves back in Belgium, whether it was seven in the morning or eleven at night. The time difference obviously didn't help her sleeping pattern. I got the impression that she was more interested in the phone calls than the tennis. It was no surprise when she was knocked out early.'

Martina Hingis was the second-round executioner, winning 6–3, 6–3, although Justine's turbulent personal life meant that she had beaten herself almost before she went on court. Something had to change, and soon. As they flew back across the world, father and daughter knew it was only a matter of time before the tension in their already strained relationship boiled over into something more decisive.

In February, Justine was due to play in the Open Gaz, an important indoor tournament in Paris. On the day she would make the short journey from Belgium, her grandfather, Georges Rosière, came to see her off. As well as being the father of her beloved mother, Rosière had also taken over as Justine's number one fan. But he, too, had felt the sudden impact of Justine's love affair with Pierre-Yves.

José explained, 'You have to bear in mind that Georges had already complained to me, on six or seven separate occasions, that he never saw Justine any more. Now he had come to give her a warm send-off and she simply wasn't there at the appointed time. He was becoming agitated, so I thought I had better do something about it. We both knew where she would be – round at her boyfriend's house. In the end, I ran out of patience and went to fetch her. I found her sitting on Pierre-Yves's lap, in a short skirt, without a care in the world – she had forgotten her responsibilities to the rest of us. When I told her she was late and that her grandfather was waiting to say goodbye, she finally tore herself away from Pierre-Yves and came back with me.

'When we got there I told her how selfish and unprofessional I thought she was becoming, because her kit wasn't even packed and ready. I also scolded her for keeping her grandfather waiting so long. What shocked me then was that Georges, whose agitated state had contributed to the tension, suddenly took Justine's side against me. He defended her and made excuses for her, effectively undermining everything I had said to her. I couldn't believe it. I had tried to make sure she did the right thing, in order to please him as well, and now I was suddenly the bad guy in everyone's eyes.

'Eventually, Justine and I got in the car and drove off to Paris. But I had made up my mind that this was going to be the last time I ever escorted her to a tournament, and I think we both knew deep down that was it.'

* * *

If Justine hadn't already come to the same conclusion, she soon would. The tournament started well enough with her win over the better-known Magdalena Maleeva in the first round. Then she came up against the might of world number six Nathalie Tauziat, and lost the first set 5–7. What she produced next shocked many observers, who witnessed a ferocious comeback against her more fancied opponent. As Justine took that second set 6–2, she and everyone else watching knew that she had what it took to be massive. But it suddenly all seemed to go wrong in Justine's head. The fire went out, Tauziat was back in control and she claimed the last set 6–4. It was a match Justine felt she could have won, and it was the final nail in the coffin for her professional relationship with her father.

In the car on the way back, José said, 'I don't understand why you played to Tauziat's strengths all the time.'

'What do you mean?' Justine asked.

'You kept playing to her backhand,' José insisted.

'Well, I'm not sure I should have played to her forehand all the time,' Justine argued.

Then Carlos Rodriguez, who was also in the car, stepped in. 'I'm not sure she should have played to her forehand either.'

Suddenly, José was on the outside, looking in on his daughter's career, outvoted, undermined, and given the firm impression that his opinion no longer counted for very much at all. He had run out of patience with a daughter he now considered to be disrespectful, and she no longer seemed to have any time for him.

* * *

In March, there was a massive row in the family home. José and Justine had been building up to this moment and it didn't need anything substantial or particularly memorable to trigger the explosion. Father and daughter unleashed volleys of wounding insults at each other, in front of José's sister Geneviève. In the end, Justine asked Geneviève if she could stay with her for a week, at least until the air had cleared. Her aunt agreed that it might be the best thing, but José wasn't having it.

Later, he remembered that day with sadness. 'I said something terrible to Justine, something I should never have said and would always regret. I looked her in the eye and told her, "If you walk out of that door, you will not be my daughter any more." She walked out of the door.'

And she stayed away for more than a week. Justine moved out of José's house and went to live with his sister in another part of Han-sur-Lesse. She would return occasionally, but she would never live with her father again. His remark had given her the key to her early independence.

It also led a source in Justine's camp to claim years later, 'You must understand that it wasn't Justine who left home of her own accord, it was her father who pushed her out. He was the one who ignored her.'

On that particular, definitive day, there was an element of truth to this analysis. But in reality, it should have been obvious to Justine that what José had said in the heat of the moment was not something he could ever mean. As he remarked, 'What I said was not good, but it shouldn't have been a reason for her to break with the family as she did.'

However, family history had told her that life could be tragically short, particularly if you were female. She seemed determined to experience the high points unhindered by complications because in the back of her mind she must have realised that some dreadful low points might lie ahead. If Justine was looking for an excuse to split from the men in her family, this was it. She grabbed the opportunity with both hands, and soon it seemed as though a weight had been lifted from her shoulders. Gone was the life where, she believed, perhaps mistakenly, she had to be strong for everyone else, where she was forced to play tennis with her father breathing down her neck. Now she could be strong for herself; she could play tennis motivated only by her mother's memory and her own ambition. Better still, she could see Pierre-Yves when she wanted, and that was pretty much whenever she wasn't playing tennis. Much of her spare time would now be spent with her boyfriend and his family. She no longer felt troubled by what her father or brother might think.

And so we return to Justine's later claim: 'After my mother died it was never the same. It is wrong to say I became the mother of the family, because I didn't cook or anything like that. But I was mature very early and they all used to come to me with their problems . . . It was impossible. They would not accept my boyfriend. That is why I finally walked out and left home at seventeen.'

Was it really so simple? Thomas repeated his version: 'We were not jealous of Pierre-Yves and I didn't have some big showdown fight with her over it. For her to say that we didn't accept him, or came to her with our problems, just makes it easier for her to excuse her departure.'

Had the death of her mother placed so many heavy demands on Justine in particular, or had that tragedy left the entire family facing fresh challenges, as they all tried to fill a mother's role in one way or other?

Thomas said, 'She was young and we all had problems, the children and my father included.'

It was only a year after Justine left that Thomas did in fact have occasion to call on his sister for help. As we shall see, that plea came at a particularly desperate moment in his life, and Justine's response was hardly the one that he wanted.

* * *

Whatever the truth behind Justine's departure from the family home in March 2000, it meant the start of a decisive new phase in her life. And the rift remained unhealed, largely because so much unresolved resentment lingered on both sides. Parting shots were exchanged.

José claimed, 'She came back to visit us a few times. During one of her visits, I asked Justine, "Why are you saying I'm a bad father? A few months ago you said I was a good father. You said publicly that you were lucky to have a father like me."

'Justine turned to me and replied, "I said that to please you – but I didn't think it." It really broke my heart when she said that. I realised then that in her eyes I had just been there to work for her. I had been her "boy". For the rest, for the family, she had no respect at all.'

Thomas believed that Justine was being unfair and found all her subsequent outbursts against their father distasteful. 'It was her choice to leave and I respect that. But I do not respect the fact that she criticised my father. Sarah, David and I, we all know that our father did all he could for us. He didn't just support Justine's tennis, he found time to come and watch David and me when we played football, too. He did all he could and more for his children. He was always looking after Sarah in later years, and I don't accept what Justine said about him. It's an insult. He was always a very good father.'

Yet Justine clearly felt that her preferences and desires away from the tennis court had somehow been ignored. She also felt, quite wrongly, it seems, that her father had made a clear choice in favour of his other children and against her.

José revealed, 'Later Justine came and said, "That was a bad mistake, to choose David and Thomas instead of me and Pierre-Yves."'

If José had made a mistake under the pressure of being the single parent of four children, it wasn't this. He was not the sort of man to take sides between his children, only against an outsider who had hurt one of them. But José's course of action was certainly as costly to him financially as it was emotionally.

Carlos Rodriguez has since alleged that it was Justine who first felt the financial impact of her departure from the family home. He told the *Sunday Times*, 'And then there was the money problem. When she left home at seventeen she had nothing – not ten Belgian francs. The [Belgian] federation had to pay everything for her.'

José accepts that she might have had no money in her pocket when she walked out of the door; but then she was only going to stay with her aunt around the corner. He insisted that money had already been placed in accounts for her, in readiness for when she turned eighteen. She had a highly professional management organisation, IMG, looking after many of her interests. And as her uncle Jean-Paul said, 'The feud hit José in the pocket a lot harder than it hit Justine. He was the one who was really hurt financially.'

José strenuously denied that he had ever tried to keep Justine's tennis earnings for himself. The fact that he still had so many financial problems in 2003 and early 2004 made the idea that he had somehow hidden away her early prize money seem laughable. The companies he had set up all those years ago, with the help of others, in order to finance her training and in the hope of some future return, were now in considerable trouble.

José insisted that they hadn't been created for selfish motives: 'I never made this choice in order to take Justine's money, it wasn't like that at all. It was to help her. It took a lot of money to finance Justine's tennis development over all those years. And I had recently been working from 7.30 a.m. until 8 p.m., every day, for her career. Before that, she had almost always had a member of the family travelling with her, all through childhood, right up until she was seventeen.

'The Belgian federation paid for her bedroom and when I travelled we used to take just one bedroom, to make it cheaper. I used to pay 50 per cent, so it was actually cheaper for the federation when I was there. Every month we paid a contribution for Carlos, and one for me to travel. We paid for the car and some tax, of course. Justine wasn't supposed to receive money anyway, because she wasn't yet eighteen. A lot went towards paying back people in the family who had invested in her career, when others weren't interested. She wasn't earning the sort of money she later earned, nothing like it.'

Rodriguez claimed that Justine relied heavily on the support of her aunts during the stormy period of the split between father and daughter. He said somewhat sweepingly, 'I must say that she was helped, too, by José's sisters, Françoise and Geneviève, and another woman friend who was related to the family. They were the only ones who were kind to her.'

But it was true that the Henin family had now split almost according to gender, and José had effectively lost his relationship with his sisters, too. He said later, 'The way I see it is this: Françoise seems to think she can criticise anyone, but if anyone dares to criticise her, my God – it's a war. She's not perfect – no one is. We all make mistakes. As for Geneviève, she may be the elder of the two sisters, but she just seems to take her lead from Françoise, so I don't have much to say about her.'

When I tried to talk to Françoise to get her side of the story in January 2004, Hugues Bastin answered the door. It was raining heavily and Bastin, the man who led Justine down the aisle, seemed to take a delight in his rudeness. 'I don't talk to journalists,' he said. 'Especially English journalists.' When I tried to ask if Françoise might be more amenable, he closed the door in my face. Though more polite, Geneviève was similarly reluctant to speak out.

I have been told that Geneviève did, however, feel there might have been a chance to heal the rift between Justine and her father back in 2000, before things went too far. But it soon became apparent that her niece's mind was more or less made up, and the sisters wanted to support her in any way they could. Both aunts would now have big roles to play in sustaining Justine's push for independence. The sisters and Justine were effectively doing it for themselves. Only months from her eighteenth birthday, Justine was nearly a woman. And in broad terms that trio of Henin women was no longer seeing eye to eye with several of their male relations.

* * *

By his own admission, José was never the most efficient of business administrators, particularly now that his financial base had suddenly been thrown into chaos by the family feud. The lifeblood of the companies he had set up – the income generated by Justine's tennis –

was obviously about to be cut off, as she prepared to go her own way under the guidance of other management groups.

José suddenly found himself in considerable trouble. In such ominous circumstances, it was hardly surprising that he didn't see fit to finance what he saw as Justine's termination of their sporting alliance. Having pumped money into the nurturing of his daughter's talent for twelve years, he now felt he had to protect what little financial stability remained in his life.

'I had made some mistakes in this area and I would be the first to admit it,' he said later. 'But I did at least deserve to get back some of the money that I had put in over all those years.'

Later, Justine often seemed reluctant to acknowledge much of her father's financial outlay. At the Australian Open in 2001, she was asked the following question: 'Your family, they had to invest a lot of money when you were a kid, in order to bring you up to your level when you were fourteen or fifteen?'

Justine replied, 'Yeah, for sure, but when I was twelve, and after that, the federation helped me a lot. It continues to help me. So the federation is my best, you know, my best help.'

Once her mother had died, it was the Belgian Tennis Federation that had carried her through, or so it seemed from what she said now. Her father's contribution appeared to have been played down. There was little recognition of his considerable efforts.

But José's obligations had been very real, just as they continued to be towards his other children. He still had a younger daughter to look after, and two mature yet sensitive sons to think about and although they were a source of strength to one another, the split from Justine felt, to José, like a public humiliation and didn't help his health. To make matters worse, the past came back to haunt him and caused another blow to his difficult relationship with his elder daughter.

José revealed, 'Some tactless person chose this moment to tell Justine about some of the problems that had existed in my marriage to her mother. The one-sided way the story was told gave Justine a further excuse to do what she wanted. But I repeat, not a day goes by when I don't miss Françoise. And whatever happened in our marriage, I really did love her and she loved me.'

Justine didn't seem to want to consider the fact that life isn't always as simple as we would like; that perhaps her mother might have been at least partially responsible for any complications in her marriage.

As her uncle Jean-Marie put it, 'She looked upon her mother like a saint and still does.'

If surviving relatives unwittingly threatened Justine's vision of the past, it seemed she simply didn't want to know them any more. She had the memory of her mother instead. And that memory would remain perfect, for who would ever dare to speak ill of the dead? Justine would continue to feel inspired by her mother, who wasn't there to question whether her daughter was doing the right thing by the rest of the family.

Justine would later complain, '. . . they all used to come to me with their problems, my two older brothers and my young sister. But it became difficult. I lead a very special life – I have to. But they didn't understand . . .'

And that was just the point. It was Justine's tennis talent that turned common family tensions into insurmountable barriers. José and Thomas, in particular, had made great sacrifices to help her nurture that talent. They had adored her; and perhaps José had also staked his own claim on her sporting adventure.

Jean-Marie told me, 'José was always a sportsman, and maybe he lived some of his sporting dreams through Justine, like his protégée.'

Now that Justine was preparing to pursue those dreams with others – Pierre-Yves and her coach – it was the Henin men who felt cheated, since they were the ones who had previously opened the way for her.

* * *

Many family rifts can be bridged, frayed ties repaired. But the world of professional tennis doesn't necessarily lend itself to the regeneration of fractured family relationships. The entourage closes in around the player, who can easily become convinced that only a 'tie-break' from that troublesome family can clear the path to glory. A sense of responsibility to the past can become blurred, particularly when the loved one who mattered most is dead; and when surviving family members don't behave in a convenient way, it seems they can simply be wiped off the emotional map.

CHAPTER 8

Only a Baby

Fundamental changes in Justine's personal life during those first months of 2000 meant she would take time to settle down to the business of climbing the tennis ladder still further. It was during this period that her contract with IMG ran out, and in June, when she turned eighteen, she signed up with a Luxembourg-based company, Vincent Stavaux's Management and Consulting.

The move went against her father's advice, and seemed to strengthen the position of Carlos Rodriguez as Justine's coach even more. A mighty international force such as IMG had many talented coaches of all nationalities at its disposal, and Justine's promise was attracting interest worldwide as well as closer to home. While he had still been in a position of influence, José had discussed the possibility of replacing Rodriguez. But it was José, not Carlos, who was to be cut out of the loop. The new allegiance to Stavaux seemed to provide greater long-term stability for Rodriguez, a man who had done so much good work for the Belgian federation. In truth, however, it didn't matter who was supplying the management, because the removal of José from the backroom line-up was proof enough of the enduring bond between coach and player. No one could have turned Justine against her mentor at this stage. She left her father and didn't regret it.

She later told the *Observer Sport Monthly*, 'When I took the decision to leave, it was probably the best thing I did for years. I am not afraid to lose now. But before I left, I was under a lot of pressure. Everybody was taking the decisions that should have been mine.'

Rodriguez was clearly her preference, and he was to remain one of the few constants in her life. The coach's next task was to set about getting Justine's mind and body right for a new assault on the summit of world tennis.

For a while they seemed trapped at base camp. A nagging elbow injury meant she was forced to withdraw from Antwerp and the all-important French Open at Roland Garros. Still rusty, she was knocked out in the first round at Wimbledon, although she gave the highly rated Arantxa Sanchez Vicario quite a fright during a topsy-turvy 1–6, 6–1, 1–6 defeat.

To add to her woes, Justine was forced to retire from a tournament in Filderstadt and then withdrew from Quebec City as a result of inflammation of the toe joints. But it was at the US Open that she really found her feet and gave a further indication of what was to come. She beat twelfth-seeded Anna Kournikova, ranked fourteenth in the world and the game's most glamorous player. That put Justine in the top 50 for the first time.

She was ambivalent in her praise of Kournikova afterwards: 'I think she is a really nice girl. She likes her look, and everybody likes her look. But I am not here to do cinema. I am here to play tennis and I think that's the most important.'

But Justine's tennis wasn't yet strong enough to beat the big guns. She ran into Lindsay Davenport, who was simply devastating in front of a patriotic crowd, and took the match 6–0, 6–4.

A shell-shocked Henin went off to learn the lessons of that drubbing with her coach. She might be on the verge of the big time, but she wasn't there yet.

Still, a place in the last sixteen was enough to suggest that one day soon she really could make that ultimate breakthrough.

* * *

In her personal life, big changes were afoot. Justine was so happy with Pierre-Yves that they moved in together, taking a simple flat above a butcher's shop on the rue de la Station in Marloie, near Han-sur-Lesse. It was quite a step for the young lovers to take, but how else could they maximise their precious time together, away from the pressures of the tour? Much as Justine adored her aunts, she was eighteen now and felt it was time to strike out on her own.

Pierre-Yves decided to sacrifice his studies, so he could dedicate himself to supporting her on tour in any way he could. The alternative would have been to live apart for half of each year, and neither of them wanted that. They were falling more and more deeply for each other, and although Pierre-Yves risked compromising his own independence by building his life around Justine's, it was a risk he was prepared to take.

For José, however, this development looked like a confirmation of all his worst fears. He also felt Pierre-Yves didn't deserve his new lifestyle. José, after all, had spent more than a decade on tour with his daughter, spending all the spare cash he had – and plenty he didn't – to help put her on the verge of sporting greatness. Now that she was so close, and he saw hope of a return on his huge expenditure, José had been cast aside. The frustration was almost too much to bear and he seethed at what he perceived as the injustice of it all.

What José couldn't see, and might not have wanted to contemplate in any detail, was that Pierre-Yves was making Justine ecstatically happy in a way he never could. Pierre-Yves was an integral part of her new life, her new identity – her independence. In the long run, that meant he would be incredibly good for her tennis, too. But José couldn't know that, not at such an early stage. He worried that if tennis had a rival for Justine's attentions and there was no 'narrow focus' as before, she could never hope to take the next step and rise above Davenport and the rest to become a true champion.

In fact, Justine was as focused and as ambitious as ever; Pierre-Yves had helped enhance all her hopes and remove the emotional complications in her heart. The more defined the new family boundaries, the better Justine played, or so it seemed. And the better Justine played, the more frustrating it was for her family to be excluded.

Her 2001 campaign took off in Australia, where she won tournaments on the Gold Coast and in Canberra, beating world number thirteen Chanda Rubin on her way to ten straight victories. It was the first time since Pam Shriver in 1988 that anyone had taken successive tournaments prior to the year's first Grand Slam. Her long lay-off the previous summer had left her fresh and hungry, although she was feeling the pressure of such an incredible start by the time she reached Melbourne for the big one.

Even so, the victories kept coming. She outfought Tatiana Poutchek, winning 6–4, 7–5 in the first round of the Australian Open; and Sarah Pitkowski-Malcor proved an even easier opponent in the second. After that 6–3, 6–2 triumph, Justine was relaxed enough to give an extremely revealing press conference.

'Mentally I think I am not afraid to lose now,' she explained. 'I am not so nervous as last year and I think I can play without problems in my head. I had injuries and I had personal problems last year and now it is in the past and I can do my best on court . . . I am here with my coach and fiancé.'

So for those who didn't yet know, the secret was well and truly out.

'When are you getting married?' she was asked.

'Married?' She said it almost as though that wasn't what a fiancé was for.

'Yes,' the interviewer replied simply.

Justine smiled and answered, 'I think in the next two years.'

And so it was that Justine told the media at a Grand Slam event something she hadn't even mentioned to her father.

She claimed a third-round win over the fourteenth seed, the French girl Sandrine Testud, whom she had already beaten that year. This time Justine needed to take time out in the second set to have a blister treated, but the opportunity to have a break and collect her thoughts worked in her favour. She won 6–2, 6–4, to notch up an incredible thirteen straight victories for the year so far. It also paved the way for a titanic battle against the fiery and formidable Monica Seles in the fourth round.

Here she was in a Grand Slam, about to face Seles, the girl she had watched as a ten-year-old spectator at Roland Garros alongside her mother. Although Monica wasn't quite the force she had been when she beat Justine's heroine, Steffi Graf, in that French Open final, she was still seeded number four. So she was stunned when Justine took the first set 6–4. At that stage, it looked as though no one could bring a halt to her early 2001 momentum. But Seles struck back, almost every shot accompanied by her trademark unnerving yelp. The American took the second set 6–4 and maintained momentum to close out the match by the same margin in the last.

Justine and Pierre-Yves returned to Europe, where the proud husband-to-be announced their engagement to the Belgian media. Absorbing the news he hadn't been given personally, Justine's father said, 'Whatever problems we've had, my place is with my daughter on that day, leading her down the aisle. That's where I still hope to be.'

Ignoring such complications as best she could, Justine went on to play more tennis in Nice, but lost to Magdalena Maleeva. Even so, she knew that her life was progressing at a furious pace. Recently her career and her personal life had taken such huge strides that her family was struggling to keep up.

Excited, Justine crossed the Atlantic to the USA, for tournaments in Scottsdale, Indian Wells and Key Biscayne. Then quite suddenly, inexplicably, things started to go wrong. She was knocked out in the first round at Scottsdale by the little-known Spaniard Magüi Serna, who won two tie-breaks to seal victory.

Henin thrashed Kim Clijsters 6–1 in the first set of a third-round tie at Indian Wells, only to lose the next two 3–6, 4–6. It was a result that was to return to haunt her sooner than she suspected. Closing out a match against her younger rival seldom came easy after that first, emphatic thrashing she had administered to a shell-shocked blonde child in Ostend.

The Ericsson Open at Key Biscayne began well enough. Justine had a bye in the first round and then beat Elena Bovina 6–2, 6–2. She was based in a hotel in Miami and was surprised to receive, right out of the blue, a call from home. It was her brother, Thomas. In a faltering voice, he broke the news that his six-week-old baby son was dead. Justine's nephew, the infant she had never held or got to know, had fallen victim to lung failure.

* * *

Even in 2004, Thomas and his girlfriend, Vanessa, still found it difficult to utter their baby's name, such was their lingering distress over what happened. Through Thomas, Vanessa requested that I respect her private grief by omitting the baby's name from my book. Naturally I have complied with her wishes, although Thomas still wanted to tell me the extraordinary story of how his sister responded when he asked for her support in his darkest hour.

José supplied the background to this bleak moment. He said, 'Thomas had woken at about four in the morning, looked at his baby and seen immediately that something was seriously wrong. By seven o'clock I received a phone call from Thomas at the hospital, and he sounded distraught. I feared the worst and went over immediately. His baby had died of lung failure. Thomas fell into my arms and the very first thing he said was, "I want Justine to come back."'

'But I warned Thomas not to call her, that she would not say the things that he needed to hear, that she would not be there for him as he had been for her in the past. I warned him it might cause him even more pain. But he made the call anyway, he felt he had to.'

At first he did hear the words he hoped to hear from his sister. He recalled, 'The initial conversation was very good, considering everything. She said she wanted to be near me. I asked her to come. I said that we were waiting for her. Her reply was that she had a match to play the following day and she would see if she could come. But she didn't. I think the other people close to her didn't want this.'

Thomas rejected the idea that his bereavement coincided with a crucial moment in her career and that she simply couldn't return home. 'We always knew she had talent, and her talent was always going to come out, it didn't depend on that moment in time,' he said.

Justine probably felt obliged to respect her professional commitments, although Thomas failed to see how such pressure could have excused her subsequent silence. He added, 'I have a heart but I don't know if she has got one. I can't understand why she didn't have the time to write to me. Not one letter or one word. Nothing. No call. She is really another girl. She is an individualist, which may be normal, but not in this context.'

* * *

You can almost understand Justine's dilemma. Her relationship with Thomas was now significantly less important to her than her relationship with Pierre-Yves. She was free from the past, doing things her way. She knew she could make her tennis dreams come true, but suddenly a fresh tragedy threatened to pull her back into the old world, the old order. Whatever her reasoning she tried to focus on her tennis, supported by her coach. But she lost 3–6, 1–6 to a little-known Italian called Tathiana Garbin.

As far as the Henin men were concerned, there should have been no dilemma at all – and no match. Justine's grandfather, Alphonse, later summed up the family's feelings when he sighed and said, 'Thomas was there with his son dead. And she told him she had a tennis match the next day. As if a tennis match can count in life like a death.'

And three years after this disturbing episode, Jeanne Henin, Justine's grandmother, was clearly still struggling to come to terms with the family's loss, just like the infant's parents. Her voice faltering, she said, 'He was only a baby and he died so quickly.'

So the Henin family grieved without Justine and tried to come to terms with the scarcely believable reality of another infant death; another merciless twist of fate on top of all the others.

* * *

Justine remained absorbed by her career. There were spring tournaments to play when she returned to Europe, and soon there would be the ultimate challenge of Roland Garros. Now that she was ranked twenty in the world, she was getting some real respect at last. Big-name opponents didn't seem to fancy taking her on any more, and she wanted to build on her growing reputation.

In early May, she played the Eurocard Ladies German Open in Berlin. She beat the South African Joanette Kruger and the German Jana Kandarr, before facing the might of world number two Venus Williams in the third round. It was their first meeting, and the Williams family didn't quite know what Venus was letting herself in for. The outcome of that third-round showdown sent shockwaves through tennis, putting Henin's name on everyone's lips for the first time. Despite being dwarfed by the American, Justine pulverised her opponent 6–1 in a truly breathtaking first set. Before Williams could recover, she found herself having to shake hands and take a shower. Henin had taken the second set 6–4 and the tennis community struggled to find an explanation.

To her credit, Venus wasn't about to make excuses. In fact, she made a remark as generous as it was prophetic: 'If Justine played like this every day, she would be number one in the world.'

Henin accepted that she had played like a number one to register 'such a big win'. As for reaching top spot one day, she said, 'I am eighteen and have many years before me. I must wait. Today was a big success, but I must become more consistent. But it works well at the moment. I played wonderful tennis. I hit many balls to the middle of the court, which Venus doesn't particularly like.'

Miriam Schnitzer, a German outsider who had progressed to the quarter-final on home ground, was brushed aside 6–4, 6–2, and suddenly Justine was in the semi-final against the highly talented Jennifer Capriati. Henin stormed to a 6–2 first-set win, but lost the second 6–4. With the match in the balance – in the third set she was actually leading 2–1 – a sprained right ankle halted her progress. It wouldn't be the last epic battle between those two. The pain barrier would become familiar to both in virtually every big match they played against each other.

But it was a different kind of pain from the one still being felt in the Henin family. Bereavement, combined with Justine's distant attitude to many of her relatives, made for a stressful time. José's parents, Alphonse and Jeanne, struggled to understand it all, particularly the seemingly selfish way their granddaughter had reacted. Tennis was not a matter of life and death, and they were shocked by what she had done. But Justine was young, and one day she would see the error of her ways, they felt. Since tennis was her chosen course, and her talent God-given, her grandparents would not ignore her big matches. They would follow her progress on television and see where it took her.

The next destination was Roland Garros, Justine's theatre of dreams. The French Open would soon be upon them.

CHAPTER 9

Alphonse

It was like a dream. Justine Henin had stormed into the French Open semi-final and she was playing well enough to make that outrageous promise to her late mother come true. She wouldn't be playing on the famous Court Central, now known as the Court Philippe Chatrier. The venue for her semi-final would be the other great show court at Roland Garros, the Court Suzanne Lenglen. And Justine's opponent would be her friend and compatriot, Kim Clijsters. Someone up there would be looking after her; this was just meant to be.

Sure enough, Justine came out like a whirlwind and Clijsters had no answer. In no time, Henin had taken a 5–1 first-set lead, with the sort of crushing tennis no one can counter. Then the heavens opened and the rain fell, giving her opponent temporary respite. It didn't alter the course of the first set, though, and when they resumed Justine took it 6–2.

* * *

Back home, her 81-year-old maternal grandfather, Georges Rosière, was ecstatic. In the past, he had lost his wife and daughter so tragically and prematurely to cancer. Now he was comforted to see Justine making the most of her sporting opportunities. It seemed they were closer than ever, and, unlike the other men in the family, he had accepted Pierre-Yves. Many Sundays spent together had shown him how happy the young man was making Justine. But perhaps nothing could make her quite as content as the prospect of keeping that promise to her mother, Françoise, to play in a final at Roland Garros.

At the end of the rue de Grottes, Justine's other surviving grand-parents, Alphonse and Jeanne, were with their sons, cheering 'Ju-Ju' all the way. Family recriminations were on hold. This was a huge moment in their granddaughter's life and they were going to enjoy it as though they were actually in the stadium with her.

Justine saw her dream within touching distance and reached out to grab it. She broke Kim again early in the second set, and although the magic wasn't quite as evident as it had been before the interruption for rain, she had her opponent on the run at 4–2. With fate and perhaps even her mother's will on her side, it seemed that nothing could take this triumph away from her now. She looked ready to forge further ahead and put her Flemish friend out of her misery. She was cruising, and then she took her foot off the pedal.

At that moment, it all started to slip away, and she didn't know why. Three more break points were squandered. Mentally, for all her new-found independence, Henin was growing weaker by the second. Clijsters must have sensed what everyone could see with their own eyes – Justine was 'choking'. Not the prettiest of terms, it is the one chosen by tennis professionals to describe what happens when the finishing line is in sight and the enormity of the achievement dawns on the player about to win. Suddenly, they start going backwards, the occasion becomes too much for them and nothing in the world can alter the new, cruel course of the match.

Clijsters battled back from nowhere to take the second set 7–5, when she and everyone else knew she ought to have been in the showers, having wished Justine luck for the final. Justine's magic had evaporated. Where was her mother's inspiration now? What was happening to her strength, her determination? Try as she might, she couldn't seem to find a foothold in the final set either.

* * *

Back in Belgium, the blood pressure rose among the family elders. No one could believe what had now begun to unfold. Georges Rosière knew better than anyone what victory would mean for Justine if she could just turn the tide, and how devastated she would feel if her promise to her mother were not kept. Like all Henin supporters, he must have experienced a sick, sinking feeling in the pit of his stomach, and a sense of utter helplessness.

Down on the rue de Grottes, Justine's other grandfather, Alphonse, had watched with horror as Justine's game disintegrated. He willed her to perform to her true potential; he played every point with her, trying to lend her his own strength. But there was precious

ABOVE: Florence Henin, Justine's sister, who was tragically killed before she reached her third birthday.

MAIN PICTURE: Perfect memories: Justine and her father José enjoy a family holiday in beautiful Canada.

BELOW: The joy of a second daughter: Françoise Henin with Justine at José's local football club.

LEFT: Just married! José and Françoise Henin are a picture of happiness on their wedding day.

ABOVE RIGHT: Four generations: Alphonse, baby Florence, Julienne, who survived the dreadful car accident, and José.

BELOW RIGHT: Jeanne and José with Florence, this time held by Marie, who died soon after her great-granddaughter.

OPPOSITE (MAIN PICTURE): In her element: a nine-year-old Justine is already showing off her tennis talent.

INSET (ABOVE RIGHT): Justine is already the centre of attention alongside José and her brothers, Thomas and David.

INSET (LEFT): A family united: David, Justine, Thomas, Sarah and Françoise, proudly photographed by José.

LEFT: Don't step on my red suede shoes! Justine shows some early rhythm on the dance floor.

RIGHT: A proud mother: Françoise watches over Justine and Sarah on another family outing.

BELOW: Still a loving couple: José and Françoise are all smiles alongside a ten-year-old Justine.

RIGHT: Football was Justine's first love and, as a seven-year-old, she looked the part.

LEFT: The first of many: Justine, alongside fellow Belgian child-star Olivier Rochus, shows off an early trophy. A decade later, Rochus attended her wedding.

RIGHT: Georges Rosière, who died hours before his granddaughter's Wimbledon final, pictured here with Sarah and Jeanne.

LEFT: Friends and early rivals: Justine Henin and Kim Clijsters, aged eleven and ten years old respectively.

BELOW: Doubles partners and compatriots: in their early teens, Justine and Kim used to room together.

Winner and loser: as Justine savours
glory at the US Open, 2003, Kim can
only gaze longingly at the trophy –
not for the first or last time at a
Grand Slam final.

LEFT: Calm before the storm: Justine's coach, Carlos Rodriguez, and her father, José, once got along just fine.

RIGHT: Inseparable sisters: Justine and Sarah were so close until tennis got in the way. Perhaps they will become friends again.

BELOW: First taste of true stardom: Justine Henin wins the Junior French Open at Roland Garros in 1997.

little strength left in either grandfather or granddaughter; and the more Justine's form slipped away, the more anxious Alphonse became.

Meanwhile, at Roland Garros, Kim swiftly put Justine out of her misery. She had pulled off one of the great Grand Slam comebacks to win the final set 6-3, and her compatrict's dream was shattered.

Justine tried to collect her thoughts and fight her despair. Even after such a soul-destroying defeat, she was anxious to understand what had happened. Hadn't she said earlier in the tournament that she had learnt how to play the pivotal points in a match? What could she offer by way of explanation, if she were asked what on earth had happened out there?

In Han-sur-Lesse, the Henin family was carrying out a similar investigation into what had gone wrong. Alphonse recalled, 'Jean-Marie, Justine's uncle, was particularly animated, to the point of being angry because she had lost. I was agitated as well, because she should have won it, and we were arguing about what had gone wrong. Then something happened to me.

'Suddenly, I was staggering around and slurring my words, talking as though I were drunk. Jean-Paul's wife, Clelia, thought I really was drunk. But it was actually the blood clots forming on my brain.'

Jean-Paul soon realised there was something seriously wrong with his father. He helped Alphonse gently into his car and rushed him to hospital in nearby Dinant. Jean-Paul was frightened by now and recalled, 'I was driving along and he was talking rubbish about how pretty the Christmas lights were. It was June and he was actually talking about the lights on the motorway.'

* * *

Unaware of the makings of yet another family tragedy, Justine began her post-match press conference. 'It was almost perfect,' she said wistfully. 'But mentally I was becoming weak . . . It was in my head. At this time I perhaps thought nothing could happen.'

Was it possible that she felt so strongly that her mother was with her, and all this was meant to be, that she thought she could simply sit back and let destiny do the rest? Momentarily, she had forgotten that you make your own destiny in sport, as in the rest of life. Clijsters had needed only a moment, a small flicker of hope, to carve out her own destiny on the day.

Having already sacrificed one winning advantage in a less important match against Kim Clijsters at Indian Wells, there lurked in Justine the suspicion that she had begun to develop a mental block when it came to beating her compatriot. 'Maybe I have problems concluding matches against Kim,' she conceded. 'If it had been another player as my opponent, I might have won 6–2, 6–2 . . . Playing a player from your country is not easy . . . It's not a question of being friends with her. It's simply that I was on the point of doing something great, to be in the finals of a Grand Slam tournament. Maybe if it had been somebody else, it would have been easier, obviously.'

The Clijsters jinx would have to be addressed and conquered sooner or later. But even at this apparent professional low point, Justine was reassured by the fact that she had reached the top ten for the first time. She wasn't about to give up now.

* * *

Alphonse wasn't a quitter either. The doctors in Dinant identified the problem – blood clots on the brain – quickly and managed to save him. He had been down and almost out, but he had found enough of the famous Henin willpower to survive his ordeal. Although it would take several weeks in hospital before he would recover sufficiently to leave his bed, Alphonse was still alive. He couldn't speak properly, and it would be a while before the ability to form clear words returned. But he had time to reflect upon the fact that tennis, though not in itself a matter of life and death, had very nearly caused his own sudden departure from his family's troubled world.

Meanwhile, Justine was still preoccupied with her tennis, and talked in some depth with her coach, Carlos Rodriguez, about what had gone wrong at Roland Garros. Both were determined to ensure that it would never happen again. Did the fear of failure, the feeling she sometimes used to experience when her father was in closer attendance, still lurk somewhere within her? Had it left her too afraid to relax and win when victory was there for the taking?

Next time she would be perfectly conditioned to seize her opportunity. Within 48 hours, therefore, she was back in training. For the first steps of her sporting recovery, she chose a synthetic surface in Belgium, the closest she could find to grass, pre-Wimbledon. That also gave her the chance to visit her grandfather as he made his slow recovery.

Alphonse smiled when he remembered: 'She came to the hospital in Dinant with Geneviève. We talked, although I couldn't really get out many words. I didn't say it had happened because of the match. I didn't want to hurt her.'

In their own different ways, Justine and Alphonse had just faced critical moments in their lives, and each had survived to fight another day.

Perhaps humbled for a while by the pain of Roland Garros, Justine's attitude to her father José softened for a while. José recalled, 'She was down after the defeat to Clijsters and she came to see me twice. She even brought along Pierre-Yves. We went to see some houses in the country near Rochefort with a view to Justine buying one, and we got on well. She was going to play a grass-court tournament at Rosmalen in Holland and said she would call me from there. She didn't do it, but of course it was nearly time for Wimbledon then. I didn't call her or push it, I was just happy that we had enjoyed that contact together away from tennis. I heard later from someone that she had told her coach how much happier she felt after our meeting.'

Now Justine's father had reason to hope that he would be able to play a principal role in their wedding plans after all. She was remembering her family again at last. Perhaps the worst was over.

* * *

Before the warm-up tournaments for Wimbledon began, Justine also found time for Georges Rosière. His unconditional support and acceptance of Pierre-Yves meant that 'Papy', as Justine called him, would continue to enjoy a prominent place in his granddaughter's life.

Like everyone else, he had felt the first impact of her love affair with Pierre-Yves and had noticed how he had started to see less of his favourite girl. While some elderly men in his position might have complained about the selfishness of youth, Georges had found the perfect solution instead. He invited the young lovers around for lunch whenever Justine was free, and with his warmth made it a pleasurable experience for Pierre-Yves, too.

This was the faith and recognition Pierre-Yves had been seeking from Justine's family. Georges didn't judge him and he didn't tell Justine what to do. He merely loved her, and followed her matches with a passion equal to that of the younger grandfather, Alphonse. Georges couldn't wait for Wimbledon; he savoured every minute of her meteoric rise. Here was another big stage on which Justine might emulate and perhaps even surpass her remarkable run at the previous Grand Slam in France.

CHAPTER 10

Wimbledon

Even though Justine took confidence from a victory over Kim Clijsters in the final at Rosmalen, she must have known deep down that the match had been relatively unimportant to her opponent after what had gone before. And Henin really shouldn't have got anywhere near the Wimbledon quarter-final, having trailed in the second round against Kristie Boogert, 5–7, 1–4, with a break point against her. But then Justine's famous never-say-die spirit came into play, and she hit back to win 5–7, 7–5, 6–2. She wasn't the finished article by any means, but what she lacked in polish and consistency, she made up for in guts. Deep down, Henin must have begun to realise that she was still mentally stronger than most of the other girls on the circuit and that no situation was irretrievable. Opponents who had the upper hand also knew that one mistake against Justine could leave them on a slippery slope to defeat. Having been on the receiving end of such a dreadful semi-final experience in Paris, Henin was fast becoming the queen of comebacks herself.

Meanwhile, in Belgium, Justine's grandfathers had been to hell and back watching yet another cliffhanger of a confrontation. What her sporting return from the dead had done to their blood pressure was unknown at this time. After what had happened to Alphonse during Roland Garros, both men knew that supporting Justine, especially at their age, could be a perilous business indeed. On the other hand, what else were they supposed to do? Should they potter about in the garden during her big matches and pretend that their beloved granddaughter wasn't doing battle in one of the biggest tournaments of her life? Not knowing how she was faring would probably make them feel even worse.

Part of José hoped that his daughter would call home. Five minutes of her time would allow him to feel more involved with her Wimbledon campaign, if only from a distance. What harm could it do? José knew he had made mistakes, pushed Justine too hard, been intolerant of her boyfriend, too demanding himself. Most daughters have to break away from their parents to establish their own identity. He understood that, and he didn't begrudge her her new-found independence, on which she seemed to thrive. He hoped that she and her brother could be friends again one day; and he wanted her to understand that he wasn't taking sides. José loved all his children equally and he didn't want to lose any of them, especially not after what had happened to Florence.

He felt sure that he and Justine could enter a new era, and forge a fresh understanding based on the fact that she was now an adult. If that meant a father-daughter relationship on her terms rather than his, then so be it. He would keep his distance and give her space, and he certainly wouldn't go to Wimbledon. A phone call would have been nice, though, considering the fact that the tournament was going so well for her now. But José had been disappointed by his daughter's behaviour before, and he wasn't exactly staring at the phone, waiting for it to ring. As it turned out, that was just as well. Justine was concentrating on her tennis

In the quarter-final, she struck her very best form to annihilate the highly respected Conchita Martinez. The Spaniard didn't know what had hit her and the 6–1, 6–0 scoreline bordered on humiliation. Henin's game, already renowned for its punishing backhand, had moved into overdrive. What really impressed observers during this match was the way Justine's forehand shone through to equal her favourite shot in lethal force. When her racket was flowing on both sides, the girl from Belgium was simply unstoppable.

Now the whole world was talking about her. She had reached her second successive Grand Slam semi-final and claimed the nightmare of Roland Garros had only made her stronger. She explained, 'Now I have more experience. I will enjoy this moment more . . . I was 6–2, 4–2 up in Paris and I didn't win the match. Maybe if I have the possibility here, I will not make the same mistake.'

In the rarefied atmosphere of the last four, Justine needed to adapt quickly. Her climb towards the summit of world tennis had come at a frightening pace. She was asked, 'If someone had told you at the beginning of the year that you would be in two Grand Slam semi-finals this year, what would you have said to them?'

Justine answered, 'I wouldn't have believed them, for sure, because I was ranked 45 at the beginning of the year. I was 100 one year ago. So everything was so fast. I played so well this year.'

* * *

Her talent was pushing her into unknown territory. She needed a dose of normality, if indeed anything could be normal in her life.

Back in the gateway to the Ardennes, Georges Rosière picked up the phone. While many wanted to speak to Justine at this special time, unconditional love found a way through. There was nothing emotionally draining or complicated about talking to a man who had supported her so gently since the death of her mother, his daughter. Besides, Justine was as keen to hear a wise old man's perspective on these heady times as her beloved 'Papy' was to congratulate her.

The conversation must have been particularly sweet. It was always an extra delight for Justine to know the happiness her success had brought him, the pride he felt in her achievements. At the same time, a familiar voice from home brought welcome reassurance.

Georges might have been old and wise, but he was as excited as anyone over her march to another Grand Slam semi-final. He knew what it would mean for her future. He could feel encouraged by the fact that she now seemed to be on the verge of a truly glittering career, and was swept away by the sheer thrill of it all. Georges was happy for Justine, pleased that all her hard work had paid off with two massive tournaments in as many months. But they both knew what her triumphs would have meant to Françoise, too. In many ways, she was still the driving force behind Justine's breakthrough into the big time. Maybe, somewhere up there, Françoise was savouring these moments, just like her father and daughter.

* * *

Justine's amazing tennis journey, however, wasn't quite complete. Was she ready to take the final step? She had already surpassed all expectations and therefore anything more here at Wimbledon would be a bonus. As she stepped out for the semi-final, no one knew if that mind-set would work in her favour or not.

Perhaps Jennifer Capriati picked up on a sense of disorientation in her opponent. Sensing a chink in the Belgian's psychological armour, she strode on to Centre Court and began to demolish Justine. The American was faster than ever, while Henin struggled to read the bounce. She was suffering from a horrible blister on her right foot. That in turn brought on extra nerves, and suddenly she had lost the first set 2–6. She thought about quitting, the pain was so bad. To make matters worse, she was soon 1–2 down in the second. The match was beginning to look ridiculously one-sided. Capriati was clearly in no mood to be humiliated in the same way as Martinez. Already having won two Grand Slams that year, she was after the hat-trick.

Back in Belgium, the most important person in Justine's life sat shell-shocked in the Rochefort tennis club, where Justine had played day and night as a six-year-old. As her boyfriend, Pierre-Yves had attracted the attention of the local media and was pictured there in various states of anguish. As he watched the worst of the semi-final, the cameras caught his face contorted as though he, too, was experiencing Justine's pain. Limbs flailed, their young owner clearly helpless with frustration. Pierre-Yves had thrown his hands up in horror at what he was seeing, and another dream seemed to evaporate before his eyes.

Georges Rosière and Alphonse Henin, the elders of Justine's family, felt their pulses quicken once again. Whoever said it was easy when you were related to a sporting phenomenon? Multiply the passion and concern of an average fan by about ten, and you might begin to understand what Justine's grandfathers went through every time she was in trouble in a big tournament. After what had happened to him last time, Alphonse tried to take an emotional step away from what he could see on his television screen.

Across the English Channel, however, Justine wasn't quite ready to be labelled the 'nearly girl' of 2001, or dismissed as a 'choker' who crumbled whenever a Grand Slam final appearance came into sight. She remembered the horror of Roland Garros and she recalled how she had vowed to bounce back. By now she had seen the trainer to get her blister treated. A new bandage worked wonders for the mind, even though the foot still didn't look good. Justine couldn't quit now, it wouldn't be right. She decided to play on through the pain barrier. Refusing to panic, she finally found a foothold in the second set.

She knew she could beat Capriati if she put her mind to it. She thought back to Berlin, where she had taken Jennifer to a third set and only retired because of an injured ankle. She wasn't going to quit now, even though her foot was a mess. Physical pain was nothing compared to defeat, so Justine overcame it. She began to play her natural game and looked more comfortable. Back at the clubhouse in Rochefort, a glimmer of hope returned to Pierre-Yves's eyes.

Then Justine broke Capriati and even began to look confident. The American, who had previously seemed so unbeatable, couldn't find a quick answer. Suddenly, Justine was level, having hit back to take the second set 6–4. These all-conquering Americans weren't so tough when they were forced on to the back foot. They had nerves and self-doubt like anyone else if put under pressure.

Alphonse, who was still recovering from blood clots on the brain, tried to control his emotions, for fear of inviting them back. Perhaps tennis ought to come with a health warning. Down by the courts where Justine had learnt the game, there was uproar as her friends sensed the tide turning. Inevitably, the strong local beer began to flow. To add to the volatile mix, José had arrived to watch the match unfold in close proximity to the young man who had turned his world upside down. Regulars at the Rochefort club watched with interest to see whether the fireworks in the bar would match the epic developing over the water.

Back at Wimbledon, Justine's adrenaline was pumping with equal vigour. She had the upper hand now, and Capriati was beginning to wonder where her early dominance had gone. The English crowd was on the Belgian girl's side; they sensed the little underdog could cause a huge upset. Henin broke again, and soon she was on that dangerous home straight. Just as in Paris, Justine could touch a Grand Slam final; it was within her reach.

In Belgium, Georges waited to see if the match would slip through her fingers yet again, while Alphonse simply waited to see if he could get through the match in one piece. At opposite ends of the Rochefort clubhouse, José and Pierre-Yves held their breath. Although they were only on uneasy speaking terms, the two men were experiencing exactly the same excitement now. Separately, they willed the girl they both loved not to tighten or weaken.

Justine had promised that, if faced with this situation again, she wouldn't make the same mistakes as at Roland Garros. She had vowed to seize her chance and make sure she enjoyed the moment. If she needed any added incentive, there was the desolation of defeat against Clijsters in France, still such a vivid memory. Justine had talked it through with her coach, Carlos Rodriguez. They wouldn't allow such a psychological collapse to occur a second time. She was programmed now to be more ruthless, to maintain the stranglehold.

Point by point, Henin squeezed all remaining hope out of Capriati, until finally she had really done it: another legendary comeback, 2–6, 6–4, 6–2. Mission accomplished with a deadly finish. Pierre-Yves was ecstatic and now the cameras captured his joy. José also felt immeasurable pride in his daughter's courage, and hopeful for the future as never before. With that in mind, he walked up to Pierre-Yves and shook him by the hand. It was a small but extraordinary gesture, almost one of congratulation. José understood that Pierre-Yves was in pole position now where his daughter's affections were concerned. He seemed to sense this semi-final win was more their triumph than his, since he had played only a minor part in his daughter's recent life. The handshake suggested that he was prepared to accept the new order of things, in return perhaps for a little consideration. If Pierre-Yves wasn't exactly warm, he appeared to accept the olive branch for what it was. Now he would pack his bags and join her for the final. His stint teaching tennis at summer school could wait 48 hours. A Wimbledon final was not to be missed.

José, however, knew that he himself would not be there to watch his daughter on the biggest day of her career. No matter. It was more important that her build-up was uncomplicated by his presence. He wanted her to have the best possible chance. Perhaps his reward would be that Pierre-Yves would tell Justine what had taken place; explain how her father was showing signs of accepting him into the family at last. Whatever happened, he would support her from afar.

Alphonse was delighted. Justine had won and he wasn't any worse for wear. Georges Rosière was jumping for joy at home, overwhelmed by the magic of the day. He wouldn't call his granddaughter; she would have so much to deal with after such a great victory. There would be yet another press conference, more questions, more adulation. This was her moment. Let her live it to the full, and he would hope to see her soon after her return to Belgium.

* * *

Sure enough, Justine was facing the journalists yet again in the bowels of Centre Court. She said, 'I think it's a big victory for me mentally. Yes, mentally I'm stronger than Paris.'

Asked if she had been close to quitting, she replied, 'Maybe at the beginning of the second set, because it was getting worse and worse. It was time for me to call the trainer. But I did it a little bit too late. After the changeover, she changed a little bit of my tape. It was better. I stood the pain. But when I broke her in the second, I said, "Give everything that you have and go until the end of the match, win or lose." '

The next question Justine was asked was about her coach. Her answer showed how closely Carlos Rodriguez now protected her, and how he had begun to assume the paternal role.

She explained, 'We've been working together for five years now. I was fourteen when I started with him. If I didn't have Carlos, I wouldn't be here today because I think he's a coach, he's a friend, he is everything for me. I can talk with him about my personal life or tennis life. I think he knows what to say to me for myself.'

Her reply to a question about the reaction to her success back home in Belgium was even more revealing. 'I suppose it's unbelievable in Belgium. I don't want to have any contacts with Belgium now because, you know, I have an important match on Saturday. After that, for sure, I will go back to Belgium. I will feel it a lot. I am so happy for the Belgian people, too.'

'No messages yet?' she was asked by a surprised interviewer.

'Maybe to my coach, but not to me because I had a lot of things to do just after my match. For sure, this evening I will get a lot of messages. But I try to stay focused on the tournament and stay focused on the next match.'

So there it was. She didn't want to talk to anyone. And Carlos Rodriguez could filter any messages for her. When she didn't want them, she could switch those family contacts off like a light. Even her father had to speak to her coach if he wanted to get through to Justine. And if Carlos couldn't see the benefit, it just wasn't going to happen.

Justine's entourage was rising like a protective wall around her. But clearly her life was only taking this turn because she wanted it to. The tennis was what really mattered, and she wasn't about to let anything else get in the way. Not when one more giant-killing would bring her the Wimbledon title.

'Now I am in the final, I just want to win. If I play against a strong player, I am not afraid of the size. I can also be a strong player when I want.'

Nothing was going to stop Justine from walking out on Centre Court with a clear head.

CHAPTER 11

Georges

When José decided to call Carlos Rodriguez before the Wimbledon final, his reasons were threefold. He explained, 'I wanted to pass on my best wishes to my daughter for the Wimbledon final and I also congratulated him, as a coach, for getting her there. But there was something else on my mind, too. On her way to the final, he had been holding informal press conferences with Belgian journalists and telling them what an achievement it had been for Justine to get that far, after all she had been through at home. So I told him to stop talking as if her life at home had been so bad. It wasn't true, I told him; and if it had been that way, we wouldn't have enjoyed seeing each other just a few weeks ago. From his reaction, Carlos didn't even seem to know that I had seen my daughter again.'

Rodriguez has since revealed that he deliberately kept Justine's father on the line during a phone call at around this time, in order to determine whether or not there were any hidden motives behind this new contact. He told the *Sunday Times* later, 'I had a long conversation with him, deliberately long. I wanted to keep him talking to see where his thoughts would lead. And sure enough, it was the same old story – complaints about Pierre-Yves and the desire to interfere with her life again. So I warned them what to expect and, unhappily, I was proved correct.'

José disputed that version of the conversation, which took place around the time I first met him. Although there may simply have been a misunderstanding between the two men, the Rodriguez account certainly didn't sit comfortably with the sentiments José expressed to me, face to face.

Justine Henin had been relatively unknown in England before she reached the final. But the sheer guts she had shown to reach the showpiece occasion had already captured the hearts of the tennis-loving British public. Now she faced the height and might of Venus Williams on Centre Court as underdog, a state of affairs that traditionally attracted further British support.

That year, like any other, Wimbledon fans also enjoyed reading about any mystery or controversy surrounding the most successful players. And rumours surrounding Justine's fallout with her father had begun to receive attention from London-based newspapers. Surely no tension between father and daughter was beyond repair, no argument so serious that it was worth perpetuating at a time like this? Yet confusion reigned over exactly what lay at the root of their problem.

The *Mail on Sunday*, one of England's bestselling newspapers, sent me to Belgium with three objectives: to locate José, persuade him to open his heart on the breakdown of his relationship with his daughter and then, if possible, watch the Wimbledon final with him.

It was a big favour to ask Justine's estranged father on such a difficult weekend for him. And though no one could know it at the time, life was about to become much harder for the entire family, the tennis star included.

I reached the gateway to the Ardennes on Friday, the day before the final. From his restaurant in the centre of Han-sur-Lesse, Jean-Paul Henin called his brother José to ask if he would be prepared to meet me. He agreed to a rendezvous at Rochefort tennis club, where he had watched the closing stages of his daughter's amazing semi-final comeback in close proximity to Pierre-Yves Hardenne and hoped that perhaps it would signal an end to the bitterness between them.

José told me, 'I saw Justine herself three weeks ago and she told her coach afterwards that it made her feel better. I fully accept the relationship between Justine and Pierre-Yves now. We all take time to adapt to new situations. But if they get married in the next year or so, I believe it is my place as her father to be there with her.

'It would be a long time before I would consider attending one of her matches again. And even then I would only go if she invited me to do so. When she comes back to Belgium after Wimbledon, we will speak about tennis for no more than a minute. Then we must change the subject. Things will be much better between us again. I want to believe that will happen. But it must happen away from tennis. I didn't want to be on the Centre Court for her Wimbledon final.'

Did that sound like 'the same old story', as Carlos described José's mind-set at the time? José's words appeared in the *Mail on Sunday* that weekend, and contrast sharply with what Rodriguez claims to have been told at around the same time. So how could the discrepancy have arisen? If Rodriguez was manipulative with the conversation, as he himself admitted later, then is it perhaps it is conceivable that he drew José into making a less than complimentary remark about Pierre-Yves, one that Carlos then repeated to Justine's boyfriend? As for interfering in Justine's life, José simply wanted to be part of it in some way. After all, he was her father, and such a desire seemed hardly unreasonable.

José added, 'As we talked, I made it clear that I did not want to return to the circuit, and all I wanted was to have a normal relationship with my daughter, to be there for her when she felt she needed her father.'

But he later conceded to me, 'The only thing I might have said relating to tennis was that at some stage the financial situation regarding the companies I had set up for her would need to be addressed.'

Was this what Rodriguez construed as some fresh ambition of José's to assume a role in her management team? If so, he may well have been wide of the mark. The José I met had realised that the father-daughter relationship could thrive again only outside the world of tennis. But then, was it in Carlos's interests for Justine to be getting involved with her father again at all, on any level? And why would Rodriguez think it would be best for Justine, when her tennis career was going so well?

On the eve of the final, however, José and Carlos were in agreement on one thing: they knew it would be better if José stayed away from Wimbledon. But that didn't stop Justine's father from feeling a little left out. And although he insisted that he didn't want to be part of the circus in London, that didn't mean he was going to pass up the chance of some media recognition for all his years of dedication to his daughter's career. In her finest hour, he clearly felt that he, too, deserved a voice, a reward perhaps for all his supportive efforts over more than a decade. If she won, he knew that he had a right to enjoy the celebrations just like everyone else, perhaps even more.

We hit it off straight away, and Friday slowly faded into a haze of strong local beers, introductions to family friends and fellow villagers, more local beers and a family barbecue. José poured out his frustrations and revealed some of the painful events that had led to the feud. He seemed to like having a total outsider to talk to for a change; the intricacies of the closely interwoven lives above the famous caves were sometimes as claustrophobic as the darkness that lay below. We talked for what seemed like half the night, and shook hands on a firm agreement to watch the final together the following day.

Sure enough, José was waiting at his house with a big welcome on Saturday morning. Situated in the pretty little village of Hamerenne, just outside Han-sur-Lesse, the venue promised the sort of intimacy the newspaper was looking for. A *Mail on Sunday* photographer joined us from nearby Luxembourg, and Justine's fourteen-year-old sister, Sarah, closed the doors to the outside world.

Pretty soon we were all glued to the television screen, even though nothing was happening. José chose the BBC from the many channels covering the match. 'Belgian commentators are often too personal in the remarks they make about my daughter,' he said. Perhaps they were too scathing in their coverage of the 'tie-break', too.

He argued that the British were more professional in their approach; they captured the essence of Wimbledon so much better than any outsider-broadcaster ever could. Besides, he said, the plummy vowels of the British commentators always made him laugh – and he revealed a considerable comic talent for imitating an upper-class English accent.

For all the mirth and bravado in the Henin household, it didn't matter which channel you chose to watch that Saturday lunchtime – all you saw was rain. The monotony of the weather tested the skills of even the most inventive British commentators, and there seemed no end to the canopy of grey skies.

First on court, if the rain ever let up, would be Tim Henman and Goran Ivanisevic. They still had to complete their semi-final, interrupted the previous evening, before the women's final could go ahead. Only after Henman, Britain's brightest hope, had given his all in front of his home crowd could Justine step out and try to claim her place in tennis history.

John McEnroe, the 1980s tennis legend, felt the underdog had a fighting chance, especially when her backhand was the finest shot in the game. Coming from a man who had won three Wimbledon titles and four US Opens, that was high praise indeed. She was petite, not muscle-bound like many of the top players in the women's game. That seemed to be another reason why big-name commentators and British supporters alike had taken her to their hearts.

* * *

For now, José would suffer his exclusion willingly, if only Justine could turn their 'tie-break' to her advantage. She had claimed her independence; she had established her own identity and taken the world by storm. Her father understood all that. There would be time to put things right later, he hoped. For now, he would just support her quietly, from a distance. Others would have a more direct role to play.

At Justine's side in the All-England Lawn Tennis and Croquet Club would be her boyfriend, Pierre-Yves, and her coach, Carlos Rodriguez. Although José suspected both men had done much to bring about his estrangement from Justine, he also knew they would be a source of strength and inspiration to her on the biggest day of her professional life. For a start, they would make sure she was mentally prepared for the anxious long wait she must now be enduring somewhere inside the famous Wimbledon locker room. Her aunt, Geneviève, would complete what constituted her entourage in London.

Those left back in Belgium felt the mounting frustration just as keenly; perhaps it affected them even more. All their lives, Justine's relatives had hoped that her talent for tennis would lead her to a moment like this. Now the elements on the other side of the Channel simply wouldn't allow that moment to arrive.

For Justine's maternal grandfather, Georges Rosière, the tension was becoming unbearable. He adored his granddaughter, as she adored him. Georges was Justine's chosen emotional link to the mother she had known only until she was twelve. Now she was an adult, there was probably even more he could tell her, and so many fond memories they could share. Whenever Justine's tennis programme would allow, they would sit down to a leisurely Sunday meal, remember Françoise and catch up on each other's news. What made the relationship even sweeter for Justine was the fact that Pierre-Yves was also invited to these intimate occasions, and made to feel part of the family.

Georges had followed Justine's meteoric rise through the women's tennis ranks with all the enthusiasm of a teenager. Unfortunately, he no longer inhabited a teenager's body, and the stresses and strains of his fanatical support were taking their toll. He would sit helplessly in front of his television screen, unable to influence his granddaughter's game, hoping from somewhere within that she would find the strength to succeed.

He knew that the outcome of the latest match was entirely beyond his control, and now the weather only increased his feelings of powerlessness. He could imagine Justine left in the locker room, just sitting there, growing more and more nervous by the minute. That thought made him even more agitated.

'Papy' knew all about the dangers of getting caught up in the excitement of Justine's career. He was only too aware that his 'opposite number' – her paternal grandfather, Alphonse – had almost paid the ultimate price for supporting her at the last Grand Slam tournament. At a time like this, it was best to try to take a step back, to let events follow their natural course. After all, in the final analysis, only Justine could shape her destiny; only she could truly take control of her game.

The trouble was, the stakes over in England were now even higher than they had been at the French Open a few weeks earlier. Potentially, she stood just two sets away from the ultimate prize in world tennis. Georges was living the whole adventure with her, point by point. Now the day of the Wimbledon final had arrived. Matches simply didn't come any more important than this. He knew it, and he was hooked on the adrenaline.

* * *

The London skies weren't impressed by the magnitude of the occasion. They poured rain over Wimbledon in relentless torrents, smothering the sunshine with their clouds. The idea that summer showers would soon blow over was starting to lose credibility, even among the most optimistic spectators.

Back in Hamerenne, José Henin and his guests waited for a window in the weather – and then waited some more. It was almost a relief when the monotony was broken by the sound of fresh knocking on his front door. Belgian reporters had tracked down the father of the great national heroine. They were worried about how to fill their sports pages if the match was rained off for the day. The journalists probed José for a few words of wisdom and he did his best to oblige. After a brief discussion, he politely sent his uninvited guests on their way. As they left, the reporters issued a friendly warning: if there was any play in the women's final later that day, they would have to return to get his reaction.

'I only talked to them for that long because they are Flemish,' he joked after they had left. 'The French-speaking Belgian journalists are too scared to speak to me. They claim that if they did, Justine wouldn't speak to them.'

At the Taverne du Centre, Jean-Paul Henin's restaurant in Han-sur-Lesse, lunch had long since been served to a full house of family and friends. If the rain continued, it would soon be time for the host and his wife, Clelia, to prepare dinner. The big day had become a bit of an anticlimax.

After an indecisive little cameo from Henman and Ivanisevic, some definitive news finally filtered through from London. The women's final would not be played that Saturday. All would be decided on Sunday, assuming there was some improvement in the English weather.

Having stared at his television screen for the best part of a day, Georges Rosière's frustration was complete. His blood pressure had crept up with each passing hour – and all for nothing. Exasperated, he decided to end the day by doing something that he could at least control. 'I'm off to mow the lawn,' he muttered, and sprang impatiently to his feet.

* * *

At Hamerenne, I had already written a 'holding piece', detailing the Henin family feud from José's point of view. He had been so open about the family's problems that when the story reached the *Mail on Sunday* in good time for the first edition, the editors were more than happy. Match or no match, the job was done and the trip had been worthwhile.

Then came the sound of more knocking. We thought it would be the Belgian journalists, back with a new line of questioning as their deadlines approached. But when José opened his front door, he was confronted with the pale, anxious face of his eldest son, David.

Although he had been so friendly the night before, David seemed less than pleased to find the reporter from the barbecue sitting comfortably on his father's sofa. He clearly had something important and deeply private to say. Even at this awkward moment, the 27-year-old was too polite to ask his father to show me the door. And before I could offer to leave of my own accord, he ushered José and Sarah into the kitchen and delivered his grim news.

'It's Georges,' David said simply. 'He's had a heart attack. They've taken him to hospital but it doesn't look good. They may not be able to save him.'

The grandfather Justine called 'Papy' had got up to mow his lawn while there was still enough daylight to do the job. On any other day it might have been therapeutic; but this was no ordinary day. The enormity of the challenge facing his granddaughter had left his body tense and ready to rebel violently against any sudden exertion. Yet another of Justine's loved ones had fallen victim to what was starting to look suspiciously like a family curse. If José considered himself to be a long-term casualty of tennis, Georges had suffered far more suddenly. Now his life hung by a slender thread and he might not survive the night.

Sarah was already inconsolable. I had no idea what was happening until she ran to her room in tears. José put me in the picture, on condition that I promised not to write a story that night about the latest misfortune to hit Justine's ill-fated relatives.

Journalists have a rather perverse ability to ignore the consequences of the stories they write. 'Tragedy Strikes Wimbledon Finalist' might have made a powerful headline on the *Mail on Sunday*'s back page. However, no one with a conscience would have wanted a nineteen-year-old girl to find out about her grandfather's heart attack by glancing at the back of a London newspaper – especially not on the biggest day of her life. José therefore received an assurance that we would not reveal the latest twist in Justine's problematic life.

To cover myself in case the story leaked out from other sources, I explained the situation to the *Mail on Sunday*'s sports editor, Malcolm Vallerius, who agreed to cooperate fully with the family's wishes. Having put José's mind at rest, it was time to leave the Henin family to their next excruciating dilemma: when to tell Justine the sad news.

They knew how much Georges would have hated the idea that what had happened to him might in any way ruin Justine's chances of taking the Wimbledon title. If they broke the news to her before the match, it might well harm her performance. But if they let her play not knowing, how would she react afterwards? Worse still, if the news leaked out and she got wind of the story through other sources, she might never forgive those who had tried to protect her from the truth.

Calls to Carlos Rodriguez suggested that the decision had effectively been taken out of José's hands already. His sisters, Françoise in Belgium and Geneviève in London, had debated the matter with Rodriguez. Even at this highly sensitive time for the family, the ultimate decision seemed to rest with Carlos. But on this occasion Justine's father actually agreed with her mentor: she should be told about Georges only after the final on Sunday, whatever his condition by then.

* * *

Just hours before the delayed 2001 women's final, José Henin was woken by the chirpy ring tone of his mobile phone. It was the call he had been dreading. Although Georges Rosière had bravely clung to life all night, he had passed away at six that morning. Sadly, one of Justine's biggest fans hadn't lived long enough to see how valliantly she would fight on her big day.

The latest loss didn't hurt José as much as it would upset his daughter. Although he felt sorry for Georges, he wasn't going to pretend they had been the best of friends. With endearing honesty, he revealed later that day, 'In George's eyes, I was never good enough for Françoise. In fact, he advised his daughter not to marry me. When I think about my own situation with Pierre-Yves Hardenne, I suppose I can relate to that. But I never tried to turn the woman I loved against her own father, however he felt about me.'

With Sarah's blessing, José decided to join a bigger crowd to watch his elder daughter play Venus Williams. After the trauma of the previous 24 hours, he wanted to escape the sombre atmosphere in his house and tap into the positive energy now being generated by the local community. A giant screen had been erected in Rochefort's leisure centre. Some six hundred people were expected to inject new life into the party that had fallen flat the previous day.

Georges would not have wanted his death to spoil Justine's historic Sunday. There would be time for mourning after Wimbledon, her surviving family knew. But now the granddaughter Georges had loved so dearly was about to go up against a tennis giant. Somehow it seemed right that all the energies of the living should go towards willing her dream to come true. Georges would have wanted it that way and José didn't need to have been close to his father-in-law to know that.

CHAPTER 12

The Final Showdown

Before joining the throng at the leisure centre, José took a morning stroll around Rochefort. Acquaintances weren't slow to come up to the local man whose daughter was the talk of the town. They congratulated him on what Justine had already achieved and they promised that they were with her all the way. Dutifully, he smiled and thanked them for their support.

In every shop window there were posters emblazoned with the same emphatic message: 'VAS-Y, JU-JU!' The townsfolk had claimed her as one of their own. In some ways she was now more their daughter than his. To José, this hero-worship seemed a little bizarre. He was the focal point for adulation by proxy, father of a famous daughter who rarely talked to him. It was almost laughable.

Even the mayor of Rochefort, François Belot, was in on the act now. He arrived early at the leisure centre to lead the expected cheers. José nodded politely to him as we slipped into the venue and surveyed the scene. Huge kegs of beer had been brought in to set the party rolling. After making some small talk, José grabbed two glasses and led the way to our seats in the front row. Each time we dared to look back, the hall had filled a little nearer to capacity. There were television crews, press photographers, Belgian flags and a variety of patriotic hats decked out in the national colours of red, yellow and black.

Reporters crept down the central aisle to try to grab a word with José before the match began. One tactlessly mentioned rumours of a fresh bereavement in the family. We shuddered. Somehow word of Georges' death had leaked out. José was alarmed to consider what the consequences might be over in London. But gradually we realised that the Belgian reporters had decided to join the huge, benevolent conspiracy to keep the news from Justine before her final. Always a worrier, José still feared the worst but eventually he declared, 'Once she's on centre court she'll be safe, at least until later.'

Goran Ivanisevic unwittingly helped bring forward Justine's grand entrance. He wasted no time in seeing off the British favourite, Tim Henman, in the men's semi-final, carried over from two days earlier. At Wimbledon, the tension turned again to anticlimax. The local boy had crashed and burned, so the British fans would have to adopt someone else – and fast.

Justine emerged from the locker room smiling, even though the intimidating frame of Venus Williams dwarfed her as they walked on to Centre Court. Williams was 1.85 metres tall and weighed 72.5 kilos. Justine was 1.67 metres and weighed in at 57 kilos. What José saw on the big screen in Rochefort made him feel immensely relieved. Mentally Justine seemed in good shape, ready to face her biggest test yet. The leisure centre buzzed with anticipation as she went through her warm-up. At last, the maddening wait for the match to begin was finally over.

The Rochefort faithful cheered Justine through every point, falling silent only when she was outmanoeuvred by her formidable opponent. Unfortunately, that happened all too often as the American enjoyed the better of the opening exchanges. Justine had looked so ready when she first appeared on screen, but now she seemed stiff as she snatched at her shots, hesitated at vital moments and moved heavily around the court. As the underdog struggled to find her usual snappy rhythm, Venus imposed herself with a series of bludgeoning assaults, designed to shatter the confidence of the smaller girl. The favourite added intense psychological warfare to the occasion, the ferocity of which took Justine aback, for all her own mental toughness.

The Belgian girl would later admit, 'I felt a little intimidated because she kept giving me these strong, strange looks.'

Justine tried to fight back and there were glimmers of hope in that first set that she might soon find a way to hold her own. But every time she tried to force open a window of opportunity, Venus slammed it shut with her relentless power. As the American's athleticism asked more searching questions, Justine simply failed to find an answer.

'I don't understand it,' her father said. 'She has always performed so well in finals.'

But this was Wimbledon. Centre Court had already claimed a long list of victims; rising stars often froze on the big stage. Then there was another truth to contend with in women's tennis that year: hesitate, even for a moment, against a Williams sister and you were lost.

As Justine was battered to a demoralising 1–6 first-set defeat, press photographers over in Rochefort seemed almost to taunt her father. They leaped up and thrust their cameras into his face, flashing away every time he showed so much as a flicker of emotion. He tried to protest, but it soon became clear that they were thinking only of how their picture might look in the morning newspapers.

Although the photographers annoyed him intensely, José was far more concerned by what was happening at Wimbledon. Justine hadn't merely lost the first set; she had been virtually annihilated. What made it worse was that Venus had needed to do little more than go through her usual, wonderfully impressive array of shots in order to gain such ascendancy.

It was now or never; Justine could either find a way to play her best tennis or risk spending the rest of her life wondering about what might have been. Typically, she came out for the second set and fought like a tiger. Now the ferocity of her returns, particularly on her famous backhand, seemed to shock her opponent. Venus, who had enjoyed such an ominous hold on the match just a few minutes earlier, was suddenly filled with uncharacteristic doubt. Justine's venom and combative spirit had begun to come through at last.

In Belgium, the crowd leaped to its feet and José began to cheer the daughter who had all but disowned him. He exchanged high-fives with those around him, oblivious to the flashbulbs as they captured his changing mood. What did the media circus matter now? This was his flesh and blood, playing like a Wimbledon champion. Justine had broken the same Venus serve that had previously looked so invincible. She was on the verge of winning the set, and if she managed that, anything was possible. The momentum was hers and she didn't disappoint a thrilled Wimbledon Centre Court. Justine closed out the second set 6–3. Another famous Henin comeback was in full flow, and in some ways this was already a victory in itself.

As she said later, 'When you play a Grand Slam final, it's a big moment in your life. When I came back at one set all, it was a great moment for me.'

Win or lose from here, she had demonstrated her fighting spirit and given people at home something to shout about. She had shown the world what she was made of; her courage was beyond question. Understandably, José looked indescribably proud. He knew how delighted Georges Rosière would have been for his granddaughter, too. Perhaps there were now two people up there watching over her.

José realised that, after all they had been through as a family, Justine stood within touching distance of the Wimbledon title. What she had to do now, at all costs, was stay focused, and start the final set with as much venom as she had finished the second. But to maintain that sort of momentum against such a warrior of an opponent was easier said than done.

Perhaps the effort she had already expended in order to draw level had taken too much out of her; or maybe something made her lose concentration. Just when Justine needed to scrap like never before, it was Venus who found an extra gear. The taller girl sensed fresh weakness across the net and didn't need a second invitation. She broke the Henin serve immediately in that third set, and never looked back. She set about her opponent with a series of punishing winners that left Justine looking punch-drunk. The nineteen-year-old girl's brave challenge had all but evaporated. She seemed to have forgotten what she had learnt during her victory over Williams earlier that year – that the gangly American didn't like to have ground strokes aimed close to her body in the middle of the court.

The surface was different this time and you had to adapt your tactics to suit grass. But it was Venus who had learnt most about her opponent from their previous confrontation. You didn't just have to be aggressive in order to beat an in-form Justine in a big match – you had to be downright savage.

Venus had warned that Justine would soon be world number one if she was allowed to play her best tennis every time. She wasn't about to give her the confidence to take that sort of step.

* * *

Back in Rochefort, the hall fell silent as Williams produced one of the most devastating final sets of recent times. Try as she might to recover some form, Justine looked a spent force, her confidence destroyed. The crowd waited for the now-inevitable end with a touch of sadness. The match had turned from epic comeback to one-sided demolition. Venus Williams won Wimbledon 6–1, 3–6, 6–0.

Unbeknown to Justine, the afternoon was about to get worse. If she had harboured a nagging suspicion that something was wrong, she had managed to suspend that feeling for most of the day. Now she saw sympathy etched on the faces of those closest to her. Carlos Rodriguez looked particularly sad, and there seemed to be more on his mind than the final set.

Justine's spirits briefly soared again thanks to some typically encouraging words from the Duchess of Kent. Henin watched as Venus received the trophy and held it aloft, knowing just how close she had been to savouring that moment herself. Perhaps there would be other finals. She would learn from this defeat, and remember the way Venus had put her to the sword when it mattered.

Afterwards Justine was obliged to attend the post-match press conference, never a pleasant experience when a player has lost and doesn't much feel like talking. Again, she would have noted that the atmosphere seemed excessively subdued. Journalists asked her about the match, but it seemed as though they were keeping something from her. Justine had already done more than 50 press conferences, but never one quite like this.

Even so, she was determined to remain upbeat in her remarks. She reasoned, 'I will be number five in the world on Monday. This was one more experience. I will remember it all my life.'

Prince Philippe and Princess Mathilde of Belgium had flown over to be present on what might have been a historic occasion for their country. They, too, knew what had happened to Georges Rosière, but couldn't say. The royal couple tried to be as supportive as possible when they met Justine immediately after the press conference. Between them, they would do everything in their power to make life easier for Justine on her sad journey home.

Finally came the moment of truth. Justine was taken into a separate room where her entourage was waiting to break the terrible news. Justine was distraught. What could have been the greatest day of her life had ended in the worst way imaginable. Georges Rosière, the man who represented her last remaining blood-link to her mother, was gone. Life would never be quite the same.

* * *

Justine flew straight back to Belgium in business class with Prince Philippe and Princess Mathilde at her side. Despite their valiant efforts to keep her spirits up, she knew the days ahead would be painful and complicated. The funeral ceremony would bring her back into contact with people she had long since left behind – though not, as it turned out, her father. José had already thought the situation through and decided on the Monday that it would be better for all concerned if he didn't attend the funeral. Instead, he went to pay his respects to Georges Rosière at the mortuary. He claimed later, 'The funeral would have turned into a media circus.'

While José wanted to stay out of her way until the funeral was over, it was inevitable that Justine would come into contact with other relatives, including some she thought she had left behind. Her cousin Maud, for instance, had often been like a big sister to Justine, though she was actually the daughter of José's brother Jean-Paul. Maud knew she could never replace Florence, the sister fate had taken away long before Justine had been born, and she didn't want to try. Even so, everyone knew Maud to be great fun, pretty and kind. By all accounts she was an inspiration and a comfort to Justine and Sarah as the girls grew up without their mother.

Although they had lost touch of late, Maud was keen to renew the bond, regardless of the tensions between Justine and the Henin men. She explained later, 'I called Justine and told her how sorry I was that she had lost someone so close to her. I also said that our situation was stupid because we had never had any problems between us. She said that she needed time to reflect on things, and that she would call me. But she never did.'

Perhaps Justine felt that Jean-Paul, Maud's father, was still too close to her own for comfort. But Justine had many relatives, some close and others distant, to deal with at the funeral. What she didn't want was to be the centre of attention. However, certain photographers ignored her request for privacy and took pictures during moments of maximum distress. She was learning the hard way what celebrity would bring, despite the best efforts of her fiancé to protect her from the small band of paparazzi.

When the fuss had subsided, Justine and Pierre-Yves retreated to her local tennis club in Han-sur-Lesse, where he was still holding summer-school classes. Only hours earlier, she had played on Centre Court, the most famous stage of all, and had almost become queen of Wimbledon. Now she was back in touch with her tennis roots, to the delight of the local children, whose summer-school games had never included a walk-on appearance by a celebrity. Soon they were enjoying an unforgettable, impromptu tennis lesson in warm sunshine from one of the greatest young players in the world.

Word reached José of what was happening. 'Come on,' he told me eagerly. 'She's down at the Han-sur-Lesse club right now. We can go and see her.'

For all the supposed friction between them, Justine didn't seem displeased to see her father. She must have known they would probably bump into each other at some stage on the visit. Even when José introduced his new journalist friend, she smiled politely as we shook hands. Pierre-Yves glared across from the tennis court, pacing up and down like a caged tiger. But this moment belonged to just two people – Justine and her father. They had much to discuss, and I stepped away to give them some space.

From a distance, Justine appeared relaxed and respectful as they chatted; warm enough to encourage the belief that perhaps, in the near future, she might make some time in her busy schedule for her sole surviving parent. José told me later that he had taken the opportunity to express his sorrow over her 'Papy', Georges. He also congratulated her on her performance at Wimbledon. And he assured her that he had no intention of trying to regain control of her career.

He claimed later, 'I made it clear as we talked, face to face, that I never wanted to go back on the circuit. I just wanted us to be father and daughter. And she said of the previous trouble between us, "If Mum had been alive, it would never have happened like this."

'I asked her if I could call her in a couple of days, and she said yes. It wasn't a long conversation.'

Justine seemed perfectly content to listen to what José had to say, and remained positive and calm throughout the exchange. Father and daughter talked for only a few precious minutes before she returned to Pierre-Yves. But José looked so much happier afterwards; it was as though a weight had been lifted from his shoulders. To an outsider, it appeared that his daughter had finally shown him the consideration he had been hoping for since long before her extraordinary Wimbledon adventure. There was nothing to suggest that Justine was harbouring some deep disgust for her father. The body language certainly didn't speak of anything untoward. If this was a vulnerable daughter suddenly faced with a wicked father whose acts behind closed doors had left her emotionally scarred for life, then I must have missed the clues.

True, Justine knew she was in a public place with a journalist standing not far away. But father and daughter looked far more like two civilised family members trying to find some common ground, so that perhaps they could have some semblance of a normal relationship again in the near future. By the end of their brief meeting, they appeared to have broken the ice again at long last. Surely it hadn't been an act?

But before very long, the ice had formed far thicker than ever before. It seems that she spoke to Carlos Rodriguez before José fulfilled his promise to call her, and the coach advised caution. Pierre-Yves may also have pointed out the potential perils of letting Justine's father back into their lives.

José took up the sad story of his follow-up call: 'I had hardly said a word when she told me to shut up,' he alleged. 'Then she asked me what I had said to Carlos about going back on the circuit. I told her I had said nothing of the sort, and that in fact I had told Carlos quite the opposite. I told her I never wanted to see another of her matches in person again, or have anything to do with the circuit. But she wasn't having it. She didn't believe me. So that brief, friendly exchange at the tennis club was the last time I saw her.'

CHAPTER 13

No Mercy

With mounting dread, José realised that his daughter simply didn't want a lasting reconciliation. She was famous now – ranked seventh in the world. Apart from her tennis she had Pierre-Yves, who didn't seem keen to let the Henin family back into their lives. Justine wanted to look to the future, not the past. Her father represented an unwanted link with painful times. She was determined to enhance her growing reputation on the tennis court and leave any problems behind.

The perfect opportunity for more glory came in November 2001, when Belgium challenged for the Federation Cup, thrown wide open by the withdrawal of the USA because of the events of 11 September. Henin and Kim Clijsters, who was ranked above her at number five in the world, joined compatriots Laurence Courtois and Els Callens for the tournament in Spain.

Justine helped Belgium dispose of Germany 3–0 in a preliminary round with a 6–3, 6–1 victory over Martina Müller, despite falling 0–2 behind early on. Then Australia was dismissed, again 3–0. The next test would be Spain, the host nation, and Henin had to play local favourite Conchita Martinez in front of a fiercely partisan crowd in Madrid.

She won the first set 6–3 but Martinez hit back to take the second 7–5. The Spanish spectators were going crazy as Conchita raced to a 5–1 lead in the final set. Even when Henin served a fault, they cheered, and now a shell-shocked Justine was staring defeat in the face.

Just when it looked utterly hopeless, she unleashed some of her anger in what everyone assumed would be the last few, defiant points. In doing so, however, Justine suddenly recaptured something that had gone missing at the end of the first set. The crowd fell quiet and with every shot she grew more determined to punish them for their earlier lack of respect.

What followed was one of the most impressive victories in international tennis, as Justine took six consecutive games to win the final set 7–5. It was a victory that helped build her reputation as the comeback queen of world tennis.

Not content with her exploits on court and the prospect of a final against Russia, she launched into the Spanish spectators afterwards with some fierce criticism of their antics. Justine, who was still just nineteen, said, 'I understand it's the host country and all the fans are here, but you have to respect the players. When you've got to make a second serve and the crowd are all there making noise, it's very difficult for the players. It's my first experience of this type of game and I just tried to focus. I understand the crowd, but it's not really proper behaviour.'

Given the events that were to unfold at Roland Garros little more than eighteen months later, and Justine's subsequent reaction to them, there was a certain irony in her bitter complaint that day in Madrid.

Only 2,000 fans turned up to watch Henin and Clijsters defeat their Russian opposition 2–1 in the final. The first set in Justine's 6–0, 6–3 drubbing of Nadia Petrova took only fourteen minutes. Belgium was world champion, and Justine's victories had been the highlight. Afterwards, she said, 'It's a great victory for a little country with two young players and a great team.'

Back home, José didn't know whether to celebrate or not, so confused were his feelings about his daughter these days. Was he supposed to act like the proud father every time she did well? It was a dilemma he was going to have to get used to in the years to come.

* * *

Not long after her memorable Federation Cup triumph, Justine Henin was due to play an exhibition tournament with Kim Clijsters, Nathalie Tauziat, Amélie Mauresmo and Silvia Farina Elia at Ciney, in Belgium. She invited her surviving grandparents, Alphonse and Jeanne, to attend. Understandably reluctant to do anything that might perhaps be interpreted as a betrayal of family members to whom Justine had recently given less consideration, Alphonse and Jeanne declined the invitation. Besides, Alphonse wasn't in the best of health and they had seen what had happened to Georges Rosière earlier that year. The decision wasn't meant to be a slap in the face for Justine in any way; they simply preferred to stay on neutral territory until the family tensions were resolved to everyone's satisfaction. Alphonse and Jeanne assumed their decision would be respected for what it was: a natural piece of diplomacy. Jeanne took the trouble to explain things very carefully to Justine when she came round to the house one day.

As she recalled, 'She came to see us and I gave her my reasons. I said I didn't want to go into the world of tennis that had hurt us so much, and caused so much pain to the family. She seemed to accept our reasons. And when she left, she turned and waved. And she said these words – I'll never forget them: "Je vous adore." And then we hardly ever saw her again. We don't even get a Christmas card from her any more.'

Justine seemed to have taken her grandparents' perfectly understandable decision as a firm declaration of where their loyalties lay. It seemed that rather than risk their disapproval, or have to explain her attitude to their son, her father, every time they met, Justine simply cut Alphonse and Jeanne out of her life too.

* * *

Over the months that followed, only her aunts maintained regular contact. And Justine would soon let the rest of the Henin family know where they stood in her list of priorities. The date for her wedding had been set for 16 November 2002. Most of her relatives had heard the news in the same way as the average man on the street – through the media. She certainly hadn't taken the trouble to tell her father, who still feared the worst about his chances of involvement in what should have been one of the proudest moments of his life.

He repeated, 'My place should be at my daughter's side on the big day, walking her down the aisle. She did not see fit to give me her news personally, and I still don't even know if I'll be invited to the wedding at all. Even if I'm not invited, she has my best wishes. I'll send flowers.'

His fears were well founded, as were those of other close relatives who hadn't been given any positive indication that their names would appear on the final guest list.

Soon, however, there was a more pressing concern for one of those recently set adrift by Justine's increasingly ruthless 'tie-break' with her family. Alphonse Henin was told he had prostate cancer. Sometimes the Henin family wondered how much more they could be expected to take.

* * *

Meanwhile, in January 2002 Justine gave a creditable account of herself in the Australian Open, but lost to the more highly rated Clijsters in the quarter-final, 2–6, 3–6. Losing to Kim was starting to become a habit. She would need to get over that mental block if she were ever to achieve true greatness.

José later told me, 'Justine had always been worried about Clijsters and her rise through the ranks, ever since she was about nine. I told her not to worry. I told her she just had to accept that Clijsters would always be a big rival. I told her Clijsters would probably have a picture of Justine on her wall as motivation. So accept the challenge, I said. Accept it – and then beat her.'

But 2002 had begun exactly as it would finish – with Justine too ready to accept Clijsters's apparent superiority, along with the dominance of the Williams sisters – and not enough groundbreaking victories to open the way for her to claim the highest ranking in women's tennis.

* * *

When his daughter returned to Europe from her Australian campaign, José decided to visit her – not to talk tennis, but to see if he could lay the foundations for what he still hoped would be a harmonious wedding day at the end of the year. Naturally he wanted to be involved, as any normal father would. He craved a healthy, loving relationship with his elder daughter, and the chance to show that he had learnt the lessons of his previous mistakes. After all, he continued to enjoy a good relationship with Justine's sister, Sarah. Why couldn't they all just be friends again, before it was too late?

José walked down the rue de la Station in Marloie and stopped by the butcher's shop, above which Justine now shared a modest apartment with Pierre-Yves. He rang the doorbell, full of brave optimism for the future, despite the pouring rain. If he was positive in his attitude, he was confident he could build some bridges here and make life better for everyone.

Pierre-Yves answered the door and José politely asked for his daughter.

'She doesn't want to see you any more,' was the abrupt reply.

José remembered this terrible moment vividly. 'He was smirking,' he told me later. 'It was as though he was really enjoying the moment. I asked if she could come down and tell me herself. He just stood there and repeated the words: "She doesn't want to see you any more." A terrible anger welled up inside me, because he looked so self-satisfied, and I must admit I felt like doing something I would later have regretted. But I kept my self-control and I simply walked away.'

Shattered and humiliated, José feared the worst. This had been a definitive moment in the deterioration of his relationship with his daughter, and yet she hadn't come down to tell him face to face how she felt. How much of this had been his daughter talking and how much Pierre-Yves? He didn't know for sure, but he began to suspect that his chances of walking Justine down the aisle were very remote indeed.

* * *

That summer, another impressive run at Wimbledon, including a first victory over Monica Seles 7–5, 7–6 in the quarter-final, was ended by a seemingly inevitable semi-final defeat to Venus Williams, 3–6, 2–6. This represented Justine's best Grand Slam showing of 2002, for it was a year in which she had crashed out of the French Open at the very first hurdle, falling victim to illness and a little-known Hungarian called Anika Kapros.

Although she tried to deny it, the emotional enormity of her forthcoming marriage was bound to have been playing on her mind on some subconscious level. Justine didn't get any further than the last sixteen at Flushing Meadows, and she voiced her own suspicions, ultimately unfounded, a few months later: 'I know the marriage is not the best thing for my career. But I just did it for myself. I thought it was the right moment for me.'

She suffered two more crushing defeats to Clijsters only days before the biggest occasion of her life. On 8 November, Kim beat her 6–2, 6–1 in the quarter-final of the WTA Championships. 'Maybe that's the worst I've ever played against her,' said Henin. 'I was really tired. I completely forgot that I'm getting married next week so that wasn't the reason for this.' (Clijsters went on to beat world number one Serena Williams in the final.) Then on 14 November, the Thursday before the wedding, the Belgian girls played an exhibition match in Brussels and

Justine was trounced again, 1–6, 4–6, and even joined in the crowd's Mexican wave. To console her after her defeat, Pierre-Yves gave her a passionate kiss and a red rose.

* * *

The wedding day passed off smoothly enough if you were on Justine's side of the camp, though it meant torment and humiliation if you were an outcast. Perhaps the most admirable aspect of the day was the couple's request that fans donate money to charities helping children with cancer instead of spending it on flowers.

In the following weeks, there was precious little time to settle into the routine of traditional married life, although Justine did say with a revealing smile not long afterwards, 'I feel more like a woman, and I've found that I've grown up a little bit more since my marriage.'

As far as Justine was concerned, however, the more conventional ideas that often went with marriage, such as starting a family, could wait for another ten years or so. She was more interested in pushing herself beyond all previous limits, in order to become the best tennis player in the world. To that end, she enlisted a fitness coach with a fearsome reputation for putting his charges through torturous physical training regimes.

Pat Etcheberry had worked with Pete Sampras, arguably the greatest player of the modern age, Jim Courier and a host of other tennis players. He was director of the Etcheberry Sports Performance Center at Florida's Saddlebrook Resort, and that's where Justine Henin-Hardenne, as she was now to be known, went in search of whatever physical power might still have been missing from her game.

'Obviously we do strength work, but we also need to improve her endurance,' Etcheberry said then. 'Her goal is to win a Grand Slam event, and to do that you need to be in shape for seven matches.'

Through most of December, Justine was given a punishing routine that involved sprints, shadow hitting and side lunges for muscle conditioning and lateral movement. But then the pain really began. There were leg raises while holding a medicine ball between her legs, and pullovers with a dumbbell to strengthen the muscles she used to serve. One day they worked intensely, the next day was slightly less agonising. Just when she thought she was starting to recover, Etcheberry piled on the agony again, until Justine was finally on the point of tears.

'You'll thank me when you're lifting the trophy at Roland Garros,' he said. But gratitude wasn't exactly what she felt for Etcheberry while he put her body through a living hell. Even so, she stuck at it and did as she was told. 'She always gives 100 per cent and she always wants to win, whatever we're doing,' he said.

* * *

When Justine Henin-Hardenne finally emerged from her self-imposed pain, it was to start the 2003 season in Australia. There had never been much wrong with her technique. Now she was stronger and fitter than ever before.

So it was something of a setback when she lost her semi-final in the Adidas International in Sydney, a key warm-up tournament for the Australian Open in Melbourne. If the margin of defeat – 2–6, 3–6 – was disconcerting, the identity of her conqueror was even harder to take. Yet again, Kim Clijsters had put paid to her compatriot's immediate hopes of taking her game to another level.

Justine began well at the Australian Open, with straight-sets wins in the first three rounds. Then all that hard work with Etcheberry was put to the test in searing temperatures against Lindsay Davenport. Justine drew first blood 7–5 and had chances in the second to close out the match. Instead, she let Davenport back into the action, and soon the American levelled with her own 7–5 success.

The war of attrition in the final set tested the endurance of both players, with neither prepared to give an inch. Finally, at 7–7, with Justine serving and 0–15 down, she was hit by a serious attack of cramp. She took an injury time out and called the trainer. Against the odds, she returned to take the match 9–7 and book herself a place in the quarter-final. Her fitness work had seen her through in the end, but it had been hard going.

The Spanish girl Virginia Ruano-Pascual was efficiently dispatched 6–2, 6–2 in the next round and then it was the formidable Venus Williams again in the semi-final. Henin-Hardenne was seldom in the match and crashed to a highly disappointing 3–6, 3–6 defeat.

'I think that Venus played much more aggressive than me,' she admitted afterwards. 'I have to play more aggressive against this type of player.'

However, she seemed surprisingly satisfied with her start to the year: 'I was in the semis in Sydney, in the semis here, and I played good tennis. It's just that today there was a better player in front of me.'

That didn't necessarily satisfy her coach, Carlos Rodriguez, however, who soon confronted her with the facts. Over the previous year or so, she had played six matches against Kim Clijsters and the Williams sisters without taking a single set. In the past she had shown herself capable of beating even the very best players in the world, so what was happening now? Did she really want to be the best, or had she settled for a top five spot? If she still wanted to be number one, she was going to have to sort out her attitude and become ruthless. It was all very well having a great backhand, a sound all-round technique and new muscular strength. But unless Justine truly believed she could beat those ranked above her on any given day, she was wasting her time. The first mental block to get over was Clijsters, the girl she had pulverised in Ostend when they were small, but had struggled against with every passing year.

Even much later, Rodriguez refused to reveal exactly how he turned Justine's psychological block on its head. 'I'll say something about that when her career is over,' he said. 'I am a polite, pleasant man, but I can also be a "son of a bitch" if I feel it's necessary to provoke, in order to take [Justine] to the objective she herself has chosen.'

One can only speculate whether or not there's a connection, and it could be entirely coincidental, but Justine's father claimed that he once had a strange phone call from his daughter in which she said accusingly, 'You enjoy it when I lose matches, don't you?'

Whatever it was that Rodriguez said to put new fire into his player, the coach appeared to have provided the final piece in the jigsaw. It cleared Justine of any mental block she may have been harbouring about those above her in the rankings. To go with the technique and strength there emerged a new weapon – the killer instinct all champions need. She was going to be meaner on court than ever before. From now on, it was win at all costs and her opponents had better beware.

CHAPTER 14

Beyond Sport

On 5 June 2003, Justine was back where she had made the promise to her mother eleven years earlier. The soft red clay of the Court Philippe Chatrier, Roland Garros, was about to stage yet another titanic struggle. Justine Henin-Hardenne vs. Serena Williams in the semi-final of the French Open might not produce as pure a vintage as Monica Seles vs. Steffi Graf in 1992, but the match would be every bit as unforgettable.

Wherever she looked, the stands towered above Justine, each tier brimful of passionate fans. Many were Belgians, waving national flags of black, yellow and red. Some wore weird hats in the same colours, and the remainder were mostly French, though just as keen to support the French-speaking underdog, affectionately known as Ju-Ju.

Only a tiny minority of American fans and neutrals made up the 14,000 gathered that day beneath a burning Parisian sky. High clouds softened the sunlight every so often, bringing temporary relief to the crowd below. But such respite was only temporary, and there would be no escape from the heat or pressure for the gladiators now.

Dressed in a white cap, white top and grey skirt, Justine cut an undistinguished figure as she marched out behind the favourite. In the bright afternoon glare, her skin looked pale and blotchy and, to anyone unaware of her extraordinary fighting spirit, the impressive surroundings and the sheer magnitude of the occasion might have seemed too much for her.

Serena's outfit celebrated her love for innovative sportswear design. One shoulder strap was pure silver glitz, the other orange, like her top. Her skirt was the same striking orange, and she oozed glamour and confidence. Even her footwear was orange and white, and although traditionalists might have considered the look to be excessively flashy, Serena was taking the game into another age.

Unlike Anna Kournikova, however, this wasn't a case of a woman's style surpassing the substance of her talent. Serena's outfit merely served to highlight the feminine side to a relentless sporting warrior. Her artistic leanings contrasted sharply with the brutal power that had helped her win 31 of her 33 matches so far that year. Serena had the look and the punch behind it.

On paper, the match was already a foregone conclusion. Serena had won four successive Grand Slams – the 'Serena Slam', they called it – and remained in the form of her life. On her way to the semi-final, the American had dropped only nineteen games in five matches. At 1.78 metres and 64 kilos, Serena was shorter and lighter than her sister Venus, but very much the giant of the game that year. The intensity on her face as she strode purposefully on to the court showed that she wasn't about to rest on her laurels now. Anyone who had witnessed her 6–1, 6–2 quarter-final demolition of the French giant Amélie Mauresmo could be in no doubt of her intentions.

Yet there were still reasons for Justine Henin-Hardenne to feel confident, even if she might have been intimidated by the aura surrounding her opponent. The winter fitness training stood her in good stead. She might not be as statuesque as Williams, yet her deceptive power could still take her where she wanted to go. She had won the Dubai Open in February by defeating Monica Seles 4–6, 7–6, 7–5. Having watched Seles win at Roland Garros as a ten-year-old, perhaps that victory in the Gulf was an omen, a precursor to Justine's own French Open glory. And she had beaten Serena on the green clay in Charleston, South Carolina, 6–3, 6–4, to pick up a cheque for $189,000 and send a message to the world. Miss Invincible could be beaten after all, even on home territory. She was only human.

If carried by the vast crowd, Justine was capable of anything. This was her domain and Americans, even true superstars like Serena, weren't necessarily welcome. Some would say this was payback time. Serena, like her sister Venus, could be hugely intimidating on court. Theirs was a legitimate kind of sporting intimidation, though strangely shocking when first experienced. Justine herself had talked about the withering impact of the Venus glare during the Wimbledon final of 2001. It had been unnerving, even though deep down she knew that in tennis psychological warfare was acceptable. Perhaps now it was Justine's turn to show what mind games she could play.

But there were other reasons for thinking payback time might be just around the corner. Serena's emphatic victory over Mauresmo had amounted to something of a kick in the teeth for French pride. Justine might come from across the border in Belgium, but in a sense she could bring the host nation a kind of revenge. After all, it was French she would speak to express her pain or joy on the day. Player and crowd shared a common bond. Never mind borders, she was one of them now. If the Parisians shouted loud enough along with their Belgian guests, they might just help the match unfold the way they wanted.

Two wider-ranging factors pointed to the crowd being the toughest opponent Serena had ever encountered. First, there was the political dimension. She was an American and, in some respects, she was in the wrong place at the wrong time. George Bush Jr had recently tried to humiliate the French for their refusal to support his invasion of Iraq. He had gone as close to insulting the French nation as diplomatic language would allow. The Parisian fans couldn't get hold of Bush, the warmonger now encouraging a boycott of French goods across the Atlantic. But they could certainly vent their fury at America's final representative in their beloved tennis tournament.

Then there was the racial element, also hard to quantify. Was it possible that their hostility might prove to be more intense because Serena was black? The far right had often enjoyed a shocking amount of political support in France, and for many years Paris had been a city troubled by high levels of racial tension. Though France, and even French tennis, had its share of black sports stars, perhaps some fans still couldn't see past their own prejudice in a game with predominantly white roots. Would that same prejudice fuel some of the taunting that emerged from the safety of a huge crowd? Cowards traditionally operate in such a way.

Whatever the reason, Serena Williams, at 21 the same age as Justine, had walked into a cauldron containing highly volatile elements. And Portuguese umpire Jorge Dias would be hard pressed to maintain order and dignity around the Court Philippe Chatrier as the day wore on. This clash would be about as brutal and gladiatorial as tennis ever got. Sport? Some encounters burst through such confines, unleashing darker forces in those gathered to watch. Even a player could forget that this was just a tennis match between two young people.

Up in the privileged seats, Carlos Rodriguez waited nervously alongside Pierre-Yves Hardenne. They knew just how hard the tennis was likely to be for their golden girl. Serena led their head-to-head confrontations 4–2, but they hoped that Charleston would give Justine something of a psychological edge.

Her recent record was impressive. She had won 25 of her 27 matches in 2003, not a bad way to respond to the distractions of early married life. Her fourth-round loss of concentration at Roland Garros against Patty Schnyder had almost ruined that impressive run, but she had eventually won through 6–3, 2–6, 6–2, and gone on to defeat Chanda Rubin in straight sets in their quarter-final, 6–3, 6–2. Having come this far, she would give almost anything for victory here, and the chance it would provide for her to fulfil that long-standing vow to her mother at last.

As they loosened up, it was hard to imagine two more highly motivated tennis players. Both had been hardened by adversity and were unbelievably strong – so steely it was almost scary. Serena's tough upbringing and her ongoing battle for acceptance in the predominantly white world of tennis meant it would take something special to pierce her armour in a match as big as this. For Justine, Roland Garros was the stage upon which she wanted to triumph more than any other. This clash of wills was sure to spark fireworks.

Serena started with an ace but stuttered and found her first service game broken by a stunning backhand pass. Justine held her own serve with a disdainful forehand winner and already Carlos Rodriguez was nodding with satisfaction. She was playing out of her skin, and put Serena off balance with another sensational forehand pass. The Belgian girl didn't just break the American's serve a second time; she did it without her opponent winning so much as a point. The crowd went wild and the chant of 'Ju-Ju, Ju-Ju' could already be heard all around her. It was 3–0, a start beyond Justine's wildest dreams.

With a series of smashes, Serena broke straight back and screamed loudly as she sent her opponent scrambling all over the court. At 3–2, Pierre-Yves was pictured with his head bowed, a young man clearly feeling the tension as much as his wife. To his relief, however, it was

Serena's act that fell apart again, Justine winning her next service game to love. Still the favourite stuttered, giving Justine hope of a further break with a sixteenth unforced error. At deuce, the women fought out a punishing thirteen-shot rally before Serena netted and Justine clenched her fist. The taunting look she gave her opponent seemed to work. Serena hit long on break point and Justine was 5–2 ahead.

Justine's backhand, arguably the best the women's game had ever seen, gave her two set points in the very next game. Under immense pressure, Serena came up with a superhuman forehand pass, and even Pierre-Yves had to smile. When Justine only found the net on her next set point, the situation suddenly became more serious. Surprising power on her forehand gave Justine another chance to close out. And when it mattered, she came up with an ace.

Pandemonium broke out all around Roland Garros. In half an hour, Henin-Hardenne had brought the world number one to her knees. With twenty unforced errors, Williams was in turmoil, and one more set like that would end the match more quickly than anyone had expected. Perhaps Justine allowed herself to think ahead to a place in the final against her arch-rival, Kim Clijsters. With the American ripe for the picking, she made a series of unforced errors and lost momentum. Serena held serve and took a 0–30 lead in the next game, but Justine soon hit back with a serve of 173 kph. The crowd went crazy.

Any line call that went against Justine sparked howls of protest. And any time Serena dared to stick up for herself, she was shouted down almost before she had started. Stretching and sliding on the soft clay, Justine held serve, clenched her fist and shot Serena another taunting glance. The match was moving out of the realms of sport.

When Serena double-faulted in the next game, the crowd actually applauded. But Justine squandered two break points and the American held serve for the second time that set. Justine then struck a cleaner blow with a service game to love, and was outgunning Serena with an average serving speed of 162kph to the favourite's 156kph. But Williams responded by stepping up a gear to win a series of bludgeoning rallies. She roared like a lioness as she went 3–2 ahead, but Justine soon equalised and began to test Serena's mental strength. As if playing to the crowd, Henin-Hardenne questioned the accuracy of a Serena serve. Umpire Dias ruled in favour of the American and the crowd howled their displeasure. Ignoring the provocation, Williams held her nerve to take the game, and celebrated defiantly. Replays showed that disputed serve had clearly hit the line.

They had been playing for 65 minutes and Williams led 4–3 in the second set.

For the first time, Justine was under real pressure, but she responded well to lead her own service game 40–15. Inexplicably, though, her serve, reliable so far, suddenly slowed and Serena pounced with some blistering returns. When the American questioned a good call, the crowd jeered mercilessly. Undaunted, Serena forced one break point after another, until finally Justine cracked. As the Belgian misjudged her last shot and fell 3–5 behind, Serena screamed with delight. 'Come on!' she yelled, as if no one else in the arena was supporting her. And she was almost right; apart from her mother, Oracene, virtually no one else was.

Serena could do nothing about a searing cross-court backhand winner that gave Justine hope of breaking back immediately. But the Belgian's aim erred on the next point and it was left to the crowd to unsettle her opponent. They clapped long and hard to delay the Williams serve, and then cheered loudly when Serena made another unforced error.

Justine soon put her own pressure on the Portuguese umpire, insisting that he come down off the chair to examine the spot where she felt a Serena serve had landed long. When Dias agreed and overruled the original call, Serena chose not to complain, perhaps fearing what the crowd's reaction might be. On some subconscious level, it seemed the bigots were starting to get to her at last. Seizing the moment, Justine fought like a tiger and clawed her way back into contention, winning a sixteen-stroke rally to break back at 5–4.

At the changeover, she covered her mouth with her towel, seemingly lost in thought. She looked up to Carlos and Pierre-Yves for inspiration, knowing she needed only to hold serve to achieve parity in the second set. But a brutal backhand return soon gave Serena the initiative, and, try as she might, Justine couldn't break the American's stranglehold. Before long, she was facing set point, and she had to run her heart out just to keep her hopes alive. All the time, however, Serena controlled the point, sending her opponent from one side of the court to the other in a series of desperate dashes. At last, the Belgian could run no more, and her final shot crashed decisively into the net. Ominously, Serena didn't even celebrate winning that second set 6–4. She knew that what really mattered was about to begin. Until now, they had simply cancelled out each other's talent.

Serena double-faulted to hand Justine a break point in the first game of the final set and the crowd cheered the American's mistake loudly. With admirable defiance, Williams refused to be broken until Justine became frustrated and lost all accuracy. She had let her opponent off the hook.

A game ahead, Serena declined to take a breather as they changed ends. Justine towelled down briefly and came out to do battle. If she messed up now, she would find herself two behind and there was no guarantee she would ever recover. Once again, the Henin-Hardenne serve, so strong earlier in the match, became wobbly. Serena had the chance to go 0–30, but carelessly sent her return into the net. At deuce, an amazing 22-stroke rally saw Serena aim too low at the last. Justine followed up with a sizzling forehand to clinch the second game.

Roland Garros erupted as though Justine had won the match, and she responded by playing her worst game so far. Serena shot her a withering look as the Belgian surrendered three dreadful points and barely competed. The American was 2–1 ahead and seemed to sense her big chance had arrived. Justine responded to the crisis with a double fault and more tired stroke-play. She grimaced, stared into the distance and slid into an unconvincing backhand. As it drifted into the net, Serena celebrated a 3–1 lead in the final set.

Justine looked on the brink of despair. How could she do this again in a Roland Garros semi-final? What would her mother have thought of her wasteful ways in their own special place? Yet there was still time to prevent this particular story from ending as sadly as the one that still haunted her from two years earlier. Justine dug deep and turned mean. If Serena thought she was home and dry, an amazing cross-court backhand under pressure flew past to make her think again. Shaken, Serena began to make her own unforced errors, and failed to win a single point on her key service game. It was 2–3, Justine was back with a bang and the crowd was determined to lift her further.

Even the line judges must have been feeling the pressure. When Justine's shot dipped just out on the first point of her next service game, there was no call. Serena pointed to the dent in the powdery clay, but the crowd just jeered. Bravely, umpire Dias pronounced in Williams's favour, and now Henin-Hardenne was up against it. Later in that same game, the biased crowd claimed that Williams had hit too long. The majority of the 14,000 people present vented their fury, even though television replays backed the officials – the shot was good. If prejudice had brought about temporary blindness in most of the spectators, there was no mistaking Justine's mistake with her next wild swipe. This one was genuinely overcooked, and suddenly she had offered up her own crucial service game without claiming a point.

At 2–4 in the final set, Justine's long-held dreams were evaporating before her eyes. She was truly a desperate woman. Up in the box, where, from their own seats near the umpire, she had once promised her mother a privileged place among the elite, Pierre-Yves's face was a picture of pain. Judging from his colour, he looked as though he was about to be sick.

Serena moved in for the kill, and Justine battled for her life. A sixteen-stroke rally reminded tennis lovers what a magnificent match these two had provided, and just how much talent there was to celebrate out on court. But Justine was first to fail, sending her backhand wide on the run. Serena clenched her fist and screamed as she sensed that another key moment had gone her way. In contrast, Justine allowed her head to drop as she shut her eyes, perhaps in prayer.

They squared up again with a new series of pulverising blows; but Justine's accuracy under pressure deserted her again and a forehand flew fractionally long. This set in motion a chain of events that was to give the semi-final a controversial place in tennis history. Even though Serena clearly gestured to her opponent that the ball was out, pointing to the mark with her racket, Justine walked over to umpire Dias and exercised her right to request that he examine for himself the spot where the ball had landed. Dutifully, he stepped down from the chair and walked towards the end where Serena was waiting. The American advanced slightly, quite willing to show him the mark, but he motioned for her to keep her distance while he conducted an independent investigation. Serena threw her arms out in despair, as if insufficient respect was being shown for her own sporting reputation. In an instant, Dias backed Serena's original claim and returned to the chair. The television replay had confirmed that the ball was out. Serena shook her head, obviously hurt that her word had been so blatantly questioned.

When Dias announced the score to be 30–0, the crowd erupted in fury yet again, their whistles and jeers an indication of Justine's perilous predicament. At 4–2 and 30–0, it was almost all over. Widespread dissent could still be heard as Justine crouched down in readiness to receive. Blanking out the wall of noise, Serena threw the ball up to take her next serve. At that precise moment her opponent raised her left hand, and the Williams serve dipped into the net. Now the jeers turned to cheers at the American's failure, and no one seemed keen to acknowledge the fact that Serena might have been distracted by Justine's belated gesture.

All the umpire did was to say, 'S'il vous plaît' ('If you please') in a bid to silence the rowdy crowd.

Serena raised a ball in the direction of Dias and said, 'First serve.'

Dias looked confused.

'First serve,' a dumbfounded Serena repeated. '*First* serve.'

'What?' The umpire didn't understand why.

'She had her hand up,' Serena explained patiently, glancing across at Justine, as if for verification.

'Sorry?' Dias was slow on the uptake. The crowd, also struggling to understand, fell relatively silent for a moment.

'She had her hand up,' Serena repeated, looking at Justine again, the glance turning into a glare.

'Yeah?' Dias asked, as though he almost wanted Serena to say it a third time.

And now they both looked at Justine, who simply stood silently, her arms flopped by her side.

Was it possible that some distraction, or conversely the sheer intensity of Justine's focus, meant that she hadn't heard one word of Serena's complaint to the umpire? Could she have forgotten what she had just done, or otherwise felt no moral obligation to come to Serena's aid?

Justine was given one last chance to contribute.

'I didn't see that,' Dias admitted, glancing at both sides of the net.

'*What?*' Serena's expression suggested that she could hardly believe what was happening. She looked at Justine with what looked like a mounting sense of outrage. Yet there appeared to be something more than anger written in her expression – hurt. Was it hurt because a fellow warrior had seemed to show so little honour in battle? Had Henin-Hardenne allowed her hunger for the prize to obscure what sport was supposed to be about?

'I didn't see that,' Dias repeated helplessly.

Serena shook her head disdainfully, and here's where she made her biggest mistake. Had she asked one simple question of her opponent, within earshot of the umpire – 'Did you raise your hand?' – the Belgian girl would have been forced to respond.

But Serena didn't do that. She was already being jeered, and obviously she didn't want to spark a verbal confrontation that would have encouraged further anarchy in the stands. To put it more simply, she appeared to have been intimidated.

So why didn't she ask the umpire to put the question to Justine? More important, why didn't Dias take it upon himself to ask Justine directly? You can analyse such moments for ever. But, as we saw later at the Australian Open, officials under pressure don't always respond in the way you would expect them to.

Had the score been different, Serena might have acted more ruthlessly and risked the consequences. But she was 4–2 and 30–0 ahead in the final set. She still had one serve left, and even though she might have to rely more on spin than her customary power to fox her opponent, she was still in a commanding position – if only she could just keep her head. She would stay on the moral high ground. It wouldn't be the first time in her life that she had risen above the provocation of people who should have known better.

But Serena's dignified reaction backfired as Justine displayed the instincts of a trapped animal suddenly shown an escape route. Having gained the psychological edge over her opponent, Justine went into physical overdrive. She latched on to that spinning Serena serve with total conviction and took instant control of the point. Her technique never wavered until Williams fired into the net. There was no sign of guilt for any part she might have played in the confusion. Instead it was Serena who showed signs of strain. She sliced a backhand into the net, paying the penalty for an absurd shot selection under pressure. Her next serve was a fault. The crowd cheered. This wasn't tennis. It was more like mortal combat. Another misdirected Serena shot never made it over the net. Break point. Another fault. More cheers as the crowd smelt blood. 'S'il vous plaît' was all the feeble umpire would say. He had lost control. With a superb forehand winner, Justine finished the game. She had broken back at 4–3.

The crowd raised its favourite cry: 'Ju-Ju, Ju-Ju.' Neutrals were finding the whole thing grotesque; a few hardy souls even applauded a Justine fault at the start of the next game to make their point. 'S'il vous plaît,' said Dias mechanically. Justine wasn't going to let this chance slip away, though. She lifted her game to further heights, matching Serena's power with two incredible returns and a breathtaking backhand smash. A ten-shot rally ended in more uproar, and it was only 15–0. Serena drew level with her own stunning return but two strong serves and a truly awesome backhand brought Justine back to 4–4.

Although Serena fought hard to move into a commanding 40–15 lead in the next game, she caught the net when she might have closed out. From up in the box, Carlos Rodriguez nodded at Justine, sensing the makings of a new opportunity. Serena double-faulted for the third time in the set, an error greeted by deafening cheers. Her mind seemingly in turmoil, she hit long and gave Justine the advantage. But an equally nervous Henin-Hardenne squandered her chance by aiming too low on break point.

Soon another unforced error from a jittery Serena gave fresh advantage to Justine. Stunned by an extraordinary piece of defiance from her opponent, Serena tried a drop shot, only to see Justine cover the court with lightning speed and whip away the winner.

It was 5–4 and Justine was about to serve for the match. A cautious smile spread across Pierre-Yves's face.

A Mexican wave started up in the stands as 14,000 ecstatic and savage spectators sensed the end. At that moment, when Justine took a few breaths and contemplated victory, something changed in her. The killer instinct was suddenly overwhelmed by anxiety. Two double faults and two unforced errors later, she had lost her service game to love. When it really mattered, she had choked again. What on earth was happening? She couldn't do this to herself here in a second semi-final. She mustn't.

Serena still wasn't focused, and fired long to give Justine the early initiative in the next game. Then the American double-faulted and the crowd cheered again. Serena paused to change rackets, wondering what she could do to turn the tide. When Justine squandered an opportunity to take a 0–40 lead, she looked furious with herself. But Serena made another mistake and let out a whine of frustration. From somewhere, she found heart, her forehand punishing in its depth, exerting pressure all the way back to deuce. The next few moments would probably decide who would win a battle that had proved fascinating and tarnished in equal turns.

Justine's swish of the racket sent the ball long and she held her head in despair. But when Serena missed the chance to win the game with a basic volley, the Belgian punished her with a forehand winner down the line. It was deuce again, and Henin-Hardenne must have known how lucky she was to have been let off the hook. Amazingly, given the tension, she poked out her tongue as she flashed a furtive smile in the direction of her entourage. These were the moments she lived for.

Not surprisingly, Serena was now feeling the pressure that little bit more, and overcooked from the baseline again. Justine clenched her fist and screamed her delight to underline the significance of the moment. Break point yet again, and she was closing in for the kill.

Disgracefully, Serena was forced to hesitate on her next, vital serve swing to more unsporting noise from the crowd. When she was finally able to continue, Justine returned with relish and produced a series of wounding blows that forced Serena into the fatal error. It was 6–5 and chaos broke out around the Court Philippe Chatrier. Henin-Hardenne had earned herself the right to serve for the match yet again.

In this unpredictable drama, such an inviting chance was still no guarantee of victory. It would need a cool head to close out, so Justine sat down and hid her face in her towel. She glanced up at Carlos, who shot her an emphatic nod, his expression seeming to invite no further visual dialogue. It looked as though he was telling her that enough was enough. The match was hers for the taking, and it was time she seized control of her fate.

No one could take any more, least of all Serena. She failed to nail a smash on the first point, which Justine won with an unlikely lob. Henin-Hardenne followed up with a mighty serve, allowing the American no meaningful reply. Another fierce opener forced Williams to return long, and suddenly the underdog had three match points.

With Serena at the mercy of its favourite, the crowd yelled its verdict – thumbs down, she had to be put to the sword.

A crescendo of screams and shouts forced Justine to hesitate as she prepared to deliver the killer thrust. The serve went wide. For the same reason as for the first, Justine's second attempt had to be delayed. When she did let the serve go, it flew over the net like a bullet and Serena's backhand return landed out.

An unseemly mess had been clinically concluded. Game, set and match, the public execution of a proud champion carried out with relish. The will of the baying mob had been done, and sport was almost forgotten. A colossal, brutal struggle, streaked with flashes of sublime tennis, was finally at an end, though some of the scenes had left a nasty taste in the mouth.

Justine pumped her arms in the air, having achieved her aim. She was through. In the box, Pierre-Yves hugged Carlos, and then they looked down lovingly at the winner. If a game of tennis hadn't given rise to so much ugliness on the day, their moment of triumph would have been touching.

Serena forced herself to accept Justine's cursory handshake and prepared to leave the arena. She heard herself jeered loudly by the merciless Roland Garros crowd. To make matters worse, she realised that she had forgotten to shake the umpire's hand; now she had the added worry that her error might be misinterpreted by those hoping to make her humiliation last a little longer. Whatever she felt privately, she didn't want a genuine oversight to tarnish the occasion any further. She went back to Jorge Dias and made amends. As Serena left the court, she waved, only to be greeted with more jeers. At least the spectators were consistent. It was their motivation that seemed questionable. Had this really been only about patriotism and a common language?

CHAPTER 15

The Aftermath

The Belgian flags waved triumphantly; the silly hats were thrown in the air. Justine signed autographs and prepared to explain. Strangely, there seemed to be an element of whitewash about her perspective on what had happened. The first question at the post-match press conference was short and to the point: 'What did you think about the crowd?'

To listen to Justine's first reply, you would have thought the spectators had been saintly in their behaviour that day: 'I think the crowd gave me all the support I needed to win the match. It was unbelievable playing in this atmosphere. So I was happy they were totally behind me. And, you know, when you have to fight like this at 5–5 in the third set, it's so important that they are behind you.'

So the girl who had complained so bitterly about an unsporting crowd in Madrid only a year and a half earlier was asked, 'Was it a fair crowd?'

'Sorry?' she replied, as though the question were absurd.

'Was it a fair crowd? Don't you think it was a little bit too much against Serena?'

'Yeah, sometimes it could be a little bit too much. It's true that when she was missing first serves, yeah, they were . . . But, you know, that's tennis. It's like this. I think they wanted so much that I won this match, so I understand them. And I also say, "Thank you" to them, but it's true that sometimes it was a little bit too much.'

And this was as far as Justine was prepared to go in condemning one of the most shocking afternoons professional tennis has ever seen. Often it hadn't appeared to be about tennis at all.

Justine's mother had died long before the scenes that surrounded her daughter's semi-final. What she would have thought about the manner of victory that day, it is impossible to know. But Serena's mother, Oracene, had witnessed her own daughter's nightmare, and Justine couldn't have been comfortable when a question soon quoted her.

It was put with considerable dignity: 'A tremendous victory. I don't mean to diminish it in any way, but Oracene, Serena's mom, was talking about the crowd. She said the crowd always roots for the underdog. But also she said that there was a lack of class in terms of the booing, the cheering of errors, and that there was a total ignorance of the etiquette of the game. Could you comment on that?'

Justine seemed to want to evade the question. 'I didn't understand everything,' she replied.

But ignorance was a French word, as was etiquette, and the journalist was having none of it. 'I'll repeat,' he countered.

Suddenly, Justine indicated that she had understood. 'OK. Yeah, I think, yeah, like I said, it was sometimes a little bit too much. But maybe if I have to play in the States, it's a little bit the same kind of situation. I don't know why exactly, I don't have to answer to this, to this question. You have to ask the crowd why they did this. I don't want to make any comment about this.'

'Did Serena say anything to you at the end.'

'No.'

But she said plenty afterwards. When asked about the crowd's sportsmanship, or lack of it, Serena replied, 'It was just a tough crowd out there today, really. Very tough – story of my life.'

Serena had been living with discrimination almost since she was born. Another journalist picked up on her remark: 'You said "story of my life". Why do you think that is?'

'I don't know,' Serena said, and suddenly burst into floods of tears. The prejudice and the cynical gamesmanship had been too much to take. 'I'm not used to crying,' she added almost apologetically, as if all this had somehow been her fault. And it wasn't long before the key question was posed, direct and searching: 'Were you upset with her at the end of the match? You usually go up to the net and shake someone's hand. You walked around the net. You did shake her hand. It seemed like she had to come to you. Was it because she had put her hand up on that first serve and then didn't allow you to take the first serve again in the third [set]?'

Again, Serena's attempts at diplomacy soon crumbled: 'Well, I mean, obviously I'm not upset with her. Actually, OK, I was a little disappointed with her because . . . you know, it wasn't the turning point of the match – obviously I probably still should have won the game. It definitely didn't turn around the match. But I think, to start lying and fabricating, it's not fair. I understand that, you know, people want to win these days, but . . . I don't know. It's just . . . it's just, whatever, you know. I understand this is just a tournament, and I'm looking forward to the next time already.'

What she didn't understand was that, for Justine, it wasn't just a tournament. It was a promise – a promise to her late mother, a promise she had been in severe danger of breaking.

For all that, in her own post-match interview Justine had still tried to demonstrate that she understood the greater importance of life beyond sport. She explained, 'It's fantastic to beat Serena in the French Open, but there are many other important things in life. At times, you're living good or bad times, that may be more important. The day when I got married was the nicest day of my life. I cannot compare that to a victory like today. So you have to put things in perspective. Tennis is a beautiful sport. It's fantastic when you can win, especially with this type of ambience, but you must realise that there are things in life that are much more important.'

Especially with this type of ambience? Had she lost the plot so completely? Her opponent was in tears owing to the naked prejudice of that 'ambience'. And if Justine was prepared to behave as she had behaved on court for something that wasn't of paramount importance, how far was she prepared to go to protect something that was?

Serena continued to air her dissatisfaction, 'I think it's bad when people start booing in between serves, you know, or other people are egging them on by doing ridiculous things. So that gets a little tough, you know.'

She was asked, 'Did it get worse when you questioned a couple of calls?'

'I didn't question any calls,' she pointed out.

'The umpire, the chair came down?'

'The balls were clearly out,' she stated.

'It seemed to get worse after that,' the journalist maintained.

And Serena took the bait: 'Yeah, for some reason . . . I don't know. Like, you know, when a player circles a ball, I can see that it's out. I don't necessarily call the umpire and say, "Go check it." The point is not going to change the match.' Then, remembering to maintain her dignity, she added, 'Like I said, she played very well today and she probably deserved to win. She was the better player today, really.'

But those two points at 4–2 had indeed changed the match, and deep down Serena must have known it. Justine was now setting her sights even higher and there was virtually no stopping her.

She almost said as much: 'Winning matches like this means I'm starting to believe that one day I could be at the top, really at the top. And I'm playing good right now, you know. It's sometimes very difficult to explain why I'm doing better, like I've been doing in the last six months. But I was able to make the right decisions and I have good stuff around me, and I'm feeling very good in my private life, so it's helping me to be 100 per cent on the court.'

* * *

Back in Belgium, José had watched his daughter's match on television. He wasn't entirely proud of Justine's conduct. Later, he said, 'If Serena had served an ace while Justine had her hand up, I suspect my daughter would have confessed to putting her hand up. In my opinion she was wrong in what she did. But maybe that's why she won. If she had given Serena two serves, as she should have done, imagine if Serena had served an ace. It would have been 4–2 and 40–0 in the third set. That would have changed a lot of things. But she did it and so she at least had to explain herself.'

The following month, Justine spoke out about the episode: 'I have no regrets right now. Everybody was excited. I did hold my hand up, for sure. Everybody was nervous. I can't change this. It didn't change the result. I think I am a fair player.'

CHAPTER 16

A Promise to Keep

Justine later revealed that she was woken by noises in the corridor outside her hotel room at three in the morning of the final. She tried to get back to sleep, but Pierre-Yves kept coughing. The hours passed. Finally, she drifted off again, but she had run out of time. It was morning and soon she was awake again, although still feeling tired. In her head, she spoke to her late mother. 'You'll have to give me the energy to win today,' she told her.

Then she had a quiet word with herself: 'You'll have to win. You'll have to do it for Mum. Fight all the way. You can't let this escape you.'

She talked it over with her husband. He knew how much pressure she was under to fulfil her dream, and the promise she had made to her mother eleven years earlier. But Pierre-Yves also knew just the right thing to say. 'It's not everything if you win or lose,' he began. 'It doesn't matter. We're very proud of you anyway.'

Somehow those remarks removed a little part of the fear of failure that lurks in every finalist's heart. But it didn't make Justine Henin-Hardenne any less determined to win the French Open. It had been a burning ambition for a very long time and her mother's death had only intensified her desire.

On finals morning, when it is still eerily quiet, each player is allowed practice time on the Court Philippe Chatrier. For Justine, these moments were more special than for perhaps any other finalist the tournament will ever welcome. She looked over to the seats not far from the umpire's chair, where she had sat with her mother. As she practised, her gaze kept returning to them. She could almost see herself sitting there, an awestruck ten-year-old, watching her first major tournament live. To be courtside and so close to her heroine, Steffi

Graf; to watch her play a final in the flesh against Monica Seles. What a day that had been. The only disappointment was Steffi's defeat. But the quality of the final and the drama of the last set, won 10–8 by Seles, had made it one of the best French Open finals ever seen.

What had left the biggest impression on Justine that afternoon was the sheer determination of both players – their pride, their refusal to bow to the will of the other. Justine had taken much of that on board and underpinned her own game with a similar street-fighting spirit. Even without Graf and Seles as role models, she would probably have become that type of player. Given her mother's great courage and willpower, how could it ever have been otherwise?

Justine remembered the words she had spoken to her mother: 'One day I'll be on this court and I'll win.' Françoise wouldn't be out there waiting for her in the Tribune des Joueurs that afternoon; but Justine was convinced that her mother would be watching from somewhere, giving her the energy to succeed. This final was always meant to be. No one could take it away from her now. With one last look at the seats, she finished her practice. She was ready.

* * *

A few hours later, that same arena was packed, beneath a cloudless Parisian sky, and Justine prepared for an all-Belgian final against her conqueror from two years earlier, Kim Clijsters. She would have given anything to be able to look up at the box where the players' loved ones were gathered and see her mother smiling down at her. Instead, her husband was there, with her coach, Carlos Rodriguez, and his little son, Manuel. Her aunt Geneviève was also given pride of place in those privileged seats. But her father, who claimed he had also been promised such VIP treatment by the ten-year-old in 1992, wasn't there.

He was back in Belgium, in his rented house in Hamerenne, where together we had waited for the Wimbledon final two years earlier, only to be greeted by the terrible news of the death of Justine's grandfather. Now he felt compelled to watch. José, too, thought of that day eleven years earlier, when he and his son Thomas had also been at Roland Garros to see Seles beat Graf. He remembered what Françoise had told him Justine had said as they filed out of the arena after the epic match. 'She told me you and I would be in the players' seats,' his wife had confided with a smile. 'She told me she would be out there playing.'

Well, that was his daughter out there, even though she didn't seem to think of herself in those terms any more. She was in the final at Roland Garros all right, but José wasn't there to watch her. He wasn't in the special seats. He hadn't been invited. He wasn't in any seat, apart from his armchair in his own home, but still he couldn't turn his back on events in Paris. That was his daughter. Perhaps, at some point in the future, things would be different between them, and they would be able to share some sweet memories from this day.

* * *

As she loosened up on the Court Philippe Chatrier at Roland Garros, Justine was completely focused on the business in hand. Nevertheless, she was bolstered by the knowledge that her chosen entourage was present, ready to support her in every way. To her, even royalty, celebrities and fanatical fans could not have been as important as Pierre-Yves and Carlos. Nonetheless, they had all turned up. King Albert and Queen Paola of Belgium were looking down with excited smiles. This time, of course, their loyalties would necessarily be divided between Justine and her amiable compatriot, Kim Clijsters. Belgium simply couldn't lose. Thierry Henry, one of the greatest soccer stars of all time, added a touch more glamour to the occasion, along with many other rich and famous figures from the French-speaking world.

Not that Justine was interested in glamour. She dressed in the same basic way she had chosen for the semi-final – wearing a white cap, white top and grey skirt. It was almost as though she wanted to keep her feet on the ground and let her tennis do the talking.

Kim Clijsters was more eye-catching in a red top, white skirt and white cap, but that was hardly a fashion statement either. What talked most for Clijsters was the record she had built up going into the final. She had dropped only one set, a 6–0 blip against Magdalena Maleeva, although she had swept aside that opponent so comprehensively in the last two sets – 6–2, 6–1 – that it scarcely seemed to matter.

In the crowd sat Kim's boyfriend, one of the hottest tennis stars in the men's game. In his black baseball cap and sunglasses, Lleyton Hewitt cut a charismatic figure, and the Australian seemed like a good psychological weapon for Kim to have in her corner.

Clijsters hadn't won a Grand Slam yet, but she had won just about everything else, and came into the final as the slight favourite. She had won tournaments in Indian Wells and Sydney, and she had reached the semi-finals of every tournament she had played that year. The early exchanges would determine whether Justine's recent form or that wounding Clijsters win over Justine at Roland Garros in the 2001 semi-final would be telling factors when it mattered.

Kim was early into her stride on serve and took a 30–0 lead. An immense forehand from Justine helped her back to 30–30. Clijsters landed a useful psychological blow when she came out of a long and bruising rally on top. In the box, the tense expression on Pierre-Yves's face suggested this wasn't going to be easy. Kim had always been a formidable adversary.

On the next point, however, a fizzing backhand pass from Justine seemed to knock the stuffing out of her opponent. Deuce. She followed up with an emphatic smash and suddenly it was break point. Another fierce Justine return had Kim hitting too long: Henin-Hardenne's raw aggression had struck first blood.

Pumped up with adrenaline, Justine began to play wildly on her own service, and suddenly Kim was back in it with three break points. When Henin-Hardenne played a courageous backhand drop shot, beautifully disguised, one of those break points was saved. Again, Clijsters seemed so nervous that a single telling blow appeared to shatter her composure. Two unforced errors soon meant she had squandered all three break points. A third gave Justine the advantage, and Kim screamed 'No!' – horrified at what she had done. Henin-Hardenne made a careless mistake of her own, but forgave herself more easily. With a superb smash she made amends and followed up with an emphatic ace. It was 2–0 and Kim had blown her big chance.

Clijsters' head failed to clear in time for her next service game, and before she knew it she was three down. Her boyfriend, Lleyton Hewitt, looked on helplessly and braced himself for more punishment. Instead, it was Justine who imploded with inexplicable unforced errors to give Kim three more break points. A foothold to steady her nerves was only a winner away. Clijsters couldn't squander a second opportunity, not so soon after the first. She had to make this count.

As usual, Justine fought like a tiger when cornered. A colossal serve wiped away the first break point. Two massive forehands bludgeoned Kim into submission on the next, leaving Clijsters clinging to one last chance at 30–40. Justine was now playing like a woman possessed, and at deuce a stunning series of strokes from the baseline, some executed with both feet right off the floor, earned her breathing space – except that she didn't seem to want to take it. More power play gave her advantage, and a final serve struck the line and stayed a little low. Game over, 4–0, and poor Kim was in turmoil.

Justine looked invincible now. Even at 0–40 on her own serve, she had twice demonstrated that she could retrieve the game with ease. Nothing could have made Kim feel more impotent. Her confidence was crushed, and it would get much worse for her before it got any better. In the next game, Justine anticipated Kim's drop shot superbly and whipped away a winner on the backhand. Thinking her opponent would fail to anticipate the same type of shot so soon, Clijsters tried another. This time the ball hit the ribbon at the top of the net and bounced back on her side. Some force seemed to be working against her. Advantage Mrs Henin-Hardenne. When Kim needed big serves, she produced two turkeys to double-fault on break point. It was 5–0 and they had hardly begun.

Pierre-Yves rested his head on his hand and tried not to look too content. After all, when the two Belgian girls had clashed at Grand Slams in the past, it was Kim who had always come out on top in the end. Today, though, any sort of mental block Justine might have had about beating her rival seemed like ancient history.

Justine swept relentlessly through the next game until she had two set points. The crowd applauded rhythmically, anticipating the kill. On the first point, she hit an extravagant backhand far too long. She conjured a stunning drop shot on the second, so well disguised that Kim was left helpless. The cheers masked any disappointment in the crowd that a Grand Slam final could turn out to be such a complete mismatch. The first set had gone to Mrs Henin-Hardenne 6–0 in just 26 minutes.

Clijsters realised this couldn't go on. She had lost a set 6–0 earlier in the tournament and still won. Why shouldn't she do it again? Clawing her way back, Kim took the first game of the new set to great cheers of sympathy. At last, the humiliating run had been broken. Since she was ahead in the second, it no longer seemed to matter how heavily she had lost the first. What she needed now was composure and a steely determination to match Justine's.

On the vital first point of the following game, Kim looked disgruntled when her opponent's shot wasn't called out. She went to the spot where the ball had landed, realised she was wrong and wiped the mark away. The crowd applauded her tremendous sportsmanship, a breath of fresh air after the ugly atmosphere surrounding the semi-final. Henin-Hardenne remained focused and was soon smashing the ball so hard that it almost bounced out of the arena. A killer volley made it 1–1; the chance for Clijsters to inflict some early pain had passed her by.

It seemed nothing could stop Justine. Soon she was marking a spot where Kim's shot had gone out, and it was break point yet again. Since Justine had the Clijsters drop shot nailed by now, she dashed in to whip her usual winning reply. At 2–1, Justine was a whirlwind, and Kim hadn't woken up in time to take evasive action. A smash, an ace and two more unforced errors gave Justine a love game and now she was cruising at 3–1. Lleyton Hewitt went crazy in the box, trying to shake his girlfriend into a comeback before it was too late.

Kim certainly took control of the next game with a dream of a drive volley, followed up by an unanswerable smash. Justine struck back with two winners of her own, but this time Kim's nerve held, and she gained something of a foothold at 3–2. That action finally gave her the confidence to play some of her best tennis. And at her finest, she had always been good enough to give Justine nightmares. The Flemish girl began to hit freely, and found that she was at last outgunning Henin-Hardenne. Suddenly, Hewitt was off his seat, and his girlfriend had two break points. Perhaps we had a match on our hands after all.

Facing a third test of character, Justine passed yet again with flying colours. An unexpected drop shot helped her wipe away one break point; and Kim hit the ribbon of the net to squander the next. The gods seemed to be conspiring against Clijsters; she had thrown away another chance to break Henin-Hardenne's unusually fragile service. The unforced errors that soon lost Clijsters the game suggested that she knew just what a fool she had been. The problem was made worse by an apparent unwillingness to forgive herself.

At 4–2, Justine was on the home straight. And yet she had lost to Clijsters before from this sort of position, right here at Roland Garros, and perhaps the past began to play on her mind. With nothing to lose,

Clijsters now showed the force and precision that had made her such a great player in the first place and came back into contention at 3–4.

Feeling the pressure and troubled by sudden gusts of wind, Henin-Hardenne began to misfire on her own serve, as massive Clijsters forehands probed her defence. Now Justine was hitting either too long or too low. Doubts crept into her mind, memories of a winning position wasted two years earlier. If she allowed those negative thoughts to snowball, she would soon be facing a dreadful case of déjà vu. When yet another Justine shot floated helplessly into the net, Kim was level at 4–4.

Everyone could sense the makings of another dramatic comeback, Kim included. Here was proof that Justine was still human after all, vulnerable under pressure like anyone else. Kim must have known her opponent would be shaking inside, given what had happened to her here in the semi-final of 2001. Now was the time to break her resolve completely.

But Justine had learnt from her last nightmare at Roland Garros. And instead of beating herself up over wasting a winning position, she seemed to forgive herself. It was as though she looked at what she had just squandered and told herself it was all right to make mistakes, even in finals. She became visibly more relaxed, and with that her confidence returned. Just when Kim thought she had her opponent where she wanted her, the tables were turned.

At a time when most players would have crumbled under the pressure of Clijsters' force, Justine dug in with some desperate returns. Then, out of nowhere, she produced a vicious cross-court backhand, and clenched her fist when she saw Kim was beaten. Staring across the net at her opponent, the little warrior knew what a telling psychological blow she had delivered. Sure enough, Kim's mind seemed to have gone. Two unforced errors later, she had gifted Justine three break points. She saved the first with some belated defiance of her own. But Justine wasn't about to let her off the hook now, not with her childhood dream so close to coming true. This time, she blasted a forehand cross-court winner that brought the house down.

Henin-Hardenne was about to serve for the match. She could see the finishing line. And then, inexplicably, she served a double fault. She won the next rally, but her coach clearly thought she had done so more by luck than judgement. When she glanced up, his forefinger jabbed a warning as if to say, 'No! That's too tentative!' Then he smacked his fist into his other hand. The message seemed unmistakable: 'Be ruthless! Make it yours!'

It wasn't so easy with the winning post in sight. Justine needed a second serve at 15–15, but Clijsters failed to make her pay. It was the Flemish girl's forty-fourth unforced error, and she couldn't expect many more chances. Henin-Hardenne responded to her coach's call for one last burst of aggression, and in the next rally a superb forehand set up her winning volley. Eleven years down the line, Justine was almost there. She had two match points with which to fulfil the vow she had made to her mother.

Clijsters returned the next serve with power, but the ball struck the ribbon of the net and rebounded high into the air. It might have landed just over the net, which would have left Justine no time to come in. As if nudged by a force from above, the ball came down on Kim's side instead. It was over, a lifetime's ambition realised in 67 minutes.

There was a split-second of silence before Justine and the rest of Roland Garros realised she was champion. Then she threw away her racket, turned her back on Clijsters and cradled her head in her arms. As she looked up, in those first moments, there can be little doubt that she was thinking of her mother. In the Tribune des Joueurs, where José's wife would have been sitting had she still been alive, Pierre-Yves tried to hug Carlos. But the coach didn't really want to know – he was too busy punching the air in triumph. So Justine's husband did the same, shaking one fist and then both at the same time, wild lunges in the direction of the court. Pierre-Yves finally got to hug Rodriguez around the same time that Clijsters sportingly hugged Justine at the net.

Kim knew her opponent's history and she realised just what this meant to her. Clijsters had wanted victory badly; but deep down she might not have wanted it quite as much as Justine. Perhaps only tragedy can give you that kind of hunger. Luckily for Kim, she hadn't known too much of that in her life, although in 1999 she came perilously close to suffering a bereavement to mirror that of her arch-rival. Her mother, Els, a former champion gymnast, had contracted a cancer that also appeared to be terminal. She was even given just two months to live, and survived only thanks to a last-ditch liver transplant.

Clijsters once said about that, 'When you compare those things to losing a tennis match, it's nothing. I'm happy to go home or call after my day and hear my mum on the phone.'

However, Justine couldn't do that. She had lost her mother and won a tennis match. But could she feel her mother's presence? She thought so. Now she looked close to tears, and glanced up at Pierre-Yves and Carlos. Not wanting to wait a moment longer to be with them, she disappeared down the tunnel, to the slight confusion of the crowd. When she suddenly emerged among the seats that she had once promised her mother she would occupy, in pride of place, everyone understood.

Pierre-Yves had gone, but he reappeared just in time to save his wife from considerable embarrassment. She hugged him as hard as she could, and she hugged Carlos, too. Soon all three were hugging as one, to rapturous applause from the Roland Garros crowd. They had been a team. Their bloody-minded determination to succeed had excluded many, at considerable emotional cost. But they were a winning team now, and no one could take victory away from them.

Justine broke free briefly to embrace her aunt Geneviève before falling back into the arms of an ecstatic Pierre-Yves. Though he didn't seem to want to let go, he knew she had to return to the court below to receive her trophy. Her defeated opponent no doubt wanted to get the formalities out of the way.

There was a big cheer for Clijsters as she received the runner-up plate and two kisses from King Albert of Belgium, in his khaki suit. But an even bigger cheer greeted his kisses for Justine, and in the moment when she raised the Suzanne Lenglen trophy high above her head she must have worn the widest grin in Paris.

There was a sense of expectation when Justine took hold of the microphone to speak to the crowd. 'Thank you,' she said, pausing for more cheers. 'I'm very honoured to be here with you at Roland Garros, a place which evokes such powerful emotions inside me. Thank you for your support. The first Grand Slam is for you all.'

Having complimented Kim on her performance and thanked the officials and sponsors, Justine came to those matters closest to her heart. 'I'd like to give my personal thanks to two people now. They are true companions when the going gets tough. Pierre-Yves, my husband, and Carlos, my coach.'

As the crowd applauded, Pierre-Yves smiled through his tears and then had to look down, clearly overcome. But this was just the beginning. Both he and Carlos, who had his son, Manuel, sitting on his shoulders by now, must have known what was coming.

'I want the last words I say to you to be about my mother, to whom I dedicate this win. My mum is looking down at me from Paradise. I hope you are very proud of me, Mum!'

As she spoke these words, Justine put her hand on her heart and her eyes filled, although as always she maintained her self-control. Up in the box, Pierre-Yves promptly burst into tears and covered his face.

Kim added to the beauty of the moment when it was her turn to speak to the crowd. 'I'll try to speak in French,' the Flemish girl said, to huge roars of approval. 'I know how much this means to Justine. Well done to her. And to Lleyton, thank you so much for staying to support me. I'll try to come back and play better next year.'

Justine kissed the Suzanne Lenglen trophy like a long-lost friend and posed for the hordes of photographers. The dream had come true. Most of her life had been lived for these unforgettable seconds. These moments of glory were the culmination of a longer, more inspirational story. In the context of her troubled life, they were truly dramatic and deeply moving. When someone as rock-hard as Justine Henin-Hardenne reveals such emotion, it somehow carries extra power. The woman, the warrior, the breadwinner, holding aloft her prize while her partner, the man of the family, simply melts in tears. It was a feminist's dream, as complete a reversal of roles as ever you could wish to see.

Yet there was no disgrace in Pierre-Yves's tears; they enhanced the moment and showed how much he loved his wife. Whatever Pierre-Yves had done to José Henin in the past, he was not to be condemned for his conduct at Roland Garros. His quiet support and carefully chosen words had helped his wife become a winner, even if his coughing the previous night had been less than helpful. He was entitled to be moved by Justine's beautiful victory speech – beautiful for everyone except José and his family.

Justine's father described how it felt to listen to her: 'It was right that she spoke about her mother and the others, I have no argument with that. But I was hoping she would find a way to thank me, too, perhaps even without mentioning me by name. She could just have said that she wanted to thank other people who could not be there for whatever reason, people who had helped her in the past. And I would have understood that she also meant me. But there was nothing at all.'

At the post-match press conference, it got worse for José. For most of the interview, Justine revealed how it had been for her before and during the final. Of her mother, she said, 'I think she gave me all the energy I needed to win the match.'

Later, she was asked about her father. Though the question was put in the nicest possible way, it didn't provoke a particularly warm answer. She may have learnt to forgive herself for errors on court, but she hadn't yet learnt how to forgive her father for his imperfections.

'I don't mean to ruin at all your joy,' the interviewer began. 'But I remember, a few years ago, Mary Pierce won a tournament in Australia and some people asked her about her father. She said that her father had also been part of her win, even if she was not talking to him any more. Now, here, we always hear you dedicating your win to your mum and your coach and everything else. Are you thinking there is any way to reconsider about your situation? I mean, today, on the day of your joy, your bigger enthusiasm, do you have anything to say?'

'No, not at all,' Justine replied bluntly. 'I don't have anything to say about that. I just took decisions a long time ago. I took the right decisions. I have the people I want around me. That's the most important, you know. In life you have to make choices, even if they're hard. You don't live in the past. The right moment is the most important thing. And I just try to bring something very solid. That's what I did with nice people around me and that's my personal choice, and I think everybody has to accept that.'

Her uncle Jean-Marie heard that remark and didn't accept it. He said, 'To me, she sounded like a dictator. That's the sort of thing they say, isn't it? "It's my choice and everyone must accept it." Why should we accept it when we think she is talking rubbish?'

Some things José had to accept for now, as he watched television coverage all alone at home in Hamerenne. He certainly greeted the result with enthusiasm – his daughter was champion of Roland Garros. In spite of everything, he was still happy that Justine had won – and very proud. Every bit as proud, in fact, as Justine had hoped her mother would be in heaven.

CHAPTER 17

Payback Time

With barely a flicker of emotion, Justine took the question from the *Sunday Times* head on. Not that it was even a question as such, more a statement of fact: that two weeks earlier, she had won the French Open without her father or brothers having been present to share the special moment.

'I'm very happy about that,' Justine replied. 'I am happy they didn't come. I am happy my father has not contacted me since my victory. At least they are giving me the respect I asked for. They are giving me the space to lead my life the way I want. They refused to understand my ambitions and my determination to become a top tennis player. They could not understand the time and dedication it takes and they hurt me very much.'

It seemed an extraordinary thing to say, since José had, if anything, been guilty of pushing Justine too hard on her road to tennis stardom. Could she have been talking about Thomas and his request for comfort when his baby died? If they, the Henin men, had hurt her over Pierre-Yves, she had certainly hurt them too. And what she said now suggested that they had stayed away from Roland Garros because they had disowned her. But she must have known that José would surely have dropped everything to go there to see her fulfil her dream, if only she had invited him. After all, José had been there in 1992, with Thomas, when Justine had made what seemed to be an outrageous promise: that she would win the tournament and her parents would be sitting in the VIP seats on the Court Philippe Chatrier to see it happen. Was she seriously suggesting that José hadn't wanted to be there on the day when the dream came true and his wife's memory was so perfectly honoured? The whole thing seemed ridiculous.

Perhaps because of the manner in which he had been excluded, José objected strongly to the way Justine appeared to monopolise the grief and suffering felt by the entire family since Françoise had passed away.

He said later, 'When she won the French Open, she said it was for her mother and she said she missed her. That's fine, I understand. But in my opinion she gave the impression that it was harder for her than anyone else. That's simply not true. She has a busy life; she hardly has time to think. I have every day to think about my wife. And I miss her every day. Everyone wants Justine to shut up about her mother now. It's as if she is the only one who has suffered.'

Those words may seem as harsh to the outsider as Justine's. The difference is that José's outburst was born of rejection, whereas Justine's was motivated by an apparent desire to leave the family 'tie-break' exactly where it was. She was sending out a clear message that she didn't want any contact as she prepared for the most famous tournament of them all – Wimbledon. As before, she wanted to focus on her tennis and see how far she could go.

But Justine nearly didn't get to Wimbledon at all in 2003. While playing Kim Clijsters at a warm-up tournament in Rosmalen, she sprained some fingers on her left hand. She called the WTA Tour trainer, a move that seemed to interrupt Kim's flow and worked in her favour for a while. As Kim regained control, the pain appeared to return to her opponent's hand. This time, Justine chose to retire from the proceedings completely, sparking concerns that she might have to miss the big one. Those fears proved unfounded, however, and there was certainly nothing wrong with her by the time her campaign at the All-England Club began on 24 June.

Justine didn't drop a set all the way to the Wimbledon semi-finals. Then came the deliciously dramatic realisation that she would face the woman she had beaten in such controversial circumstances at the same stage a month earlier at Roland Garros – Serena Williams.

To say that Serena would be looking for revenge was something of an understatement. Justine knew she would have her work cut out. Although she had beaten Serena three times on clay, it would be tougher on grass, and tougher still owing to the recent history between them. Sure enough, Serena showed her little mercy. Whether or not, on some subconscious level Justine still felt uncomfortable about what had transpired during their last meeting. She later admitted she had been nervous at the start of the match. Whatever the reason, she fell 0–4 behind in the first set before she managed to settle. Although she broke back twice, Serena took control again to close out the set 6–3. The American then broke Henin-Hardenne's serve in the first game of the second set. Justine had three break points to strike back straight away, but she wasted every opportunity. She clearly wasn't feeling right mentally, and it wasn't hard to imagine why. As neutrals suspected, Justine couldn't live with Serena's thirst for revenge. Williams won 6–3, 6–2, and Justine faced the added humiliation of a painfully direct 'question' at the press conference.

She was confronted with the following: 'Someone just said that you told your coach you didn't admit to the hand-raising incident in Paris because Serena is arrogant and haughty.'

Justine was annoyed and replied, 'Why are you coming back all the time with what happened in Paris? We are here at Wimbledon. You know, when I talk with my coach, it's nothing to do with that. We didn't talk about this problem. So, I mean, I don't understand your question, really.'

It had been a legitimate point for the journalist to make, as it seemed relevant to the pre-match mind-set of both players. But Justine didn't like it, and the press conference was terminated. However, Justine's father was adamant that her defeat had been a natural case of 'what goes around comes around'.

José said, 'Both Williams sisters were very angry with Justine and that was the result. I don't think she was in a good mental condition for the Wimbledon semi-final. Sometimes it is easier to control a situation after a previous defeat than after a victory. In this particular case, that is what Serena did.'

She went on to defeat her sister Venus in the final, too, and no one who remembered the recent events of Paris could have felt anything less than delighted for her. It was the last chance either sister would have to play Justine in a Grand Slam that year, since both subsequently suffered injuries before the US Open.

* * *

In the run-up to Flushing Meadows, Justine was more worried about the injury her husband might do himself if he continued to indulge his passion for motorbikes on public roads. In his spare time away from the tennis circuit, Pierre-Yves Hardenne loved to ride his Honda 900. Justine understood that, but she also knew all about the statistics that pointed to a shorter life expectancy for petrol heads on two wheels. She had known enough death in her life.

'She detested the idea of me riding that motorbike on the roads,' Pierre-Yves told me in 2004.

But he wasn't about to give up his pride and joy just like that, not when he found the Honda so supremely liberating. It acted as a thrilling release, albeit temporary, from the pressured world of the tennis circuit, and a life dominated by his wife's career. On the bike, he was master of his own destiny, and it would take something special to make him reconsider. Negotiations seemed to have hit an impasse, until Justine came up with an idea that would bring added motivation to her latest Grand Slam challenge.

'What if I win the US Open?' she asked. 'Will you reconsider if I take the title in New York?'

Pierre-Yves decided to play along. 'She got me to promise that I would no longer ride my motorbike on public roads if she won the US Open,' he later confirmed.

Justine now knew that if she could pull off another unlikely Grand Slam triumph, she would effectively control the keys to the Honda, and at least determine when and where her husband risked his neck. With tragedy already a feature of her past life, she sensed a chance to have some say over the destiny of a loved one after all – but only if her tennis proved good enough.

* * *

As Justine packed her bags for the warm-up tournaments prior to Flushing Meadows, Pierre-Yves could have been forgiven for forgetting all about that deal. The Acura Classic in San Diego soon gave his wife new food for thought, too. It was the first time in seven years that she had turned up at any tournament without her coach, Carlos Rodriguez, who was unable to be there.

As she said later, 'I didn't know what to expect coming here alone without Carlos. I really enjoyed my week here. It was my first time here. People are so nice here.'

She sounded almost surprised that she could have thrived outside the cocoon of her Argentine mentor's protective guidance, the bubble that had kept most of her family out for so long.

At any rate, she reached the final, where she faced the familiar but formidable challenge of Kim Clijsters, who was a regular at the San Diego tournament and had been a quarter-finalist the previous year. A capacity crowd of 6,500 turned up to watch in the sunshine. Without Carlos to prepare her mentally, Justine started nervously against her compatriot and lost the first four games. She staged something of a comeback, but Kim was flying and took only 32 minutes to win the first set 6–3.

Clijsters' momentum was destroyed when Justine called the WTA Tour trainer during the break between sets to tend to two blisters on her right foot. To be fair to Justine, she had suffered a similar problem against Elena Dementieva in the third round. But an irritated Kim still resented the timing of the attention her rival was now receiving for what she seemed to regard as a very minor matter. Clijsters promptly lost concentration, and soon she was serving at 2–5 to stay in the second set. She double-faulted at 0–40 and the match was even.

Justine had the chance to break at 4–3 in the final set and did so after an amazing fourteen-point game. Her final service game was more of a formality, and a sweet cross-court drop volley gave her victory, 3–6, 6–2, 6–3. Apart from striking an important psychological blow before the US Open, Justine picked up a cheque for $165,000.

Although Kim was generously rewarded with a $94,500 runner-up prize, she was still far from happy, and the tournament will be remembered most of all for her remarks after the match. Asked about the unscheduled time out, Clijsters said, 'I'm sort of getting used to it. She's probably [called for a trainer] in every match that I've played against her. It's just a matter of knowing if it's really for an injury or if she's doing it for [another reason]. It didn't look like it was hurting. I think she was still running quick. I don't want to say anything bad about her, but it's not the first time that's happened. Those are moments that you know that she's not feeling her best and she has to try to do different things.'

As we shall see, some months later Kim qualified those remarks by insisting that she didn't blame Justine for anything she did on court. She had never accused Justine of feigning injury, she maintained. And anyway, it was Henin-Hardenne's right to open up a psychological front, just as it was any player's right, since tennis is a mental game as well as a physical one. But that climbdown came much further down the line and back in San Diego, it wasn't long before Justine heard that Clijsters had questioned her conduct. 'She can think whatever she wants,' she responded. 'I had to change my tape. It's very easy to talk about that, but at this point in the match I had to. I have no problem with my actions, not at all. When you're not in this situation, you cannot understand what it is to play with a blister. I almost had to retire in a couple of matches in the past for blisters, so I'm pretty comfortable with what I did.'

Back in the players' lounge, the small talk between Clijsters and Henin-Hardenne might have been a little less comfortable after that edgy exchange of views. But Justine had won, so why should she care? She politely informed Kim that she and Pierre-Yves were off to see a Celine Dion concert in Las Vegas, and forgot all about the accusations – for a while.

* * *

Still flying, Justine stormed to her sixth title of the year a fortnight later at the Canadian Open in Toronto. She crushed a nineteen-year-old Russian called Lina Krasnoroutskaya in little more time than it took to say her opponent's name. The 6–1, 6–0 scoreline was all the more satisfying since Krasnoroutskaya had dumped Clijsters out of the same tournament a few days earlier.

Justine hadn't lost since that thrashing from Serena at Wimbledon. In 2003, she had won the Dubai Open, the Family Circle Cup – an irony if ever there was one – the German Open, the French Open, her first Acura Classic in San Diego and now the Canadian Open. But the biggest remaining challenge of all was still to come: the US Open in New York.

CHAPTER 18

Match of the Century

They say that what goes around comes around. When Justine Henin-Hardenne first saw Jennifer Capriati dressed in all-American red skirt and blue top with white stars, she must have known the crowd would be as partisan as the baying mob in Paris whose unsporting antics had helped her through her last Grand Slam semi-final.

But this was the US Open, not the French, and the Flushing Meadows fans would be cheering for the girl on the other side of the net. Justine had chosen white, but under the bright floodlights that evening she definitely wasn't cast as the heroine of the piece.

Capriati's story was almost as remarkable as Justine's. She had first reached the US Open semi-final some twelve years earlier, the year before Justine went to Roland Garros as a child with her mother. Twice she had served for the match against Monica Seles, before losing the final set in a tie-break.

Jennifer, who had always believed in herself so completely, was shattered by this defeat to a fellow newcomer, and some suggested it had far-reaching consequences. Before long, she had descended into a world of substance abuse, only to emerge for another semi-final appearance a decade later against Venus Williams. Once again, she was denied at the death, and 2003 very possibly represented her last real chance to take the title.

Justine had never been past the fourth round before, and she didn't have much more support in the Arthur Ashe Stadium than could be supplied by her husband and her coach. No wonder Pierre-Yves had cancelled his flight back to Europe the previous Tuesday. Justine would need him more than ever now.

In addition to the thousands of American fans cheering Capriati's every move, Jennifer would enjoy the support of Matthew Perry, star of the hit television sit-com *Friends*. Then there was her father, Stefano, a big bruiser of a man, flat-nosed, the sort of person you'd want on your side in a fight. Whether Jennifer would find his presence inspirational, only time would tell. Justine's father continued to stay away from the circuit.

Kim Clijsters had sailed through the other half of the draw, and awaited the winner in the final. Now it was Justine's turn to try to give her arch-rival a rematch. Although she slipped and hurt herself on the very first point, the pain clearly didn't last. She exploded into a 4–1 lead, her two breaks of serve temporarily silencing the huge crowd.

Capriati struck back, an awesome forehand pass and a deadly smash helping her to break point in the very next game. Justine's first serve was a fault, and an American fan applauded. As Justine feared, the events of Paris hadn't been forgotten across the Atlantic. Unsettled, Henin-Hardenne squandered a great chance to get out of trouble, hitting inexplicably long. Capriati was back in the set at 2–4.

Dramatic rallies and superb volleys filled the next game, and the quality of the tennis was so high that few believed these women could maintain the pace. Evidently, the power of Capriati's flat forehand was forcing Justine to make mistakes, and the American held serve to creep closer still.

Although Justine had new balls now, fewer than 50 per cent of her first serves were finding their target, and the eighth game led to deadlock. When a brilliant drop shot from Justine caught Jennifer napping, the American kicked the ball away in disgust and berated a baseline judge for not calling one of her opponent's earlier shots out. The umpire, Alison Lang from Newcastle, UK, looked far from amused.

Capriati appealed again on the next point, claiming the ball was out. This time, the umpire overruled her baseline judge, who hadn't called, and handed Jennifer the point. A computerised replay showed that Justine's shot had hit the back of the line, yet the Belgian had shown enough self-discipline to accept the decision. Again, what goes around comes around. In Australia a few months later, Justine would benefit from a similar, yet far more important, overrule at a crucial stage of a big match. This umpiring mistake looked bad enough, though. A wild backhand soon saw Henin-Hardenne broken for the second time in succession. It was 4–4 and Jennifer's turn to serve. After so much fantastic tennis, neither woman had established supremacy, yet the crowd was captivated.

With power and subtlety in varying turns, Justine's backhand helped her to a 0–30 lead. But Capriati's all-round game was looking equally formidable, and she hit back to win her fourth game in a row, clenching her fist in triumph. A twelve-stroke epic in the tenth game confirmed the breathtaking quality of this second semi-final. Gripped by hysteria, the crowd screamed 'Out!' mid-rally, as Justine's pass flirted with the line. Another Henin-Hardenne shot flicked the net, allowing Capriati to take control of the point. Justine resorted to a desperate backhand on the half-volley, but Jennifer raced up to kill the point to huge cheers. Now she had two set points and the Belgian knew she was under pressure.

Justine's first serve was a fault, and this time more of the crowd dared to applaud her mistake. Capriati latched on to her second serve to force more pressure and Justine hit long when it really mattered. The stadium erupted; the all-American girl had somehow claimed five games in a row to take the first set 6–4. Her father was on his feet and even Jennifer allowed herself a smile during the break. Free of such family interaction, Justine stared her granite stare, bit her lip and planned her comeback.

Henin-Hardenne broke serve immediately at the start of the second set. Capriati, however, was soon over the shock and back with more scintillating tennis. She defended herself brilliantly against what looked like a winning smash, pounced on a drop shot and came up with the winning pass. In no time, Jennifer was 4–3 ahead, with Justine to serve again under pressure.

Two unforced errors took Justine's tally to 35 already, while Jennifer had erred fewer than twenty times. Another awesome Capriati forehand left Henin-Hardenne facing three break points. Having saved one, she swung wildly, and it dawned on Capriati that she would serve for the match. The American smiled again and even jumped for joy. With her fans roaring her on, it was as though the job were already done.

Although a double fault brought Jennifer back down to earth, Justine's weak return on the next point brought the all-important game level at 15–15. A wild Capriati forehand was followed by equally loose play from Henin-Hardenne. At 30–30, the home favourite was only two points from reaching her first US Open final. And had she shown the killer instinct right then, the match wouldn't have been remembered as one of the greatest in the sport's history. Or rather, had Justine failed to come up with the most daring of drop shots, at full stretch on the half-volley, the match might not have passed into tennis legend. But that's what she did: the ball crept over the net and she had a precious break point.

Capriati responded with a fantastic lob that looked unanswerable, despite Justine's attempt to scamper back in time. A girl with a bigger fear of failure – or indeed any fear of failure – would have panicked under the pressure. Somehow, Justine did more than simply reach the ball; she conjured an impossible backhand lob of her own, which so shocked Jennifer that she snatched at her next shot and sent it wide. The crowd wasn't so cocky now. It was 5–4, with Justine to serve.

Although Capriati had blown her big chance, she wasn't about to fall apart just yet. To her credit, the home favourite put Justine under new pressure and steered the next game to 15–30. Once more, the American was two points away from sending her supporters into celebration mode. Yet again, Justine tried something spectacular when others might have wavered. Her stunning backhand flew like a bullet beyond Capriati's reach, and Jennifer slammed her next shot into the net. With a desperate stretch for a backhand volley, Justine closed the game, raised both hands in the air and screamed, 'Allez!' Jennifer looked sick.

The mesmerising war of attrition continued, with an audience scarcely able to take in the quality of the theatre to which they were being treated. Capriati handed her opponent a break point and jumped about in frustration, where minutes earlier she had bounced with sheer delight. Justine was fallible, too, and wasted the opportunity with a wild return.

Whose nerve would crack first in what was becoming an epic? A straight-sliced backhand drop shot gave Henin-Hardenne advantage, and she followed up with a return that was lethal in its depth. Capriati was broken again and seemed to remonstrate with her family between games. What could she do against this sort of iron will? Was it a subconscious sense of obligation to her father that had made her tighten with the finishing tape in sight? Even without wishing to do so, families can make the pressure unbearable.

Justine swept through her service game, helped by a smash that hit the line and a punishing forehand. This time, Capriati had no reply at all and after 108 minutes, Justine took the second set 7–5. The players had claimed eleven games and one set each. They had thrilled millions of television viewers and the New York crowd, but all they had done so far in terms of the match was cancel each other out.

Capriati dashed off to the bathroom and changed into a new red top, white at the shoulders. The American stars on her original had been drenched with sweat as she gave everything she had to make her dream come true. If symbolism had anything to do with it, Justine had wiped away home advantage.

But the Belgian woman also looked as though she was already calling on her deepest reserves. She sought comfort in her towel, as if she knew the bloodiest set-piece battle in this brutal war was still to come. How long could they keep it up? At this rate, it would be past midnight before one had battered the other into submission. Sooner or later, one of these warrior queens had to lose, but which one would it be?

The first game of the final set began poorly, but it was Jennifer who seemed unable to impose herself early on serve. She volleyed long when it seemed easier to win the point, and thumped the net in self-disgust. Justine clenched her fist and made sure she maximised the psychological impact of the moment. The strongest mind would claim the spoils as both bodies ran out of juice.

When it was break point again, the Capriati volley was better directed. Except that Justine pounced to unleash an amazing cross-court backhand to win the game. With so little support in the stadium, she raised her arms again and cheered herself. The crowd fell silent, fearful that its heroine was about to implode again. In her long career, Capriati had won fourteen titles, no mean achievement. But Justine had already won twelve at the age of 21, showing just how ruthless she could be when given the chance.

Not that there was too much of the predator in Henin-Hardenne during the second game of the final set. Serving for a vital two-game cushion, she produced more unforced errors than winners. Faced with break point, she played her part in a titanic tear-up, with no fewer than fourteen strokes whipped into every corner of the court. At the end of it, Capriati set up a smash and executed coldly to bring the scores level again.

They had been hacking away at each other's resolve for more than two hours now, and neither girl had given an inch. You wondered if their bodies would withstand the pressure if they carried on like this for another set. But suddenly Jennifer looked revitalised, and when she came out on top at the end of another stunning exchange, Carlos Rodriguez shook his head in helpless admiration. An ace finished another game in the American's favour. And at 2–1, she seemed to have more left in her armoury.

Justine's mind appeared to be in temporary turmoil. At the end of another baseline blitz, she fired wide and then served into the net. It was break point. Having faulted, she was under pressure and an American fan shouted, 'Yeah! One more!'

Henin-Hardenne didn't oblige, hauling the game back to deuce. But still Jennifer wouldn't let her off the hook and conjured a magical forehand pass on the run. Now she was jumping about like a kangaroo again, as if to demonstrate her superior fitness and energy. And for once the celebration didn't turn out to be premature, because she completed the break to go 3–1 ahead. The home supporters simply went crazy.

In a match of such aggression and adventure, perhaps it was inevitable that the number of unforced errors was high. Justine still wouldn't have been happy to know that, at this ominous stage of the evening, she had committed 51 to her opponent's 31. And worse was to follow for the Belgian, who seemed for once to be running out of fight. Even when a piece of paper blowing across the court halted Capriati's service game just as she was about to close out, she refused to be riled. Instead, it was Justine who made the mistakes that led to a personal crisis. At 1–4, not even the queen of comebacks could have given herself much hope.

Scrambling for a foothold, Henin-Hardenne held her service game with the help of two sweetly judged drop shots. But the price she paid was to pull up and place her hands on her knees, as if suffering from some kind of injury. What she was actually feeling, it later emerged, were the first signs of cramp. It was 2–4 and Justine needed to win games quickly. But she didn't. An awesome forehand sent Capriati

5–2 ahead and she was still so pumped up when she reached her chair that she battered the towel as well. More ominously, she wasn't smiling any more.

In comparison, Justine looked desperate and exhaled sharply. It was as if she were trying to blow away the fatigue that seemed at last to be overwhelming her. She would need something special just to stay in the match now. And although she found enough power to go 40–15, the effort left her hobbling, as her muscles tightened once again.

In no time, Capriati had wiped away that advantage. At deuce, the home favourite was only two points from glory yet again. Justine hovered on the edge, ready to throw herself off and then holding back at the last moment. Before the eighth game of that final set was over, Jennifer had known no fewer than five times what it was like to come so tantalisingly close to victory. As in earlier crises, however, Justine came up with the right response at the right time. Finally, after more truly heroic resistance, she dug out two big serves to reduce arrears to 3–5.

But the Belgian's only immediate reward was to face Capriati serving for the match yet again. The spectators roared their approval and sensed that, this time, Jennifer would not fail them. How wrong they were. She tightened again and blew up on the vital game, firing almost everything too low. Justine had managed to hang on grimly, and now she was back in the hunt at 4–5.

But once hers was less of a rearguard action, Henin-Hardenne was just as vulnerable to a loss of concentration. Perhaps she felt she had done the hard part and the rest should take care of itself. A double fault left her only two points from defeat yet again. How long could she keep showing such superhuman defiance to prevent Jennifer from progressing to match point? To the consternation of the American public, the answer, it seemed, was indefinitely.

Just when Capriati seemed to have won the next epic rally with a crushing winner, Justine pulled out a seemingly supernatural return. With shock and wicked spin working against her, Jennifer scarcely knew which way to turn in order to play the ball. Somehow she, too, managed to swipe it back over the net in the nick of time. On they went, for nineteen stunning strokes, until Justine came up with a forehand that really did prove to be the winner. Entertainment? These were gifts from the sporting gods, and no one wanted to catch the last train back into New York City. Flushing Meadows was the place to be, even if it meant you might have to sleep rough that night.

Sublime talent and formidable willpower left both women ravaged, reminded that even well-trained bodies had their limits. By now, Justine was clearly in pain, no longer trying to hide it. Jennifer had also begun to wince with the sheer effort of staying in this epic. And what had they achieved? A wonderful tennis match, to be sure, but there was still deadlock at one set all, five games all. They would have to go on until one dropped. Short of throwing in the towel, there was no other way to end the agony.

With both women nearly out on their feet, Jennifer found the strength on serve to fire an ace past Justine, a huge morale-booster that took the score to 6–5 in her favour. In case she, too, was struck down by cramp, Capriati didn't dare to sit down in between games. It was almost as though she feared she might never be able to get up again. On they went, though both knew it must soon be over.

Jennifer had the best of the early exchanges as Justine served to stay in the match. Suddenly, Henin-Hardenne was 15–30 down and two points from defeat. A common state of affairs by now, except that she was hobbling desperately as the muscles in her left leg seized up. Could it have been gamesmanship? This time it was unlikely. The cramp looked genuine enough, given the way she was pulling up so suddenly in agony. And considering what happened later, it seems inconceivable that she could have faked her physical deterioration.

But there was no place for pity now. This was New York, a city in which the pecking order had always been decided by the maxim that only the strong survive. Capriati had to go for the jugular, to put Justine out of her misery, and march on to that first elusive final. What she actually did was make a generous, unforced error and then quietly succumb to the desperate power of Justine's serve. Six games all. Tie-break. Perhaps it was fitting that the deciding moments of this extraordinary match should be played out in the most dramatic way possible.

Many thought Justine would call a temporary halt here and see the trainer, so that she could at least reduce the chances of seizing up with cramp on the next, vital points. Perhaps fearing the crowd's reaction, she decided against it. What Kim Clijsters had said in San Diego about her alleged gamesmanship in such situations left her hesitant now. The

Bitter-sweet: instead of Justine's father, José, it is her uncle, Hugues Bastin, who leads Justine down the aisle to her husband-to-be, Pierre-Yves Hardenne.

Uneasy siblings: Alphonse and Jeanne with their five children: from left to right: Jean-Marie, Françoise, Jean-Paul, José and Geneviève. Of those pictured here, Justine was only speaking to her aunts in 2003.

LEFT: Thomas, Justine and David: she also broke off contact with her brothers during the family feud.

ABOVE: No love lost: Serena Williams can barely look at Justine after their controversial French Open semi-final in 2003.

BELOW: A dream come true, a promise kept. An ecstatic Justine honours her mother's memory with victory at Roland Garros.

ABOVE: Wherever tennis takes Justine, her husband, Pierre-Yves Hardenne, can usually be found somewhere in the background. Much of the time, he leaves the talking to Justine.

BELOW: Ferocious forehand: no one calls Justine Henin-Hardenne a one-trick pony these days. Opponents are painfully aware that she has a full array of shots in her armoury.

'The greatest shot in tennis – women's or men's!' Justine unleashes her trademark backhand, so revered by the legendary John McEnroe.

MAIN PICTURE: Keep off the grass! Justine serves with both feet well above the hallowed surface.

INSET: Preying on her mind: going into the summer of 2004, one Grand Slam title still eluded Justine – Wimbledon.

ABOVE: At Flushing Meadows in 2003, Justine served big when it mattered and reaped rich rewards.

RIGHT: She came off a drip to take the title: Justine's US Open triumph was one of the most dramatic in tennis history.

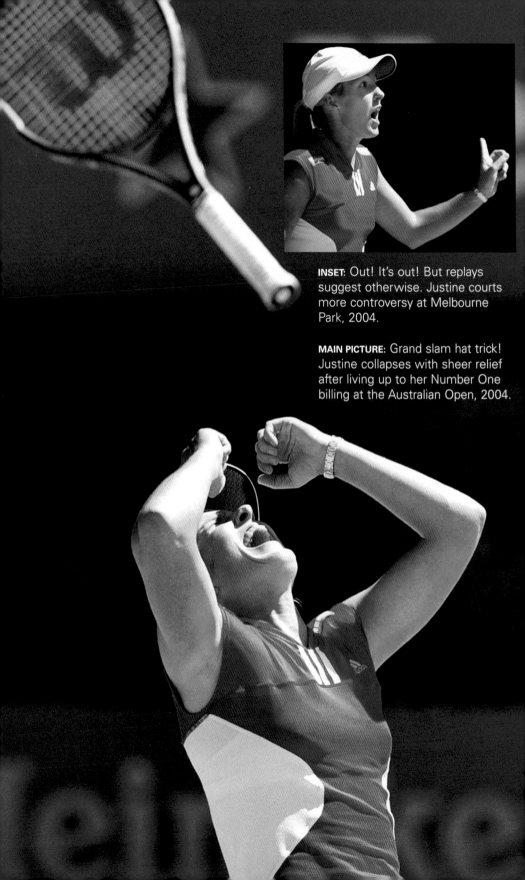

INSET: Out! It's out! But replays suggest otherwise. Justine courts more controversy at Melbourne Park, 2004.

MAIN PICTURE: Grand slam hat trick! Justine collapses with sheer relief after living up to her Number One billing at the Australian Open, 2004.

reaction in the Arthur Ashe Stadium might be hostile, especially if she won. So she gritted her teeth, rubbed her troubled left leg and prepared to continue, regardless of the consequences.

During the first three points of the tie-break, Capriati came up with a full array of shots. Unfortunately for her, they were all unforced errors. She hit low, long and wide in that order. When Justine looked up at Pierre-Yves and Carlos, genuine hope had returned to her eyes at last. She must have sensed the fear on the other side of the net as the pressure began to tell.

Although Capriati halted the suicidal slide with a winning backhand pass down the line, success was only temporary. Soon she was back hitting wild and long, weak and low with a new talent for self-destruction. What on earth was she playing at after all she had been through? Her opponent was injured, there for the taking. She didn't need to find superhuman angles and shocking trajectories any more; a percentage game would have done the trick. But there was something inside Jennifer Capriati that prevented her from taking the rewards she deserved. Soon she was 1–5 behind. Seconds later, at 6–2, Justine had four match points.

The disbelieving expression on her father's face as Jennifer threw it all away may have held the key to her story. You couldn't blame the fearsome-looking Stefano for the way he looked that night. But it was also hard to escape the feeling that Justine was at an advantage when the heat was on. These days, she had only herself to please. Pierre-Yves gave her no extra pressure. Whether it looked right or wrong to the outside world, that was the way she had organised her life. Faced with the biggest tennis tie-break of her young life, it seemed that Justine's 'tie-break' from her family was working in her favour.

Not that it seemed as though she had entirely conquered her nerves, as she blew out a breath and looked up at the dark New York sky. Was she praying? Was she calling on her mother to help her finish it? Matches had been lost from here, and would be again. Justine whipped a backhand into the net and felt new pain in her leg. She hobbled and limped, and took another serve. Capriati fought for her life and Justine's next backhand flew wide. Two match points thrown away. But, thanks to Jennifer's bizarre tactics, she still had two left.

Justine looked up at Carlos and Pierre-Yves. The coach clapped his hands together and gave her a reassuring nod. As usual, Pierre-Yves followed suit. In one final clash of wills, Henin-Hardenne sent Capriati the wrong way with a forehand down the line. Jennifer stretched to adjust her shape, and sent a lunging backhand towards the top of the net. The ribbon sent the ball back in her direction. It was over.

Justine threw her racket away, fell to her knees and held her head in her hands. Her head dropped right down, as if in thanks, until she was almost kissing the green court.

Alison Lang read out the score, 4–6, 7–5, 7–6, but no one really cared about the formalities.

What everyone knew was that this had been one of the greatest matches in the history of women's tennis – possibly *the* greatest, given that it came in the semi-final of a Grand Slam. Since we were only in 2003, people were fully entitled to describe it as the match of the twenty-first century, and that was strangely fitting. For José had called the memorable French final between Seles and Graf in 1992 the match of the previous century. And in many ways that drama represented the start of Justine's extraordinary Grand Slam odyssey.

Capriati was so heartbroken that she could barely bring herself to shake hands, and didn't seem even to look at Justine as she did so. The spectators were less bitter and howled their appreciation for an unforgettable night. Justine sat down and savoured the moment, utterly shattered. Unfortunately, the final was due to start in twenty hours.

Minutes later, Henin-Hardenne was on a drip and in serious danger of missing the final completely. On the verge of collapse, she was rushed to the US Open medical centre, the drip attached to her arm and her progress monitored carefully. The diagnosis was dehydration – not a life-threatening condition, but alarming all the same. In the early hours of Sunday, doctors were reluctant to give her the all-clear for a gruelling match that was due to be played later that same day. Time was against Justine and she knew it. Not even a supreme young athlete could be expected to recover sufficiently quickly to give a good account of herself in a Grand Slam final. What was the point of turning up if she was only a shadow of the real Justine?

She told journalists, 'I'll only go on court if I'm able to compete. Out there I was cramping on my left leg every time I tried to serve. A lot of people have talked badly about me in the last few weeks. So I made a big mistake. I needed a trainer and I will not make a mistake like that again.'

It appeared that Clijsters, with her criticism of Henin-Hardenne's gamesmanship, might have dealt a telling blow before the final had even begun. Now, thanks to a walkover, Kim stood a good chance of becoming a Grand Slam champion for the first time. Doctors rated Justine as 'possibly' rather than 'probably' capable of a sufficiently speedy recovery, but now lack of sleep threatened to become a factor hampering that recovery as that Sunday morning wore on.

For Capriati, there wasn't even the chance of an appearance in the final. At least she had quickly identified her amazing contribution to one of the great nights in women's tennis. She said afterwards, 'When I came off court, I felt the whole world was coming down on me. My heart was being ripped out. But now I look at it as a great match and I gave it all I had. For whatever reason, I didn't win. You have to give her credit for the way she was feeling out there and still trying to win. But I had the match in my hands. It was mine to win and I feel that I beat myself. I felt that I had to close out the match and she was cramping. I lost complete focus and everything kind of went off. I tried, but my shots weren't the same.'

Justine also admitted that she often felt defeat was just around the corner. She explained, 'I felt the match was almost over sometimes, but I was so proud of the way I did what I did. I think she got nervous as well. I'm so tired but I'm very, very happy. And I know my mother is fully aware of what I am doing.'

Not for the first time, Justine had voiced her personal conviction that, on some spiritual level, her late mother had contributed to her victory out on court. And considering the fact that Henin-Hardenne had been two points from oblivion no fewer than eleven times in the match yet still came out on top, it was easy to see why she felt that way.

But even now, Justine must have feared that her reward for such determination, another Grand Slam final, might yet elude her. Carlos and Pierre-Yves told her to stay positive, that she could win her race against time. She tried to believe them but wasn't so sure. Though the doctors and trainers had been magnificent in the way they had worked what magic they could, the process had eaten a big chunk out of the night. While Kim Clijsters was getting her beauty sleep, Henin-Hardenne was undergoing repairs until just before dawn.

By her own account, Justine managed to fall asleep at 3.45 a.m., but woke again at 8.30, with the Capriati epic still playing in her head. She beat the flashbacks and drifted back into a slumber of sorts until 10.30. Then, for more than an hour, she simply lay awake in bed and recharged her batteries, wondering if she would be ready.

Finally, it was time for the moment of truth. She stood up, dreading how her leg muscles would respond when they took some weight. As it turned out, she felt well enough to experience a new rush of hope. The doctors had done her proud. Now all she needed was a little more time to see if she would be able to give Clijsters her best.

By afternoon, the doctors rated her chances as 'probable'. Now Justine was less worried about her physical condition and more about how she could put the previous night's drama behind her. Normally players had a couple of days to leave the last match behind and move on, but she had only a few more hours to focus on the fresh task in hand.

At least she wasn't short of motivation. Not after the way Clijsters had appeared to call some of her previous injuries into question. Justine decided to use the psychological weapons at her disposal. She would try to carry the euphoria of the previous night through into the final. She would summon up her adrenaline again, before it had entirely receded from the last battle, and against all the odds aim for new sporting heights.

CHAPTER 19

Getting Even

That stare. Justine was like a boxer psyching out an opponent before a world title bout. She had already gone to work on Kim and they hadn't even decided who would serve first.

Clijsters was now world number one, even though she had never won a Grand Slam. She had broken Serena Williams' 57-week reign with sheer consistency, but that didn't mean she had a big-match temperament. Justine Henin-Hardenne looked determined to expose any lingering psychological frailties in the girl who had first felt her force at the age of eight.

Just how completely Henin-Hardenne had overcome her mental block against Clijsters was illustrated by the latest 'head-to-head' statistics. Although Kim was still in front overall, with eight victories to seven, Justine had won three out of the last four, and had been injured in the match she lost. She might have been seeded number two at Flushing Meadows, but Henin-Hardenne was judged underdog in the final only because she had pushed her body almost beyond endurance less than a day earlier.

Financially, the Belgian girls were in the same heavyweight league, having both won more than $2 million already that year. This was about far more than money, though. Kim was desperate to show that she could perform in a Grand Slam final, having already lost two. And Justine wanted to show that her French Open triumph was just the beginning.

Henin-Hardenne chose the same outfit she had worn for the marathon semi-final against Capriati: all white, with three lines of light blue running down her sides, her top merging seamlessly into her skirt. A white cap and ponytail rounded off the look that suited her so well.

Considering what Justine had been through in the previous twenty hours, she looked amazing and seemed relaxed.

With a ready smile, Justine had waltzed up to the stern-looking umpire, Lynn Welch, and even asked her how she was. But when Clijsters joined them, her mood suddenly changed and the charm disappeared. Justine's smile froze and faded, and she appeared to be trying to stare Kim out.

Suddenly, Clijsters was looking nervous and awkward. She had come there simply to play tennis and seemed unprepared for any additional mind games. The more she tried to behave normally, the more out of place she looked. Perhaps it was just as well for Kim that others now took to the stage to relieve the tension.

Two former champions graced the court to conduct the toss and wish both players well: Rod Laver, the legendary Australian left-hander who had had Melbourne's Grand Slam arena named after him; and Billie Jean King, who had been even tougher than Justine in her day.

Although Henin-Hardenne didn't know it then, she and King would take to the stage later that year as equals. For now, the two Belgians were the true stars of the show, and they couldn't wait to get started. Justine lost Laver's toss but looked unconcerned. With a nervous smile, Kim showed Laver that it is customary to kiss both cheeks in Europe. She didn't seem ready to recognise that she was about to walk into a war.

For the moment, it was still more like a publicity shoot, as Clijsters and her rival were told to stand shoulder to shoulder for more pictures. Bewildered, Kim even appeared to attempt a little joke at her own expense, openly wondering which way to turn for the final round of snapshots. Justine smiled efficiently for the cameras and completely ignored her opponent's casual remark. Clijsters twisted her upper body away, perhaps out of embarrassment, and shot Henin-Hardenne just a hint of a wounded glance before retreating to her side of the net. So far, the psychological battle had been a complete mismatch.

Justine seized the initiative in the first game, too, breaking Kim's serve before the Flemish girl had even begun to get into the match. For a while, it seemed that Clijsters would be given no second chance to compete. A forehand deep into the corner helped Justine close out the second game and confirm her advantage. And when a similar, bruising forehand set up an easy winner at the net, she had secured yet another early break of serve. The girl the Americans now nicknamed the 'Double H' had left her mark on her bigger, fresher opponent already. Another one-sided final was on the cards unless Clijsters could find her rhythm quickly.

That a woman could win seven titles in 2003 and reach the semi-finals of her first fourteen tournaments, yet still be short of self-belief at a time like this seemed nothing short of bizarre. Her boyfriend, Lleyton Hewitt, who had observed the early carnage from the stands, seemed as dumbfounded as anyone else by what he was seeing early on.

And then, mercifully, Kim sprang to life, using her power to force Justine into a series of errors. Suddenly, it was Clijsters with two break points, although Henin-Hardenne came up with an awesome serve to wipe away one of them. On the next, however, Justine double-faulted to show that she, too, was only human. The break gave Kim hope and now she needed to hold her serve to maintain the momentum. She did so, playing with aggression and purpose to show the sort of form that had brought her this far in the first place.

Soon Justine's serve was under severe pressure again, and she didn't seem to have the agility to see off the threat. Shots she would have made with ease a day earlier were hindered by fatigue, and she looked rather stiff and sluggish in her movements around the court. Perhaps the endless battle to subdue Capriati the previous night was finally starting to take its toll.

Before long, Clijsters had earned herself two break points to draw level at 3–3. The first she squandered with an ugly forehand. The second was in the balance when Kim's shot bounced up off the ribbon of the net. Typically, the ball landed back on Clijsters' side. Such ill fortune never seemed to visit Justine during these big finals; perhaps she made her own luck. A sublime drop shot gave Henin-Hardenne the edge in the hand-to-hand fighting that followed at the net. With advantage, she came up with an assured volley to close out the game and lead 4–2.

Kim soon seemed to be punishing herself for missing those precious opportunities. Two double faults left her next service game looking precarious, and already she had committed eighteen unforced errors to Justine's seven. But this time Clijsters kept her cool and exerted enough pressure to hold on at 3–4.

In the VIP seats, Kim's coach, Marc de Hous, and her parents, Lei and Els, knew how important the next game would be. If Clijsters could play her best tennis and break again, Justine might not be able to keep her fatigue at bay. Kim produced an awesome backhand lob from the baseline and a bullet of a forehand pass to earn two break points. Hewitt held his breath and hoped his girlfriend wouldn't waste her chance again. She fought hard in the rally that followed, Justine aimed too low with a jabbing swipe and Kim had broken again to level the scores at 4–4.

With Clijsters in full flow, Pierre-Yves chewed hard and looked more physically shattered than his wife. Carlos Rodriguez rubbed his eyes and seemed fed up as the match began to drift away from his player. Kim produced strong serves and violent volleys, defiant defence and punishing passes as she claimed her third game in a row. 'Come on!' she screamed, and clenched her fist in excitement at what she had begun to achieve at last. Now Justine was serving to stay in the set.

She looked exhausted, both mentally and physically. When she served her second double fault of the match, it was 0–30. Clijsters was only two points away from taking the first set but a loose shot let her opponent back into the game. Justine's relief was to be short-lived, however, and she miscued a forehand to give Kim two set points.

Even if Henin-Hardenne were to lose this set but win the second, it was hard to see where the energy would come from to take the match in three. So if Kim could claim just one more point, she would be odds-on to take her first Grand Slam title. The crowd applauded loudly in anticipation of the next, decisive Clijsters return. It never came. Incredibly, Henin-Hardenne chose this moment to summon all her powers and serve an ace straight down the middle.

No matter, Kim would have been able to tell herself, there was still one more chance. Perhaps she was learning at last, and she relaxed into a powerful rhythm in the next rally. Justine resorted to some desperate defence on the baseline. She knew deep down that taking the tournament depended on these last-ditch returns under heavy fire. And then, for no apparent reason, Kim snatched at a backhand and sent the ball flying a full metre too long. Justine gave her plenty of time to think about those two wasted set points before she served again.

Now Henin-Hardenne's famous backhand came into action. Her first landed deep in a corner and the second was a spectacular winner. Her mind apparently spinning, Clijsters sent her next return sailing from the court, and her chance had gone. Against the odds, a seemingly drained Justine Henin-Hardenne had saved the day and it was 5–5.

She glanced up at her contingent for inspiration, only to see a gaunt-looking Pierre-Yves clap her unsmilingly. Had he suddenly realised what this could mean for him? Was his love of motor-bike riding under genuine threat for the first time? Unconcerned by such issues, Carlos nodded in recognition of her little Houdini act, although he still looked slightly irritated that such heroics had been necessary.

But Kim's fragile confidence had been destroyed again. Gone was the flowing game that had threatened to take control of the final. Instead, she fired long three times in a row and handed Justine three break points. Clijsters came up with a memorable lob to save the first, but Henin-Hardenne's staring eyes suggested she was unfazed by the setback. A sizzling return gave Justine the chance to close in for the kill, and she sent Clijsters the wrong way with a deadly backhand volley. The vital break was hers, and she would serve for the set.

Justine took in more fluids, looked up at her loved ones, pressed her towel to her mouth and thought about the four short steps between her and the first set. When she marched out to put them into practice, the crowd buzzed with anticipation. Yet the famous Henin-Hardenne backhand dipped uncharacteristically into the net, giving Kim a glimmer of hope. But when she needed a winner to pile on the pressure, Clijsters only came up with another unforced error. Justine was off the hook, and her next backhand was a beauty, enough to bring fresh applause from the passive Pierre-Yves and Carlos.

The players did battle again, Kim's return drifted long and Justine had two set points. 'Allez!' she yelled to set off more alarm bells in that troubled Clijsters brain. Seemingly filled with anxiety, Kim botched an approach shot, seemingly thinking too far ahead. The ball didn't reach the required height, and by the time Clijsters reached the net, she had lost the first set.

Justine jumped for joy and clenched her fist. With another 'Allez!' she heralded her remarkable achievement. Two set points down at 4–5, she had somehow stormed back to 7–5, and now she might need only two sets after all. With mission impossible now half-accomplished, she dashed off for a toilet break, escorted by officials. Clijsters had ample time to wonder where it had all gone wrong.

* * *

Back in Belgium, José Henin might have been forgiven for wondering the same thing. As he sat in his newly rented flat in Marche with his youngest daughter, Sarah, he had mixed feelings about the events unfolding on the other side of the Atlantic. But this wasn't the right time to show his confusion. He had allowed television cameras to enter his domain and record his reactions, and he felt that he should put up a convincing public show in support of his daughter. Anything less would have been disloyal.

Not that José had to put on an act. He really did want Justine to win the US Open, and so did Sarah. They just didn't really know who Justine was any more. Inside this superhuman tennis player, could the girl they had once known and loved so much still have a place? Or was Henin-Hardenne someone else, a new person moulded by burning ambition and passion for her husband? The girl who had lived with them as part of the family until she was seventeen was still a vivid memory. How much of that person was there left in the extraordinary individual now dominating their television screen? This woman who had just come back from a seemingly impossible position when all seemed lost, who refused to contemplate defeat, even when she looked down and out, was a little scary. After all, they knew what she had brushed aside in order to focus so entirely on her ambitions. They knew the price that had been paid back home.

* * *

With 54 minutes already on the clock, Clijsters had to draw Henin-Hardenne into a prolonged dogfight. A final lasting more than two hours would become torture for an adversary who had spent three hours at war the night before.

At 40–15, Kim had two points for the perfect start to the second set on her own service game. When she only found the net on the next point, it was almost as though the Arthur Ashe Stadium knew what was coming. Another poor approach shot allowed Justine to whip a stunning backhand past her stranded opponent. When Clijsters aimed too low on deuce, Justine had an unlikely advantage. And the 'Double H' put enough strength behind her smash to send Kim's last shot of the game spiralling wide. Broken from 40–15,

Clijsters could only wonder how she had already managed to commit nineteen unforced errors on her forehand alone. It was usually her strongest shot.

Justine raised her game yet again to go 2–0 ahead. Kim looked totally dejected and Hewitt seemed close to tears on her behalf. Worse was to come for them. A breathtaking backhand lob under pressure took Henin-Hardenne into a 3–0 lead, and now Clijsters was reliving the nightmare of Paris. Her 37 unforced errors told a sad and unnecessary story, while Justine's more respectable count of fifteen revealed how economical she had been with what energy she had left after the previous night's exertions.

Every time Kim produced flickers of her finest tennis, Justine did something even better. She defended like a woman possessed and came up with winners, too. At 4–0 Henin-Hardenne had won seven games in a row and looked up at the sky, as if in thanks. Every time the television cameras caught Pierre-Yves, however, he looked that little bit more drained by the whole experience, as though it was his own stamina under severe examination. He continued to applaud without his usual smile, until the tide seemed to turn.

Kim had mustered some belated fighting spirit to end the long run of lost games and go 1–4. Now she had earned herself a break point, too. Faced with the beginnings of a comeback bid, Justine sensed how important the next point was. She seemed to mouth two words to herself before she took her next serve – 'Pour Maman'. Whatever source of strength she drew upon, it worked. The serve was good enough to entice Kim into overhitting her return.

If Pierre-Yves was delighted when Justine's smash gave her the advantage, he hid it well. But after his tears at Roland Garros, he seemed determined to appear less emotionally involved.

When Justine closed out the game to take a 5–1 lead in the second set, Pierre-Yves actually looked quite pleased. Perhaps he was getting used to the idea of racing the Honda around designated tracks. For a variety of reasons, Justine was clearly ecstatic about what she was on the verge of achieving. She must have been running on little more than adrenaline by now, and it was time to summon some more. 'OK!' she yelled as she jumped for joy. One more game and she could sleep as long as she wanted – perhaps even with Pierre-Yves' motorbike keys under her pillow, if the mood took her.

Clijsters seemed already beaten in her own head, and indiscipline on her serve gifted Justine two championship points. Pat Etcheberry gestured to Justine to stay calm. She looked up at the sky, as if in | new prayer, and gazed across at Kim. With the noise of the crowd ringing in their ears, Henin-Hardenne watched as Kim prepared to serve, then raised her hand. Kim didn't seem to see her, so Justine did it again. Perhaps the crowd's excitement was troubling her, though she had put up with far worse the night before against an American opponent.

Clijsters tried to ignore the hand signal and played on. Predictably, her first serve was a fault. The second serve sparked a mighty rally, with Justine firing deadly shots into both corners. She finished it with a magnificent volley on the run, and threw both hands in the air.

A double Grand Slam champion and Clijsters, her arch-rival, humbled both times. Perhaps now Kim would regret those remarks back in San Diego. Justine kissed her compatriot politely, though without much obvious warmth, and turned towards her own camp. While victory in Paris had overwhelmed her at first, this time she was clearly enjoying every moment. She laughed as Pierre-Yves hugged Carlos, and then she blew her husband a kiss.

Justine hadn't forgotten the motivation provided by the rare chance to increase her husband's life expectancy. She used mime to remind Pierre-Yves of their earlier bargain. She recreated the action of turning a key in the ignition of a motorbike. Then she gestured for him to hand over what she wanted. The meaning was unmistakable: she had kept her part of the bargain and now he would have to stop riding the motorbike she feared might kill him one day. Perhaps Pierre-Yves pretended that he didn't understand, because she laughed at his reaction and turned away with a dismissive wave of her hand.

But in early 2004 he assured me that he had been as good as his word: 'I don't ride my Honda on the roads any more, only tracks. I kept my promise, but I got to keep the bike, too.'

Back in the Arthur Ashe Stadium, Justine covered her face with her towel and tried to take in what she had achieved. When the towel fell away, she was still smiling, and an appreciative Flushing Meadows crowd was still applauding her. Those watching realised how fitting it was that Henin-Hardenne – the 'Double H' – should have taken the trophy. After what she had been through to defeat their favourite, Jennifer Capriati, she was the one who really deserved it.

But how on earth had she been able to beat the world's number one, so soon after coming off a drip? How had she beaten Clijsters, when Kim had put 67 per cent of her first serves in the right spot, compared with Justine's jittery 48 per cent? The answer lay in the other statistics, although they couldn't really convey Henin-Hardenne's sheer courage, or indeed the destructive quality of some of her work. Justine had hit eighteen winners to Kim's twelve; she had taken a ruthless six out of eight chances to break serve, while a wasteful Clijsters had succeeded only twice in eight tries. That contrast said everything about the different psychological make-up of the two girls. At the net, Justine had dared – and won – on thirteen out of twenty occasions. Despite Clijsters's towering physique, she had managed to win only six points out of sixteen in a similar situation. A total of 40 unforced errors showed how Kim had crumbled, whereas Justine had made only twenty mistakes in the entire match.

The happiest statistic of all for Justine was that she had now won two Grand Slams and seven titles in 2003, and there was still some way to go before the end of the year.

Carlos and Pierre-Yves were in fits of laughter as Justine took the microphone. This wasn't as poignant as Roland Garros, yet the US Open had been full of outrageous drama, too.

Justine said, 'Yesterday was a great fight against Jennifer and I didn't know how I was going to play today, but on the court I was feeling good.' Suddenly, there were tears in her eyes as she realised how extraordinary it was that she had played the final at all, never mind won. To the crowd, she said, 'You've been fantastic. Thank you so much.'

Then it was time to hold yet another Grand Slam trophy aloft, and somehow Justine Henin-Hardenne looked fresh and radiant. Winning does that to even the most exhausted of sportswomen. And the USA loves a winner. Against all the odds, Justine had conquered the Big Apple. And she had partially curbed her husband's daredevil spirit, too.

Back in Belgium, her father José said goodbye to the journalists who had watched the match with him, switched off his television set and struck up an easy conversation with the one daughter who still talked to him.

CHAPTER 20

On Top of the World

When Justine was asked in New York to whom she would dedicate her latest Grand Slam triumph, she replied, 'I just want to dedicate this victory to the people who are behind me, who have believed in me for a long time now. First, to my coach and my husband. I think they give me unbelievable support. You can't imagine how important they are to me. My husband was supposed to leave on Tuesday. I think he made a good decision.

'. . . I am a different person and a different player since my marriage. I'm just feeling so confident, you know. I've achieved something in my private life, you know, with my husband. It was very important for me to get married. A lot of things changed in my life.

'So he's with me almost all the time. I think it's easier. Like I said, he was supposed to leave and then he decided to stay. It's great to have a family. It gives me a lot of confidence. I'm feeling more secure. I know that after the tennis, I'll have something that's very important.'

No wonder José and his children were so disillusioned when they heard Justine say, 'It's great to have a family.' What she seemed to mean was something different: 'It's great to be able to choose your family.' Except that in reality, of course, you can't. How much life on the tennis circuit had in common with reality, though, was another matter.

Justine wasn't even going to let her hair down now, despite having done her job in such spectacular fashion. When asked how she would celebrate, she responded as though the word was almost ridiculous, '*Celebrate?*' she replied. 'Everybody knows me. I will never celebrate like maybe other people. But I want to be with my staff, you know,

178

with my husband, with my coach.' Then she said something extraordinary. 'I think about my family at home right now. They watched me on TV. I'm sure they're very proud of me, too.'

Who did she mean? Her aunts, Françoise and Geneviève? It was certainly true that Geneviève had been unable to get time off work to be there. Or did she mean Pierre-Yves's family, perhaps? If she was referring to her own closest family, such as her long-suffering father and her sister, Sarah, she was right – they had been watching on television back home; and in a way they were proud, too. But she hadn't called her father before the final, she didn't call him after the final, and she didn't call him once she got home either. Yet, from the way she spoke, you would hardly have guessed there was so much family discord behind her tennis success. Her words were misleading, though not deliberately so, and might even have given her father false hope of an imminent reconciliation.

* * *

Within hours, the girl who usually shunned the glamour and the glitz surrounding the tennis circuit was being photographed in limousines and on top of skyscrapers, arm in arm with her beloved Pierre-Yves. A glossy magazine claimed that he had practically saved his wife from her father. It had to be true, she was the new queen of America, and when she and Pierre-Yves spoke, people listened.

Little Justine had conquered the Big Apple, New York. As the Sinatra song said, if she could make it there, she could make it anywhere. She had hit the big time and now everyone wanted a piece of her. But all she really wanted to do, she said, was to go home and enjoy some peace and quiet.

However, as she landed in Brussels, she was hit by unfounded insinuations from Kim's father, Lei Clijsters, that Justine's new power could not be explained by work in the weights room alone. Others jumped on the bandwagon, and suddenly all the hard work Justine had done with Pat Etcheberry in Florida the previous winter, the punishing routines that had left her close to tears, seemed to count for nothing.

At the airport, Justine reminded the press pack just how tough it had been with Etcheberry and insisted, 'I've nothing to hide. It's thanks to my hard work and combative nature that I've achieved these results. I've proved that I was a fighter. That's all. My only drug is work.'

Justine's camp demanded an immediate retraction from Lei Clijsters and others. Sure enough, Kim's father had to lead a public climbdown the very next day.

If Henin-Hardenne needed any further motivation, her arch-rival's family had served it up on a plate. And there was one fight that Justine still had to win, if she was to round off the year in perfect style. She had told her mother that she would win the French Open, and she had. For good measure, she had even thrown in the US Open, too. But there was another promise she had made to Françoise, way back when she had hardly looked big enough to hold a full-sized racket – that she would become the best in the world. Her aim now was to topple Kim Clijsters from her perch and become world number one when the season effectively shut down in November.

* * *

With such lofty and long-held ambitions in mind, her cousin Maud's wedding on 27 September 2003 simply wasn't on her agenda. The girl who had once been like a sister to Justine found that she was snubbed by her famous relative on her happiest day. Not only did Justine fail to attend; she didn't even have the courtesy to reply to the invitation, which had been sent to her in plenty of time by Maud's father, Jean-Paul. Perhaps Justine thought that her own father, Jean-Paul's brother, would attend. But José didn't want to go either, fearing that the pain of having been excluded from his own daughter's wedding would surface to overwhelm him.

* * *

Against this backdrop, Justine remained focused, less than a fortnight later, on the next phase of her dream – to become the best in the world. At the Porsche Grand Prix in Filderstadt, Germany, she needed to beat Clijsters in the final to take her crown. She lost 5–7, 6–4, 2–6.

She might have been facing the same old adversary, but this had been a new psychological challenge. As the pretender to the crown, Justine had shown too much anxiety against an opponent playing with all the authority her number one ranking afforded her. She went away to reflect on what had happened, and prepared for a fresh assault on the summit the following week in Zurich. There was still time to achieve her aim because it was only mid-October.

The Swisscom Challenge in Zurich followed a predictable pattern right up to the semi-finals, with Justine in one half of the draw and

Kim in the other. Whereas Justine defeated Nadia Petrova 6–4, 6–4, Clijsters surprised everyone by falling at the final hurdle. Suddenly, Jelena Dokic was the girl Justine would have to beat in order to fulfil her dream.

The fact that she won the first set 6–0, in only fifteen minutes, was a perfect illustration of Henin-Hardenne's ambition. Now glory was just one more set away, although the crowd in the Schluefweg Arena was clearly hoping for more of a spectacle when the players took their positions again. Although Dokic did her best to oblige, she wasted two chances to break in the second game. And Justine was in no mood to be denied. She stormed back to serve for the match at 5–4. Her aim was true throughout that final, historic game, and when Dokic misjudged a forehand, it was done. Justine Henin-Hardenne was now officially the greatest woman tennis player in the world.

As a small child, she had told everyone it would happen. Only her mother, Françoise, had seemed to believe her. Now they had both been proved right. Justine raised both hands and tried to savour the moment. 'All my life I have dreamed about winning Grand Slams and being number one in the world. This is a very special day for me, and one I will remember for ever. It's taking a while to sink in now, and I think it will take a few days to truly realise what has happened here,' she said.

* * *

A few days were all she had. Henin-Hardenne decided she needed a rest, and she had time to reflect upon earnings so far that year of $3,277,264 in prize money alone. Meanwhile, Clijsters won her fourth Luxembourg title in five years, and suddenly Justine had been deposed by her arch-rival. She had known it would happen. She also knew that what really mattered was to be world number one at the end of the season. Whoever managed that would have weeks or even months to savour the achievement and feel the kudos that came with it. Therefore Justine concentrated all her energies on the WTA Championships in Los Angeles the following month. It would be the final battleground of the year, and the reward for success there would be sporting immortality.

The way the respective rankings points worked out, Justine didn't even have to win the LA tournament, held at the Staples Center in November. All she needed, in order to reclaim the crown, was to qualify for the semi-finals. First, she would have to negotiate a new and complicated round-robin format of matches in her particular group – Black Group.

Since the Williams sisters were still injured, and Henin-Hardenne wouldn't have to face Clijsters until the final, the main objective seemed to be well within her reach. But then Justine fell ill with a sinus infection that led to headaches, fever and a sore throat. She was due to face Anastasia Myskina in her opening match and the willowy Russian could be a tricky opponent at the best of times. Under normal circumstances, Henin-Hardenne would probably have pulled out. But there was nothing normal about this particular challenge. The stakes were too high to walk away now and she went on a course of antibiotics instead. Although they didn't really solve the problem, Justine tried to forget how she was feeling and insisted the show must go on. She stepped into the arena looking pale and tired.

Myskina spotted her physical weakness immediately and began to take her apart. In no time at all, the Russian was 5–0 ahead in the first set. Justine couldn't seem to get her timing right but managed to hang on grimly and retrieve one break to make it 5–2, even though, as she explained later, 'I was being run all over the court, and I was very nervous, so it wasn't easy for me to breathe.'

At that stage, she was apparently on the point of collapse and could feel her heart pounding against her ribcage at a frightening rate. Perhaps this was as close to a panic attack as she had ever had on court. Was she really risking her very life for the sake of that crown? She called the WTA Tour trainer, who checked her blood pressure and heart rate. She said later, 'My heart rate was so high and it made me feel nervous. With the stress and physical problems I have had in the past few days I was feeling really bad, but the trainer told me I was fine and then I felt more relaxed. I am not the kind of player to go on court and stop. I take my responsibilities and do my best.'

And at that painful moment, Justine seemed to feel that her main responsibility lay in fulfilling the promise she had made to her late mother to be the best. She snatched back the psychological initiative somehow from an opponent whose storming start seemed to be preying on her mind. For Myskina had been given extra time to think about how she was still that one tantalising game away from taking the first set. It stayed just beyond her. A revitalised Justine rattled off five more games to make it seven in a row and take the opening set 7–5.

During changeovers she had used only a throat spray. By any sporting standards, it was a miraculous recovery.

To her credit, Myskina didn't just halt the slide; she hit right back and took the second set 7–5 in front of a thrilled crowd. Now it was down to who wanted it more. And considering the indomitable spirit of Justine Henin-Hardenne, and what was resting on her ability to forget her illness, the outcome of the dramatic third set should have been more predictable. In fact, it went to the wire, and Justine only emerged the victor by the now-familiar score of 7–5.

'It was a fantastic battle,' she declared afterwards. 'We both had chances to win.'

Myskina didn't need telling. Later, she revealed, 'I didn't sleep well that night. I was thinking how stupid it was to lose a set when you are up 5–0. I was so mad at myself, I was crying for a couple of hours.'

* * *

It wasn't the first time Justine had broken the heart of an opponent, and the woman now standing between her and ultimate glory knew the feeling very well. Jennifer Capriati prepared to avenge her unforgettable US Open semi-final defeat of a few months earlier. But before she even stepped on court, she knew that the task would probably remain beyond her. While Henin-Hardenne might still be ill, Capriati had a nagging physical injury, one that presented a bigger threat to her chances of playing her best tennis. A strained hip flexor was limiting her mobility. The American decided to play anyway and give it her best shot.

Justine later assessed her own mood going into this huge match: 'I wasn't 100 per cent. But when you are playing relaxed, it helps you. There weren't too many rallies. I was calm and I wasn't afraid. I knew before the match that if I won I was going to qualify for the semis and [be] number one in the world. That gave me so much determination. Coming on the court, I was so focused.'

Henin-Hardenne powered her way to a 5–2 lead and served out the first set comfortably, dropping only one point in the last game. Capriati just couldn't seem to put her under any pressure. She took a timeout in the second set to remove a bandage that was rubbing painfully against her thighs, but it didn't seem to help her in quite the same way as Justine's timely pause in her previous match. Henin-Hardenne stepped up a gear and ran away with the set to close out the match

6–1. It was a fitting way to fulfil her dream, and now her mother's memory had been honoured to perfection.

Perhaps her opponent couldn't quite understand that sort of motivation. But there appeared to be traces of irony in Jennifer's tone when she commented on Justine's extraordinary return to health.

'I've never seen anybody recover as fast as she does,' Capriati remarked, perhaps also remembering the cramp Justine had suffered at a key moment in the US Open semi-final. 'She plays pretty good for all these things that bother her.'

As usual, Justine didn't miss the opportunity to cast herself in a positive light. 'That's what was strange this year: I always played my best tennis in the toughest situations. Mentally I have been stronger than ever at these moments, like at the US Open.'

CHAPTER 21

The Glory

It was already sinking in for Justine Henin-Hardenne. 'This feeling, winning the Grand Slams, being number one, it's just an amazing feeling and I want to keep this feeling for a long time. This season I did everything almost perfect.'

Now in Los Angeles, she had fought off illness and exhaustion to confound the statisticians who had still threatened to leave a double Grand Slam winner in second place at the end of her biggest year. Although she subsequently lost to Amélie Mauresmo in the semi-final, and therefore squandered the chance for a crack at the biggest single prize in the history of women's tennis – $1,000,030 (the thirty dollars had been added on to mark the WTA's thirtieth anniversary) – it hardly seemed to matter in the general scheme of things. Justine had millions in the bank already and she had just picked up $250,000. But money wasn't her motivation. She just wanted to be the best. She had the precious French and US Open titles under her belt, and now the year-end world number one crown. How much more did she need? And who would care about this defeat at the end of the year? In 2003, she had played eighteen tournaments, won eight titles and been runner-up three times. Even her less successful weeks had seen her reach six semi-finals, including Wimbledon, and one quarter-final.

So it wasn't the defeat against her friend Mauresmo that told the real story, but the honours bestowed on Justine immediately afterwards. As part of the celebrations for the thirtieth anniversary of the Women's Tennis Association, a parade of champions took place in the Staples Center in LA. Justine would barely have time to towel herself down and make herself look presentable before she was asked to take her place in history.

Henin-Hardenne was certainly the woman of the moment. Her victory over Capriati had clinched the 2003 number one title and confirmed her status as only the thirteenth undisputed queen of world tennis in WTA history. At the tender age of 21, she was to be honoured alongside some of the all-time-greats of the game, her talent celebrated as though she was already a legend.

Owing to the complications of the WTA ranking system, Kim Clijsters was first to be introduced as 'current' number one, even though she had effectively handed over that title earlier in the week. Technically, however, Justine would only be crowned queen at the end of the LA tournament. On the night, it made little difference. They had both joined the greats, two girls who had been battling it out since they were eight- and nine-year-olds in Ostend.

Clijsters was delighted to be first to walk on to a stage soon to be graced by the true living legends of world tennis. And then it was Justine's turn. Having hastily thrown on a red baseball cap and black tracksuit with white stripes, she began her proud walk towards the platform, rapturous applause filling the hall. The strain of a gruelling and unforgettable year seemed to fall away as she took centre stage, her broad smile beaming back at the spotlight. She was still pale, but the after-effects of her illness were the last thing on her mind now. Justine was clearly filled with excitement at the prospect of what was to come. There was still something of the child about her, the fanatical fan who had watched a final at Roland Garros with her mother and been left in total awe of Steffi Graf and Monica Seles. Sadly, neither of the 1992 finalists was present now, but their absence couldn't detract from the charm of the occasion.

One by one, many of the former world number ones joined the Belgian duo, to more loud cheers from the American crowd. The first two, Jennifer Capriati and Lindsay Davenport, were women Justine had beaten quite recently. But when Martina Hingis and Tracey Austin stepped up, the sense of history slowly began to grow. And each woman seemed to love the acclaim as much as the number one who had strutted her stuff seconds earlier. That was the beauty of it. They all seemed so genuinely pleased to be acknowledged on such a special occasion. Something genuinely humble yet very memorable was unfolding.

Martina Navratilova took her place on stage among the greats, inviting a high-five from Justine and the others as she passed along the lengthening row. Chris Evert stepped up next, sparking more cheers and high-fives. Justine's smiles turned to laughter as women more than twice her age made her feel every bit as important as they were.

How Françoise would have loved to see her daughter rubbing shoulders with the goddesses of the game. Perhaps mother and daughter would have shared a knowing smile that said, 'We told them it would happen, didn't we? We told them eleven years ago!'

Maybe the thought also crossed Justine's mind as she stood there, soaking it all up. One word summed up the expression on her face better than any other: satisfaction. This, you sensed, was when it all began to sink in. And rounding off the procession of greats was Billie Jean King, who, in her prime, struck fear into all her opponents. King's legendary force of willpower would have inspired a young fighter like Justine to even higher levels of aggression, had they been able to play each other in their prime. Henin-Hardenne was too young to remember, but King had been the first woman tennis player to seem superhuman. Justine hadn't become quite as fearsome as that yet, but they shared the same spotlight now. The link between past and present was complete.

How José would have loved to have the chance to be sitting somewhere in the arena as his daughter took her place in tennis history at the age of 21.

* * *

Those who witnessed that magical evening all agreed on one thing. The former number ones who failed to turn up, such as the Williams sisters, Graf and Seles, had missed out on something special. A simple ceremony, structured yet full of spontaneity: a perfect blend of fun, teasing, recognition and respect. Perhaps it was so charming because those who did attend really wanted to be there. To those who didn't make it, for whatever reason, it was their loss.

There would be more honours for Justine before the year was out. First, she was hailed Belgian Sports Woman of the Year, an accolade especially satisfying because it had gone to Kim Clijsters on several previous occasions. And just before Christmas, Justine was named International Tennis Federation World Champion for 2003. It served as confirmation of her stature and backed the new order of rankings. Come New Year, Henin-Hardenne was still top of the pile.

WTA Singles Rankings – 10 November 2003

1.	HENIN-HARDENNE, JUSTINE	BEL	6628
2.	CLIJSTERS, KIM	BEL	6553
3.	WILLIAMS, SERENA	USA	3916
4.	MAURESMO, AMELIE	FRA	3194
5.	DAVENPORT, LINDSAY	USA	2990
6.	CAPRIATI, JENNIFER	USA	2766
7.	MYSKINA, ANASTASIA	RUS	2581
8.	DEMENTIEVA, ELENA	RUS	2383
9.	RUBIN, CHANDA	USA	2328
10.	SUGIYAMA, AI	JPN	2235
11.	WILLIAMS, VENUS	USA	2211

CHAPTER 22

Love and Marriage

Alphonse Henin, Justine's grandfather, had a favourite saying: 'Love is blind. Marriage opens the eyes.' Having been married to Jeanne for more than 50 years, he should have known. But then he liked what he saw when his eyes were opened.

Apart from that particular piece of good fortune, I asked him if there was any other secret to his marital bliss. He smiled and said simply, 'Always listen to your wife.'

Throughout 2003, Justine Henin-Hardenne told the world how happy she was with her husband, and the fairytale endured. Pierre-Yves travelled the world as her adviser, her assistant and even, to an extent, her manager after Vincent Stavaux left her entourage that year. Besides that, he was her friend, her husband and her lover – when there was enough time away from tennis.

No one – not even the alienated José – could say that his daughter's marriage had been anything but beneficial to her game at this stage of her career. After all, she had won the French Open only seven months after the wedding, and the US Open only three months after that.

Perhaps contrary to the expectations of some relatives, it appeared that Justine Henin-Hardenne also liked what she saw when marriage opened her eyes. But still no one seemed to have opened her eyes to the plight of some inside her own family. Pierre-Yves was no knight in shining armour for them.

The Henins saw how Pierre-Yves, by now 23, and her coach, Carlos Rodriguez, sometimes basked in the glory of Justine's success, while protecting her from unwanted attention. Conquering the world didn't seem to have made Justine any more accessible to many of the males in her family. And so the feud rumbled on.

For Justine, Christmas 2003 did not involve the sending of many cards to those with the surname Henin. Her grandparents, Jeanne and Alphonse, were among many left off the list – the latest slap in the face for elderly people who had already suffered enough from her decision to keep her distance.

Alphonse revealed, 'Our daughter Geneviève comes round and says that Justine still asks after us sometimes. I hope she does think of us.'

The occasional enquiry through a third party hardly seemed adequate attention from a granddaughter. But Justine appeared to be convinced that such sacrifices had to be made. A clear head allowing her the chance to dominate world tennis was the carrot being dangled before her. Henin-Hardenne was all about the present and the future now. The past was no longer her prison. She would take only what she chose to from that troubled terrain.

José likened the process to brainwashing, with Justine a willing participant. He said, 'Justine doesn't want problems. She lives in her own world now, and from our point of view it's like she is part of a sect. I suspect that those around her tell her she needn't have any problems in her new world unless she invites those problems in. They look after her and tell her she doesn't have to worry about a thing. But real life is not like that.'

Pierre-Yves and Justine had handpicked those they trusted. 'I have nice people around me now,' Justine had said during the summer of 2003. José had not been chosen, but then families are not something that can be chosen; not like a tennis coach or a manager. Although he had been ignored for years, her father would still watch her on his television, putting up with the inevitable shots of Pierre-Yves supporting his wife from the players' box.

In Melbourne, however, where Pierre-Yves joined his wife for the first Grand Slam tournament of 2004, he soon found media attention more focused on another top star's partner. At a post-match press conference after one of the early Australian Open rounds, Justine was asked if she thought marriage would be different for Kim Clijsters because she was about to wed fellow tennis professional Lleyton Hewitt, Australia's favourite.

Dumbfounded, Justine replied, 'I'll never be in her situation, so it's hard for me to tell you!' She raised a laugh with that remark. More seriously, she added, 'I'm happy to be married to somebody who is not involved in tennis, because I think we live under a lot of pressure. But the thing for Kim and Lleyton is they can understand each other pretty well because they're doing the same thing. But I'm very happy in my couple. We talk a lot, Pierre-Yves and myself, but never on tennis.'

The fact remained, however, that they hadn't been able to enjoy much time away from tennis so far. Henin-Hardenne's pursuit of professional excellence led her to a new midwinter hell in another of Pat Etcheberry's punishing training camps. The Florida-based fitness guru wasn't prepared to be more lenient this time round simply because Justine had achieved some major goals since last they met. Under his guidance, she emerged stronger than ever in January, with her enthusiasm apparently undiminished. 'I am happy to be back on the circuit,' she declared. 'I am fitter than this time last year, and I am ready.'

She would need to be. Preparations for the Australian Open went well – despite the fact that she knew she would be seeded number one at a Grand Slam event for the first time. She won the big warm-up tournament, the Adidas International in Sydney, beating Amélie Mauresmo 6–4, 6–4 in the final. Although she didn't play her very best tennis, it still brought her the fifteenth singles title of her career.

Henin-Hardenne claimed afterwards, 'My name is at the top of the list, but to be honest I don't feel any more pressure than before.' Within weeks, though, she was saying just the opposite, as it became obvious that she was struggling to come to terms with the weight of expectations. She was human after all.

Justine's eldest brother, David, would have liked to add a touch of normality to her life, given the right circumstances, even if that only meant being at the end of a phone when she felt like a chat. Unfortunately, he had been shunned along with most in his family. He was both cautious and amusing when he observed with typical stoicism, 'It's a shame that my sister is so heavily influenced by those around her. But we who have not been afforded the slightest contact for the last couple of years will continue to get up in the middle of the night to support her.'

Just before the Australian Open, José Henin tried to deny that he would be glued to his television screen back in Europe when his daughter, now almost a stranger, went in search of her third Grand Slam title in eight months: 'I hate the big tournaments now. Justine's face and voice are everywhere. It's impossible to escape – but I'll try.'

He was almost convincing, until Justine's sister, Sarah, caught my eye with a knowing smile. We almost burst out laughing, because we both knew he wouldn't be able to resist the temptation to watch. Stranger or not, he was still Justine's father.

Until the tournament started, however, José devoted most of his attention to his younger daughter, as was his habit. And in mid-January 2004, to celebrate Sarah's seventeenth birthday, he cooked a superb chicken dinner in the rented apartment in Marche. Justine's name was very much off the menu for the entire evening. Her brothers, Thomas and David, were there with their partners. I felt lucky to have been invited to attend what was predominantly a family occasion. The evening was such a delight that it made you realise what Justine was missing.

It was still the player's choice to perpetuate the feud, not her family's. Earlier in the day, Sarah had confirmed that she would like to know her sister again, if only Justine would show her family some consideration. And Thomas expressed similar feelings when he admitted, 'I miss Justine. But it's the old Justine I miss, not the new one. The new one is a stranger.'

Then Thomas, an intense individual, came out with something even more powerful. He said, 'We've been without Justine for three years now, and our life is better than when Justine was around, because we're a real family.'

Having witnessed the happy intimacy of a family occasion 'chez Henin', it was easy to understand what Thomas was getting at. But what he really meant, I suspected, was that he wished Justine would care for her family more than she cared about her tennis, so that she could be part of the clan, too.

And I couldn't help wondering whether Justine, toiling away on the other side of the world, had even spared a thought for her sister on her birthday. There had been no card, and Sarah certainly wasn't holding her breath for any long-distance phone call. You could see why Pierre-Yves was Justine's main off-court preoccupation, but did that mean everyone else had to be eliminated for eternity, just because they didn't always behave in the way she wanted them to?

As well as declaring, 'Love is blind. Marriage opens the eyes,' her grandfather had added, 'There will come a day when Justine realises what she has done.' But her uncle Jean-Marie was equally certain that she would struggle to maintain her apparent peace of mind indefinitely. Even great tennis champions cannot play for ever. Later, they have more time to think about the choices they have made in life. And in January 2004, José's younger brother predicted that Justine wouldn't always be able to appear so comfortable with what she had done. 'There seems to be no remorse in her for now, but you can bet there will be,' he said confidently.

Even someone firmly placed in Justine's camp found it hard to reject the theory that in some ways Justine is less mature than she thinks she is. During the build-up to the Australian Open, that person chose their words very carefully, warning me not to bring up these issues with the player herself. 'Justine won't talk to you about this. But what she did, she didn't do easily. Maybe when she becomes a mother, she will understand her father better. The older she gets, the more she'll understand. I believe that when she is 30, she'll understand better. The situation is hard for the entire family. Hard for her father and hard for her, too.'

But it seemed that only Justine could end the agony for others. And here we were being told that she might not even understand the conflict herself until she was a parent. She was on record as saying that she was in no hurry to have children and wanted a full tennis career first. So where was the guarantee that, eight or nine years down the line, José, with his extra weight and enlarged heart, would still be alive? After all, he had shared some ominous news in January 2004: 'The doctor just told me that if I carry on as I am, I could die at any time.'

And what about Justine's grandparents? At the start of 2004, they also revealed that they hadn't been in the best of health. No one lives for ever, and it seemed that Justine was steering a perilous course through life, one that might later bring her considerable regret.

If there were ever to be reconciliation with her family, it appeared that Justine would have to change her own perspective before she experienced parenthood. Otherwise there was a sad but strong possibility that some of her estranged relations might no longer be around to play their part in that reconciliation.

As it was, some were running out of patience already. Hence Thomas's insistence, 'I only have one sister – Sarah.' Then he quickly corrected himself. 'No, I have two sisters. Sarah – and Florence.'

CHAPTER 23

Down Under

This was a first. Justine was hot favourite for the Australian Open and the pressure was on. Physically Pat Etcheberry had ensured she was well prepared, giving her another murderous fortnight of mini-sprints and weights in Florida before Christmas. There had been a minor ankle twinge in Sydney, but nothing serious. Other top stars appeared to be in far more trouble. Serena Williams didn't make it and Jennifer Capriati pulled out, too. Kim Clijsters had an ankle injury and wasn't expected to be ready in time. Suddenly, it looked as though only the towering figure of Venus Williams could keep Henin-Hardenne from her third Grand Slam triumph inside a year.

In the run-up to the tournament, Justine's mind wasn't always firmly fixed on tennis. During the Adidas International in Sydney, the warm-up tournament she won, she arranged for some children with cancer to come and watch her second-round victory over Conchita Martinez.

During the post-match press conference, she said, 'I have my foundation. In French it's Les Vingt Coeurs de Justine. I'm going to meet some kids who have cancer. So it's a great opportunity for myself, because I want to give them a little bit of time.'

Justine was obviously thinking deeply about others, even if most of her family still didn't appear to fall within that sphere. Sydney had given her a reminder of a world beyond tennis. Her reward was temporary respite from being the woman everyone wanted to beat. But soon it was time to move down to Melbourne to prepare for the defence of her number one ranking. She was about to mount an assault on a Grand Slam title that had so far eluded her.

If the weight of other people's expectations was heavy on Justine's shoulders, imagine the feelings of her first opponent as she stepped out into the daunting Rod Laver Arena. Olivia Lukaszewicz was a fifteen-year-old Australian who had been given a wild-card entry into her home tournament. She was ranked only 870 in the world, and even a tall, athletic build and the support of the local crowd were unlikely to alter her fate.

Justine, dressed in eye-catching red, went to work. And if anyone thought she was going to take pity and give the kid a game or two, they must have been mad. It was the dreaded 'double doughnut', 6–0, 6–0. Poor Olivia managed to win only 25 points in the whole match. To her credit, Henin-Hardenne did run up to the net at the end of this carnage, pat Lukaszewicz on the shoulder and offer a few encouraging words to the teenager she had just annihilated. But, strange as it may sound, she was probably more worried about her own game. She had served six double faults to her opponent's three. For a world number one, that wasn't acceptable.

The second round pitched Justine against French beauty Camille Pin, ranked 168 in the world. Oddly, given their ages – Camille was 22 to Justine's 21 – this was their first professional meeting. Henin-Hardenne romped to a 6–1 first-set win, and a shell-shocked Camille called the trainer to attend to some strapping high on her left thigh. She persevered and came out for more punishment.

In her white cap and red dress, Justine was looking the part as she broke serve immediately to take a 2–0 lead. Then, for no apparent reason, she became laboured in her movement and allowed Pin to break back with a forehand pass down the line. While the French girl took further treatment from the trainer, Justine now appeared to be in the more serious trouble. She clutched her stomach and looked distinctly uncomfortable. A mystery virus had swept the tour and, unknown to the crowd, Henin-Hardenne was the latest casualty.

Shutting illness out of her mind, Justine fought on, and games went with serve until it was Pin's turn again at 4–4. Suddenly, the pressure was too much for the French girl and she didn't win another point in the match. Henin-Hardenne's 6–1, 6–4 victory came in 66 minutes, and left her visibly relieved. There were two kisses for Pin before Justine strolled off to sign autographs on the huge tennis balls favoured by Australia's passionate fans.

Once more, the statistics didn't make comfortable reading for Justine. She had landed only 48 per cent of her first serves, and although she conjured 23 winners, she made just as many unforced errors. Deep down, she must have known she would have to recover her health and step up a few gears if she were to go much further.

She revealed more about her condition afterwards, saying, 'I've not been feeling well for two or three days now. I wasn't feeling well on court. I'm sure I'll feel better in 24 hours. I was already feeling a little better, but with the stress and everything it's coming back.'

What stress? If she thought that was stressful, she had only to look at her next opponent to know that more was on the way. Svetlana Kuznetsova, a thick-limbed eighteen-year-old with a grim stare and a frightening forehand, soon threatened a sterner test in round three. Seeded 30, the precocious Russian pulled out some booming serves to take the first game with ease. Melbourne's sun-drenched spectators began to sit up and take notice. This had the makings of a real match.

Justine set about breaking her opponent's spirit and serve, drawing blood in the third game with a deep backhand slice, improvised as she ran into the net. Amazing defence brought Henin-Hardenne more joy in the fifth, and she screamed a familiar 'Allez!' as Pierre-Yves and Carlos applauded. Mercifully, she had shaken off her health problems and looked to be giving the Russian the same treatment.

By now Kuznetsova was sulking, unable to forgive herself for a succession of unforced errors. Looking relaxed, Justine fired down a few 177kph serves to close out the first set 6–2, and Svetlana looked beaten already.

Whether it was an underlying faith in her ability or a bloody-minded refusal to be swept aside with such disdain, the Russian suddenly rediscovered her power and timing. Henin-Hardenne squandered four break points at 2–2 and found herself run all over the court as a resurgent Kuznetsova pulled out the heavy artillery. Not only did the underdog's clubbing forehand help her save that memorable game, but she went on to break serve with consummate ease.

When Justine broke back, it was more down to her opponent's unforced errors than her own improved stroke play. So while it made Pierre-Yves smile in the box, Rodriguez was still looking concerned – and with good reason. Henin-Hardenne's serve promptly fell apart again, found out by a series of explosive returns. Now it would be Kuznetsova serving for the second set at 5–3, and the Rod Laver Arena began to swell with those sensing an upset.

Justine had just produced an aimless backhand to leave herself only three precarious points away from conceding the set. Being the favourite didn't seem to suit her at all. She was like the fastest gun in the West, haunted by the suspicion that one day soon some kid would draw just a little bit faster. The way it was looking in Melbourne, that day might already have arrived.

Then something very strange happened to break Svetlana's concentration. A ballboy fell over the back of an advertising board, causing quite a stir in the crowd. Some spectators laughed, others whispered, and the temperamental Russian just looked furious. When play resumed, Justine found a big backhand and Kuznetsova screamed in frustration as she swiped the ball into the net. Things were never quite the same for her after that. An unusual piece of good fortune had come to Justine's aid – almost like a gift from Heaven. Kuznetsova effectively choked, Justine staying perfectly cool under fire to serve big and stay in the set. Now it was the turn of Carlos Rodriguez to smile.

Oblivious to the Russian's angst, the birds chirped happily in the Melbourne rafters, and normal service was resumed. Pierre-Yves clenched his fist as his wife broke again, and Justine returned the gesture. Before long, she had won four successive games to take the match 6–2, 7–5 in 77 minutes.

At times it had been scary to watch. Justine had landed only 47 per cent of her first serves, and come up with precious few winners to compensate. Some 27 unforced errors indicated that she hadn't particularly won the match; rather, Kuznetsova had lost it.

'It was a good fight,' Henin-Hardenne said with a measure of understatement. 'She had nothing to lose and put me under a lot of pressure.'

Justine, of course, had everything to lose, including her number one status. And in the other half of the draw, Kim Clijsters, virtually a hometown girl now that she was engaged to Aussie hero Lleyton Hewitt, had miraculously shaken off her ankle injury to swat all those who crossed her path. By the time she reached the last sixteen, Justine's arch-rival had lost only eight games.

But there was better news for Henin-Hardenne that first Saturday when Venus Williams lost 6–4, 7–6 to a 30-year-old called Lisa Raymond. Though the Williams sister had recovered from her stomach strain, she was clearly more ring-rusty than she had thought.

'I'm pretty much in a state of shock,' Venus admitted tearfully afterwards. 'I had high hopes to win here.'

More and more, it was looking as though a repeat of the French and US Open finals showdowns could be on the cards. But another supposed no-hoper stood between Justine and the quarter-finals. Mara Santangelo was a 22-year-old Italian, ranked 129 in the world, a qualifier who could scarcely believe she had come this far in a Grand Slam event. She had worked with a sports psychologist and now used every break between games to write copious notes on a piece of paper, harnessing her positive energy for the challenge ahead.

And the challenge on this occasion was formidable. When Justine raced to a 5–0 lead in the first set, it seemed that no fancy writing could rescue the Italian from her torment, not even if Dante himself had been her inspiration. Santangelo pulled one game back with an unexpected break of serve, but Justine simply followed suit to close out the set 6–1 in just 28 minutes. She still wasn't producing her best tennis, and her first-serve success rate had plummeted to 41 per cent. Nine unforced errors against weak opposition confirmed the erratic nature of her performance. However, since the Italian had done so little to take advantage, most people in the Vodafone Arena, the number two show court in Melbourne, probably believed Justine could still win even if the umpire should decide to tie one arm behind the favourite's back.

Suspicions of a mismatch were further supported by the ease with which Henin-Hardenne took her first service game, with new balls, in the second set. Santangelo didn't win a single point and her heavily strapped left thigh seemed to be hindering her movement. Still, Justine had lost concentration before during second sets here in Melbourne, and she was about to lose momentum again now, in baffling and strangely spectacular style.

Suddenly, Mara, the innocent-looking blonde, forgot she was more used to playing satellite tournaments and ripped into the world number one with a vengeance. She held serve and launched into a series of breathtaking forehands to break Justine with plenty to spare. Now she was mixing her game nicely behind an increasingly strong serve, and Henin-Hardenne looked too surprised to do much about it. The crowd roared its approval as the underdog took a 3–1 lead, then went 4–2 with the help of another booming forehand winner.

After no fewer than six deuces and three break points for 5–2, Justine finally showed enough character to hold her own serve with a thumping fourth ace of the match. Although that put her back in touch with her opponent at 3–4, she was strangely out of touch with her best form.

In the very next game, the world number one was screaming with frustration when she completely miscued a backhand, which flew into the crowd. Before long the unknown Italian had served her way to a 5–3 second-set advantage, without even having to try very hard. The crowd was growing by the minute as rumours of a potential upset swept Melbourne Park once again.

Although Justine turned on some of her best tennis to reduce arrears to 4–5, it didn't alter the fact that Santangelo would serve for the set after the changeover. Legs crossed, she put her thoughts on paper with apparent composure, then strode out to put them into practice.

A delicate drop volley put Mara level at 30–30; and when Justine hit too long it was set point to the rank outsider. Whether the words 'choke', 'must' and 'not' featured heavily in the Italian's prose isn't known. But Santangelo's carefully crafted script went out the window as she suddenly remembered who was waiting on the other side of the net. To play to her potential for a few seconds more: that was all it required for honours to be even at one set all. The underdog would then be very much in the ascendancy, with the crowd urging her on. One of the great shocks of modern tennis might have been around the corner, had Santangelo kept her nerve. But she put too much power behind a straightforward shot from the baseline, and then made two more unforced errors to throw her all-important service game away.

Still the drama wasn't over, and soon it became clear that only a tie-break would settle the issue. Justine squandered a 4–1 advantage and Santangelo started dreaming again at 4–4. But the Belgian came back with huge forehands to give herself two match points. Even then, she made hard work of what should have been easy pickings. She fired wide on the first match point and put her next serve the wrong side of the line. However, under pressure, she found a deep, spinning second serve, the perfect platform for a spectacular cross-court winner. One last 'Allez!' rang around the arena. The favourite was through. She waved in all directions before going off to try to compose herself for a quarter-final confrontation with Lindsay Davenport.

Later, she admitted, 'It's been a difficult tournament for me because it was new, being here, being the first seed. That wasn't easy every day, especially at the beginning of the tournament.'

On 27 January 2004, Justine stepped into the Rod Laver Arena at Melbourne Park for the toughest examination of her world number one credentials so far. Davenport usually beat Justine, wherever and whenever they played. The American enjoyed a 5–1 head-to-head record over her opponent. The only exception to the rule had been at the same Australian venue the previous year, when Justine had won an unforgettable match 7–5, 5–7, 9–7. Both women had been almost out for the count, with Justine suffering from cramp but then making a miraculous recovery.

Lindsay didn't look as though she wanted a re-run of that marathon. The first few games were pure carnage, as Davenport swung her racket violently and bludgeoned her smaller opponent into submission. Although Justine was world number one, she looked anything but. Lindsay produced a series of devastating winners to storm into a 4–0 lead, and it looked like a complete mismatch.

The fans around the court could hardly believe what they were witnessing – the comprehensive humbling of the best player on the planet. Justine's husband and her coach also looked shocked by the sheer ferocity of the onslaught.

To try to ease the pressure, Justine had declared herself the underdog before the match. No one had expected her to take the role quite so literally. Only in the fifth game did she finally start to use her trademark single-handed backhand to stunning effect. It earned her a break of serve and offered a glimmer of hope to her supporters. 'Allez!' she said to herself before the changeover, and a gaunt-looking Pierre-Yves urged her on.

Soon, however, Justine was facing yet another break point, and saved the day only with a winner that flicked the top of the net as it flew beyond her lofty opponent. It was amazing how many times the net seemed to intervene in Justine's favour on the big occasion. Not that she always needed such luck. The ace that clinched the game was certainly more emphatic, and Henin-Hardenne belatedly had some sort of foothold at 2–4.

Her confidence was returning and she won a third break point with a classy drop volley under pressure. Slowly, she was remembering how to play her best tennis. More defiant defence left Lindsay frustrated, and it was she who was first to crack. Suddenly, things were looking up for the number one seed – she had her second break in succession. Where heavy Melbourne rain had caused a roof closure only minutes earlier, now bright Australian sunshine filled a cloudless sky. One more game and Justine could compete on level terms.

Unforced errors and a double fault derailed the comeback. It was absurd that the best tennis player in the world during 2003 now looked so fragile while serving at the start of 2004. All Justine's efforts seemed futile as Lindsay exposed her weakness and broke yet again. Now the big American could step up and serve for the first set with a 5–3 cushion.

The world number one survived the first point with some desperate scrambling until Lindsay made a fatal error. Justine then came up with a sizzling cross-court winner to make it 0–30, and survival was suddenly a real possibility. With more disdainful stroke play, Justine put Davenport under so much pressure that she tightened and netted. The number five seed had been broken again at 5–4, and the Belgian resistance showed no signs of capitulating.

Pierre-Yves looked tense, nevertheless, and with good reason. His wife still had to hold serve to stay in the set, and she had done so only once in four attempts so far. Justine started with a double fault and soon the writing was on the wall. The first serve simply wasn't working; and Justine groaned when Lindsay sent her scrambling and sprawling all over the hard court. Attempts to reply to Davenport's power play failed to clear the net, and suddenly the favourite was staring down the barrel at three set points.

It had all happened so quickly. Try as she might, Justine was being muscled out of it, and this time there appeared to be no escape. Lindsay had three chances to make her pay for her painfully slow start, and Henin-Hardenne's margin for error on any second serve was nonexistent.

The first effort didn't fit the bill and this was no time to double-fault. Justine grimaced and unleashed a second missile, this time drawing Lindsay into a wild and wayward return. One set point had been saved, but Davenport still had two more chances to draw some serious blood. Justine connected with her next serve well, and although Davenport saw it coming at pace, she failed to find the right body-shape in time. As her return fizzed into the net, she must have begun to worry. It was more tempting to think about the two missed opportunities than the single set point that remained.

Her mind working quickly, Justine conjured a wide angle for her next, crucial serve, and Lindsay tightened as she hit her return too long. The crowd gasped audibly: three set points squandered, and the American was starting to beat herself up already. Even with six more years' experience under her belt, the 27-year-old still couldn't quite forgive herself when she made a mess of things. The next reply was too low again; advantage Mrs Henin-Hardenne. Davenport readjusted her sights and found the top of the net. The ball bounced back on her side, and Justine's amazing escape act was complete.

Justine went on to take the next two games and the set; but once again it was more as if her opponent had lost them rather than she had won them. However, Justine had dared to dream at times during the set when the scoreline suggested she had no right to do so. With sixteen winners to Davenport's twelve, no one could say she didn't deserve to take that first set 7–5 in 52 minutes of truly dramatic tennis.

It was the taller woman's unforced errors – twenty to Justine's fourteen – that let her down. Although the Belgian's action had slowly clicked into place, she had landed only half her first serves in the right place – hardly an impressive average, though a better one than she had managed in some of her previous rounds. What these statistics suggested was what Davenport already knew: for much of the set, the world number one had been there for the taking.

But Justine had refused to become frustrated with her lack of early form. She had shown courage and composure when struggling to find the answers to her crisis. In short, she had demonstrated remarkable maturity on court. In stark contrast, Davenport, though considerably older, had failed to forgive her own lack of ruthlessness. When it really mattered, she hadn't been a true friend to herself, and she wouldn't get a second chance.

Now Justine began to play her very best tennis, breaking Davenport in the fifth game. A series of aces cemented her advantage, and soon she had two more break points to go 5–2 ahead. Uncharacteristically, she squandered both, although the line calls were questionable on both occasions. And then came the moment of truth. Most players would have become frustrated by the outcome of those important exchanges, and therefore might have laid themselves open to further punishment. Justine let the past go, and replied with two unstoppable backhand winners. The familiar cry of 'Allez!' heralded her ninth game in eleven. The match was almost won.

Neither was she unduly worried when Lindsay broke back with another questionable baseline call. And when she threw away two match points at 5–3, she simply forgave herself again and got on with it. A mighty forehand winner set up a third chance, and this time Davenport had no reply. From her body language, the American had known for some time that she would end the loser. She had won only four out of twelve break points, and she had never got over it.

Justine milked the applause of the Melbourne crowd for all it was worth, turning in each direction to smile and wave like the virtuoso performer she was. It was a victory routine reminiscent of Andre Agassi's, one she would hope to use all the way to the Australian final.

After that triumph over Davenport, the words she chose told the story of her life: 'I just kept fighting and playing the best I could and I came back.'

* * *

So the comeback queen had done it again and would play a little-known Colombian called Fabiola Zuluaga in the semi-final. As it turned out, there would be less need for heroics here, since the thirty-second seed never really seemed to believe that she could pull off a shock. Since she was still being quoted at odds of 95–1 for the tournament, such self-doubt was hardly surprising.

Yet Zuluaga didn't play badly, even breaking Justine's serve in the fourth game, before losing the first set 6–2. In the second, she looked a genuine threat when she led 2–1, but Justine simply raised her game when it mattered and ran out a 6–2 winner in that set as well. As she was congratulated, it might have dawned on her that she had now reached the final of every Grand Slam event on the tour and she was still only 21.

The match had taken 75 minutes, a testament to Zuluaga's ability to hold her own in the rallies. With a little more self-belief on the big points, the South American might even have caused an upset. But her lack of obvious disappointment in defeat may have been revealing.

She had come this far and she had enjoyed the ride, but she didn't possess the confidence or necessary ambition to go any further this time.

What Justine could take from the experience was an improved first-serve success rate of 56 per cent.

As she blew a kiss and returned the applause of the Australians, she must have known that no charm offensive would alter their allegiance in her fourth Grand Slam final. For, as expected, Kim Clijsters beat Switzerland's Patty Schnyder in the other semi-final, her heavily strapped ankle holding up nicely. Clijsters had been known down under as 'Aussie Kim' even before she became engaged to local favourite Lleyton Hewitt. While Justine could expect to be reminded just how far away from home Australia was, the crowd inside the Rod Laver Arena would do everything in its power to make Lleyton's girl feel as if she was playing in her own backyard.

But was Clijsters tough enough to give that crowd the victory it craved? Before the match, she didn't sound sufficiently aggressive to avenge her defeats in Paris and New York: 'I hope I have learnt from those losses and it will be third time lucky. Justine and I have grown up together. She has gone through so many things in her life already and I admire her.'

Henin-Hardenne, meanwhile, had already created the necessary emotional distance: 'We have a really different kind of game and we are different characters.'

CHAPTER 24

Third Time Lucky

Kim Clijsters was backtracking. Some time before her third Grand Slam showdown with Justine Henin-Hardenne, she was asked about her own apparent criticism of her arch-rival's medical timeout in San Diego during the late summer of 2003.

She claimed to have been misunderstood. 'I definitely said her blisters didn't seem to be bothering her in the first set,' Clijsters told the *Observer Sport Monthly*. 'But I never blamed her for making things up . . . It's still her right, even if she would do it. Tennis is a mental game, as well as a physical one.'

If psychology was just a vital part of tennis, as Kim was now firmly suggesting, she had to learn to use it as cleverly as Justine – and quickly. They could look about as good as each other, they could play about as well as each other, but in some ways the hunger of the animal within would always be the difference between two opponents of similar sporting ability.

Justine chose her familiar battledress for the final against Kim in the Rod Laver Arena, Melbourne Park. The all-in-one effect of her red top and skirt, unified by three vertical white stripes down the back, brought out the best in her improved physique. The white side panels on her strip enhanced her shape still further, and the familiar ponytail flopped out through the back of her white cap. She looked fit and feminine.

Some ten kilos heavier, Kim was in blue with white streaks, and looked the part, too. She wore a heart-shaped necklace, and you wondered whether engagement to Lleyton Hewitt might have softened her character still further. An amazing run of fifteen successive wins suggested otherwise, but they hadn't come in Grand Slam finals.

For her part, Henin-Hardenne had notched up ten straight victories and had the most impressive record in 2004. As usual, something had to give when the giants of Belgian tennis clashed. For the first four games, however, nothing did. The fifth looked to be going with serve too, until Justine stepped up a gear and found two outrageous forehands to set the crowd buzzing. At 30–30, she raised her hand to delay the Clijsters serve, and although the Flemish girl apparently ignored her, she double-faulted to offer a break point. Under pressure, Kim crumbled and netted early in the vital rally. Justine had drawn first blood at 3–2.

More unforced errors from the local favourite allowed Henin-Hardenne to cement her advantage by holding her own serve. When Kim hit back to make it 3–4, Justine produced some of her very best tennis. A well-disguised drop shot, a courageous drive volley and a stunning forehand winner sustained the cushion, and soon Clijsters was serving to stay in the first set.

Once again, poor Kim couldn't live with the pressure, and Henin-Hardenne turned the screw with a devastating forehand. She followed up with a dismissive, swishing backhand and some brilliant all-round defence. Only one woman was showing the versatility of a true champion, and it wasn't Clijsters. Carlos Rodriguez and Pierre-Yves Hardenne were soon applauding as their golden girl earned herself three set points.

Justine groaned when she made a mess of the first. At 15–40, however, it was Clijsters who couldn't afford any more mistakes. And when it mattered most, she failed to clear the ribbon of the net. Justine had taken the first set 6–3, with ten clear winners to Kim's three.

Lleyton Hewitt, who was sitting with another Aussie sporting legend, the golfer Greg Norman, tried to put a brave face on what looked like a familiar story. And for the first six games, the second set looked much like the first. The Henin-Hardenne serve went through various highs and lows in that time. Justine hit 173kph on the speed gun in the opener, but winced as the Australian crowd cheered her first double fault in the fifth game. She recovered to hold serve and let out a defiant, bilingual shriek of 'Allez! Come on!' The locals could do what they liked. She didn't intend to let more glory elude her.

As in the first set, it was third time unlucky for the Clijsters serve, undone by a stunning backhand pass – Justine's trademark. She jumped for joy and showed improved volleying skills at the start of the next game. She was almost there, 4–2 and 15–0 ahead, seemingly without a care in the world. And then she snatched at a simple forehand and sent it flying into the net. One poor shot can unsettle a player in a final, even when that player is ranked first in the world and is one of the canniest psychological operators in tennis.

Suddenly, Clijsters was landing blows from all angles and Henin-Hardenne's mind seemed to have gone. Unforced errors, poor shot selection – you name it, Justine did it. Had Roland Garros 2001 returned to haunt her? There she had also been a set ahead and 4–2 up, only to snatch defeat from the jaws of victory. Yet she was supposed to have freed herself from self-doubt, fear of victory or defeat. Were all the things she used to blame her father for still lurking beneath the service? Now José was watching on the other side of the world and she hadn't spoken to him for years. Who would she blame if she threw this one away?

Roared on by the Australian crowd, Kim clenched her fists and produced the shots. The sadness in the eyes of her Australian fiancé turned to a wild euphoria, as Hewitt tapped into the adrenaline sweeping the stadium. From 3–4 to 4–4, from 5–4 to 6–4, the local favourite was suddenly unstoppable and Justine was a shadow of her former self, her one-set lead erased in minutes.

But now it was Kim's turn to choke again, just when she should have maintained momentum. What was it about Grand Slam finals against Justine? Clijsters fell two games behind, broken by her own unforced error, having already bounced her racket against the green hard court in disgust at her sudden loss of form. What made it worse was that Justine was still so vulnerable.

When Henin-Hardenne served her fourth double fault to more cruel applause from the partisan crowd, Clijsters let her off the hook yet again. Justine squealed with delight when she was allowed to take a 3–0 lead. Did Kim feel, somewhere deep inside, that she didn't deserve to beat Henin-Hardenne when it really mattered, because her own mother had lived and Justine's mother had died? Was there some form of survivor's guilt by proxy at play in a young woman who knew that her opponent had lived her own worst fears? Whatever the reason, Kim's temperament continued to let her down until she was 0–4 and 15–30 behind.

Justine was six points from victory when Clijsters clicked into gear with a backhand pass. Suddenly, Henin-Hardenne was sinking into the psychological quicksand again. She appeared helpless to counter the mounting power of Kim's bludgeoning forehand. Kim broke, held serve and broke again. Henin-Hardenne delighted the locals with her sixth double fault and now even Kim's miscues were finding their target. All at once, it was 3–4 with Kim to serve, and it seemed that nothing could stop her latest charge.

But Justine had other ideas. A brilliant forehand left Kim doing the splits and facing the wrong way at 0–30. Only seconds later, and somewhat cheekily, given the stage of the match, Henin-Hardenne broke into a broad grin, amused by some gesture from her camp. Had someone been making fun of Clijsters? If so, they would soon regret it. The Flemish girl came back with three points on serve, and she knew that one more would bring her level. At that moment, someone in the crowd started shouting loudly and in French. By the time he was silenced, Kim's concentration had been compromised, and she served a double fault.

At deuce, Justine's aim deserted her; but when Kim needed one good serve to take the game, she came up instead with another double fault. It seemed that neither girl had the nerve to take this final by the scruff of the neck and make it theirs. When a wild Clijsters backhand volley flew wide, she looked sick with the tension. Once again, Henin-Hardenne smiled as she nodded at her camp in recognition of a precious break point. And that's when it happened. We heard the repeated calls of 'Out!' from Henin-Hardenne as an apparently winning volley from Kim flew past her, producing no call from the official. We heard the umpire's overrule and witnessed the moments that summed up Clijsters' cruel luck. But it was Justine who now served for the match and her third Grand Slam title.

With only 49 per cent of her first serves on target, Justine's ability to close out this nerve-jangling final could not be taken for granted. Mentally, however, Clijsters had been shot to pieces by the events at the end of the previous game. She couldn't find the concentration to prevent her opponent from carving her way to 40–15 and two match points. At the death, when it mattered most, Henin-Hardenne found a massive serve, and Kim's return dribbled into the net. Game, set and match, 6–3, 4–6, 6–3. Under huge pressure, the favourite to win the tournament had lived up to expectations.

Justine threw away her racket and dropped to her knees, burying her face into the green court as if she were about to cry. As usual, she didn't, though you could understand the relief behind her gesture. Up in the VIP seats, Pierre-Yves clenched his fists, clearly still getting a thrill out of his wife's success.

Kim offered her arch-rival two kisses and Justine sat down to take in the moment, her face in her hands. She had faltered badly twice and she had found a way to recover. It had been third time lucky – for Justine. In the finals at Roland Garros and Flushing Meadows, she hadn't needed much luck. Perhaps neither woman had truly deserved victory in Melbourne. However, with 30 winners to Kim's twelve, and four aces to one, Justine had simply gone for her shots that little bit more bravely than her opponent. The Grand Slam hat-trick was really hers and, smiling, she raised three fingers to Carlos and Pierre-Yves to underline her remarkable achievement.

In financial terms, she would have needed to raise seven fingers – one for each million dollars she had made. According to the official wtatour.com website, her career earnings had now risen to $6,957,559 – not bad for a girl still in her twenty-second year at the time.

* * *

Pierre-Yves would no doubt enjoy some of the benefits, but then being a spectator wasn't easy. He said later, 'That final was the most nerve-racking of the three from my point of view, the hardest to watch.' As for the controversial overrule, he added, 'It happened, and there is no point in looking back on things like that.'

In Belgium, however, José Henin disagreed. He was proud of his daughter's triple triumph, but he was also unsettled by some of the controversy. It was the bittersweet taste of a familiar emotional cocktail.

His love for his daughter and his enthusiasm for her tennis were evident when he began, 'Justine is the best. I got up at 3 a.m. Belgian time to watch it on my own. My other children were away in various places, but I think they all watched it, too. We promised not to watch Justine again, but it is impossible. She got so far ahead that she stopped playing, and that is typical Justine. She has been doing it ever since she was small.'

But then he moved on to the issues of which he was less proud. 'She got away with a mistaken overrule,' he added. 'I don't think that was good to see, because it was the second time she has been involved in controversy. Do you remember Serena in Paris? And now we have this.'

Justine's eldest brother, David, had also got up in the early hours to watch his sister. He echoed his father's sentiments, 'Remember that big point? It made the difference between 5–3 and 4–4.'

At her press conference, Clijsters was asked whether she felt that Henin-Hardenne's 'out' calls might have influenced the umpire to overrule on that vital point. 'I'm not going to go into things like that,' she said. 'I don't want to start any trouble. Things happen.'

Kind-hearted Clijsters wasn't about to criticise Sandra de Jenken either. She added, 'I'm not going to blame the umpire, because everybody makes mistakes, but of course it is disappointing. A few people have seen the shot on television and told me it was in. So that is even more disappointing.'

Justine was busy showing off the Daphne Akhurst Trophy, named after a five-times Australian champion from the 1920s, to the posse of photographers. But it was too heavy to keep above her head for long and Justine was soon directed towards her own press conference. Asked how crucial the umpire's overrule had been to her victory, she gave this unguarded answer: 'Well, it was important because it was a break. And I needed a game after losing three in a row. The umpire took her responsibilities, and I think it was a very tough call, but I think it was just long. It's very hard to say, you know . . .'

When she admitted she hadn't seen a replay, the journalist's follow-up sounded more like a statement: 'At the time, you appeared to be pretty sure of whether the ball was in or out.'

Justine tried to talk her way out of it. 'I was pretty sure, yeah, for sure. That's why I said it was long, from my point of view. The umpire was pretty sure, too. So I didn't look at the image and right now I don't care too much about this.'

* * *

As holder of three of the four Grand Slam titles, there was no reason why she should care. The record books wouldn't speak of controversy. They would confirm an astonishing run of success. And now only one

Grand Slam title still eluded her – Wimbledon. She admitted that she would set her sights on winning the English title on grass, however long it took to adapt her game to the surface and achieve the required level of power. If Wimbledon wasn't quite the new Holy Grail, it was close. And she felt the Williams sisters were still blocking her path to the full set of Grand Slam triumphs: 'It's another goal, for sure. I know it's not going to be easy because, even though I reached my first Grand Slam final at Wimbledon, I still have to improve my game on grass, especially against the strong players like Venus and Serena. I always lost against them over there because they are so powerful and I still have to raise my level a little bit more.'

* * *

Clijsters had other, more personal ambitions, and she dropped something of a bombshell with a seemingly casual remark: 'I don't really plan to have a long career because I wouldn't mind having a family as well.'

Meanwhile, Justine's idea of family still seemed rather confused, since she wasn't talking to most of her closest relatives at the time. Even so, when asked what she was looking forward to on her return to Belgium, she said, 'Oh, just seeing my family, seeing, you know, Carlos's kids, all the people that are really important for me, and to share this moment, because it's a great moment, and I want to be with them, for sure.'

Soon after Justine's return to Belgium in early February 2004, her brother David told me, 'As far as I know, my sister has not contacted any members of the Henin family, apart from her aunts, perhaps. She certainly hasn't contacted her father or me.'

Within a month, however, that situation would change; for one member of the Henin family, unaccustomed to receiving calls from Justine, would get a surprise.

CHAPTER 25

Hurt and Hope

Not very long ago, Justine Henin-Hardenne looked at her stunning success and weighed up what it was worth in relation to her mother's misfortune. She told the *Observer Sport Monthly*, 'Even now, I think about her constantly, especially when on court or in tough situations. I would give back all the trophies and all the money to have my mum in my life right now.'

And, naturally, you believed her. But what about the parent who was still alive, though slowly dying inside because of the pain of his exclusion? You couldn't deny that Justine's decision to cut all ties with her father had worked astonishingly well for her on the tennis court. But what if there came a time when Justine herself realised just how hard it was to be a perfect parent, and reached the disturbing conclusion that José hadn't been so dreadful after all? If someone in her own camp, someone very close to her, could envisage such a change in her somewhere down the line, wasn't it already time for Justine to accept that her perspective on family issues was still painfully narrow?

One of her camp had told me, 'When she becomes a mother herself, she'll see things differently. When she is 30, she'll understand better.'

And I repeat, what if she were to arrive at a point in her life when she wanted to make peace with her father and forgive him for all his mistakes, and he simply wasn't there any more? It made you wonder whether she would ever regret her single-minded pursuit of her own dreams, and the way those who had once been close to her had suffered in the process.

Justine had looked to the skies at Roland Garros in 2003, having won the French Open, and said, 'My mum is looking down at me from Paradise. I hope you are very proud of me, Mum!'

At the start of 2004, her uncle Jean-Marie said, 'Contrary to what Justine claimed at Roland Garros, I'm not so sure her mother would be proud of everything she has done. When she died, Françoise was forced to leave behind her children, and I don't see how she would be proud that Justine has ignored several members of her family by choice.'

And back in the front room of Justine's grandparents' new house in Han-sur-Lesse, just before the Australian Open, Jeanne was of a similar mind. She desperately wanted her granddaughter back in her life, but first she had to release some of the anger that had built up over the years. At the end of the story, the impact of Jeanne's words can be better appreciated. She said, 'If Justine's mother could see what she has done, she would say, "You have been very remiss . . ."' Jeanne wanted to say something else but she couldn't. She had burst into tears. Alphonse, sitting next to his wife, finished the sentence for her: '. . . not contacting us for so long.' And then his voice gave out and he cried, too.

It was a poignant and painful moment to observe.

José chose a middle path when asked to imagine the same scenario. 'I often wonder what Françoise would say, if she came back now and saw what had happened. I think she would be very proud of what Justine has achieved in her career. But I think she would be very sad with the break in the family. Remember, a few months before she died, she told me that the most important thing was to make sure the family stuck together, through thick and thin.'

Justine would no doubt argue that her mother would understand her decision; that her mother always understood her better than the rest. She might remind us that it was her mother alone who truly believed a little girl who dared to suggest she would grow up to become the best tennis player in the world.

But surely Justine hasn't forgotten how much her mother, Françoise, appeared to value the love and care provided by José, Alphonse and Jeanne in the days before she died? Surely she accepts that her mother loved Thomas, David, Sarah and Florence as much as she loved Justine? For Françoise, there was no picking and choosing.

When I spoke to Alphonse and Jeanne early in 2004, they were obviously so hurt, but they still clearly adored their famous granddaughter despite what had happened. They just wanted the surviving family to be friends again, as one. And they were more than willing to play their part in that process. 'Our door is always open to her,' they repeated. 'The family home should never be closed to a child.'

But if her lack of contact was anything to go by, the heart of the child seemed to be closed to much of the family.

Is it right to reject certain relations if they have somehow made you unhappy? Some will say it is justified, if self-preservation and ultimate fulfilment are the rewards on offer. Others might consider such actions to appear allied to a convenient selfishness. Perhaps there is no definitive answer. Life is not made up of black and white, only the shades between.

If an emotional attachment to a member of one's family is too strong, then a 'tie-break' is no bad thing. Most people fly the nest to find their true identity; it is part of growing up. Once discovered, however, that new-found freedom usually paves the way for a different relationship between father and daughter, brother and sister, mother and son – one where healthier boundaries can define a new and basic respect between adults.

For some reason, this particular journey hadn't ended with much mutual understanding between Justine and José. And by early 2004, I knew just how badly José craved the chance to talk to Justine properly and, for the first time, explain some of his feelings.

One of Justine's uncles, Jean-Paul, believed that initially she had been right to make a push for professional independence and personal space. He reckoned that what followed was the real shame of it. The chance for a more mature and balanced relationship between father and daughter never came.

He said, 'José smothered her a bit, she needed to assert her own personality. I think it was necessary to create a sporting distance. When Pierre-Yves came along, José tried to tell Justine that her tennis was her priority. He was too rigorous, and that was like digging his own grave.

'But when people say she had a bad childhood, it's just not true. She had a good childhood, and everything in the family was designed so that she could have a good time and develop her tennis. When her mother was ill, she was strongly supported by the whole family. She was never abandoned in her hour of need. Some people try to suggest that José was a bad father. It's not true. He had a lot of good qualities and still does.'

Jeanne agreed: 'That expression "bad childhood" is a damaging one, because it can be construed to mean anything. She had everything, including wonderful holidays in North America, happy times that some children only dream of.'

Deep down, Jean-Paul doubted whether Justine would give her father a chance to show what he has learnt from their tie-break. He claimed, 'She is in a bubble, influenced only by the people who motivate her. And I believe many people have influenced her not to have a relationship with her father. She has allowed her character to become so hard, and she is always so sure that she is right. As a child, she had such a good heart and she was very family-orientated. The Justine we hear about now is not the same person as before. I don't know how she could have changed so much.'

As we spoke, her uncle didn't see any light at the end of the tunnel. Instead, Jean-Paul only offered this: 'When she reflects on what she has done later, I hope she will look at things differently. But I don't think she is going to change, or start to think about certain members of her family again, until she has finished her time on the professional tennis circuit.'

Justine's aunt Clelia, Jean-Paul's wife, agreed, adding, 'She is in a world of her own. And it will be about ten years before she comes back to the real world again. By then it might be too late for José.'

Jean-Paul claimed, 'The two people in our family that Justine listens most to these days are our sisters, Françoise and Geneviève. If anyone could do something, perhaps it is those two. But I don't know any more.'

I have been told that at least one of those sisters thought there might have been a chance to influence Justine's attitude before it hardened. But the moment apparently passed everyone by, and any subsequent attempts to ease tensions were regarded as futile.

At the time of writing, José wasn't convinced that he would be given the chance to make peace with his daughter before he died. And perhaps Jean-Paul's next remark was the most shocking of all. He said, 'I don't even think Justine will go to her father's funeral. I don't believe she has any feelings for him at all. If things stay as they are now, I don't think she will go anyway. Remember, she didn't even go to her little nephew's funeral.'

The worrying thing was that Jean-Paul said this without any bitterness, almost in a matter-of-fact way, as though the die was already cast. He genuinely bears Justine no malice, and I believed him when he said, 'If she came into my restaurant now I would make her perfectly welcome. The family would welcome her back as a whole, if only she showed willing.'

But at the time of writing, it didn't seem that Justine was willing to forgive everyone in her family and step back into the fold. You can partially understand her all-consuming desire to fulfil her own dreams in life while she can. Perhaps what happened to her mother has made her acutely aware of her own mortality. In the Rosière branch of her family, Françoise wasn't the only woman to fall victim to cancer. Now all the survivors have been alerted to the potential risk posed by the family genes.

* * *

José revealed, 'My other daughter, Sarah, has tests every two years to make sure she is clear and Justine should be doing the same. She suggested soon after the "break" that she was doing this. "I'm OK for two years," she told me one time when I saw her in that period. These days, that's her problem. But I hope she still does those tests. It's certainly better for her that she does it.'

Whatever happens in her future, Justine Henin-Hardenne has been a winner in tennis, and some day she might go down in history as one of the all-time greats. And yet, while getting to know the Henin family a little, it was hard to escape the feeling that Justine was also a huge loser. Surely her understanding of the fragility of life should have helped her appreciate her surviving family even more?

As an outsider, I can only say that I never met a single Henin I didn't like instantly. When they spoke harsh words about the most famous member of their clan, it was only because they felt, rightly or wrongly, that they themselves had been treated so much more harshly. But they were all sufficiently generous of spirit to forgive Justine for her part in the feud since neither side in that stand-off can claim to be perfect, if only she would do the same for them.

In early February 2004, I put the most worrying scenario to Pierre-Yves Hardenne: 'What if José were to die before a reconciliation takes place? And what about Justine's grandparents? Don't you think she might regret her decision later?'

'She doesn't want me to talk about this,' he replied. 'But unfortunately I don't see any immediate change in the situation.'

I wanted to talk to Justine, to put these points to her.

'She is too busy with other commitments,' Pierre-Yves said. 'She has her training and the tour.'

And suddenly I realised how hard it might be for anyone to burst the bubble and make her see things differently. There seemed no end to the feud in sight – only more dramatic tennis matches, more hungry battles for shining trophies and world domination, and more misery behind the scenes in a family who, rightly or wrongly, felt neglected.

Yet perhaps there was still time. Those Justine used to love were still alive, and prepared to love again. In truth, they had never stopped. Sport, as Justine once claimed to realise, isn't everything. You could only live in hope that she would return their love again one day, and the bitterness would disappear. Perhaps first she would need to air her own grievances more fully since no one has tried to deny that, on occasion, she has had reason to feel aggrieved.

Some of this sorry tale is likely to hurt Justine – there is no getting away from that. But if the pain helps her look at some aspects of her life in a new light, perhaps it is no bad thing. People say that we journalists like to stir up trouble, and sometimes we do. But in this particular case, nothing would give me greater pleasure than to be able to add a happier ending some time soon.

Epilogue

Towards the end of February 2004, one phone call offered a glimmer of hope. No one was getting carried away, but it did seem that a happier ending, previously only a distant wish, suddenly might not be so unlikely after all. To her credit, it was Justine Henin-Hardenne who made the call to her sister, suggesting that they meet up. Cautious but receptive, Sarah agreed to the idea, and now it was just a question of timing.

The only stumbling block was Justine's tennis schedule. She had to fly to the Middle East for a tournament in Dubai, in the United Arab Emirates. A week or two after that, she was due to play at Indian Wells in the USA. Between Dubai and California, however, there would be a window of opportunity, and Justine suggested that they take it. She would call again so that they could fix a specific day.

Sarah was delighted, although she knew that such a dramatic development might cause more conflicting emotions in her father.

José harboured no real hope that Sarah's proposed meeting with Justine would have any positive repercussions for him. Indeed, he feared the reverse – that Sarah might come to see him in a different light if she listened too closely to Justine's views on their family's problems. He wondered whether his relationship with Sarah would ever be quite the same, yet he knew how wrong it would be for him to discourage his younger daughter from going ahead with the meeting. Others might just benefit in the long run, even if he himself feared further isolation.

'I still think I'll die without having the chance to make up with my daughter,' he insisted. 'But who knows, perhaps in time this meeting might offer some sort of hope that Thomas and David could know their sister again. It's difficult to say. We'll have to wait and see.'

Aware of her father's insecurities, Sarah tried to reassure him, insisting she would simply change the subject if Justine attempted any criticism of him. As far as Sarah was concerned, this meeting was about two sisters getting to know each other again, and nothing else should be read into it.

Mature beyond her years, eminently sensible and yet still very sensitive, Sarah both deserved the opportunity to know Justine again and was well equipped to deal with whatever delicate issues might be raised. On balance, no one in the Henin family thought it was anything other than a good idea for the sisters to meet up. It was their right, and peace was long overdue.

But first there was the small matter of the circuit to be considered. On 28 February, Justine won the Dubai Tennis Championships in some style, beating Svetlana Kuznetsova in the final. The Russian teenager, who had set alarm bells ringing in the early stages of their Australian Open clash in Melbourne, did so again before she was finally subdued. Justine needed a tie-break to win the first set, but she continued her winning streak with a 7–6, 6–3 victory. Still unbeaten for the year, Justine now came under pressure to play another tournament, the Qatar Total Open in Doha.

She agreed, and the meeting with her sister was put on the backburner. In the semi-finals in Doha, the familiar form of Kuznetsova waited on the other side of the net, and it was easy to assume that the underdog's temperament would fail her as it had done before when Justine had put her under sustained examination.

But the powerful Svetlana won the first set 6–2 and this time she didn't crack, not even when Henin-Hardenne stormed back to take the second 6–4. Instead, Kuznetsova became sufficiently angry to bring the Belgian's sixteen-match unbeaten run to a surprising end, winning the third and decisive set 6–3. On 5 March, Justine's perfect start to 2004 was interrupted. The young Russian had proved that a previously invincible world number one was still vulnerable and human after all.

Perhaps in some strange way it was for the best. Defeat at a relatively unimportant venue not only removed the illusion of perfection but also took away a little of the burden Justine carried as undisputed queen of world tennis. She was still the best, but for a moment she had come crashing back down to earth, perhaps to rise again in time for the Grand Slam events at Roland Garros and Wimbledon.

And it seemed possible that a gentle reminder of her sporting mortality might give Justine further occasion to reflect upon other areas of her life, not least the importance of that meeting with Sarah.

In the tense few days between Doha and Indian Wells, Sarah waited for her phone to ring in case her long-anticipated reunion with her big sister could still be fitted into Justine's demanding schedule. But the call didn't come. And all too soon Justine was back fulfilling her responsibilities to the tennis tour in sunny California.

'Sarah was very disappointed,' José confided in March. 'But perhaps the meeting will still happen.'

'I hope she will call me after California,' Sarah told me as she tried to hide that disappointment. The WTA circus was due to move to Miami straight after Indian Wells and remain there for the rest of the month. Even so, Justine's sister hadn't given up on her. 'I hope this is still something positive,' she maintained with a confidence that bordered on defiance.

And then Justine announced that she would skip the Nasdaq-100 Open in Miami, where the Williams sisters would be back in action together for the first time since their respective spells out of the game. And you wondered if there was fresh reason for Sarah's optimism since there would be time, in theory at least, for the consideration of family matters before the end of March.

First there was Indian Wells to think about, and after that blip in Doha, Justine was determined to reassert herself as the best in the business. Following a bye in the first round, she brushed aside Samantha Reeves of the USA and Spain's Marta Marrero, dropping only seven games in the process. She then entered the record books yet again with a 6–3, 6–4 victory over the Czech girl, Barbora Strycova. The guaranteed income for reaching the quarter-finals meant that Henin-Hardenne became the fastest woman to earn $1 million worth of prize money in any given year of professional tennis.

But what meant more to Justine, you suspected, was the quick chance to avenge that Doha defeat at the hands of Kuznetsova, who waited ominously at the next stage. Sure enough, the 'Double H' came out with all guns blazing to take the first four games and the opening set of that quarter-final 6–4, almost before a shell-shocked Svetlana found her stride. However, it was a very different story in the second, when Justine needed all her nerve and determination to close the match 7–5, and she might easily have been forced into a tricky third set. At one stage, Carlos Rodriguez had been so concerned for his player that he actually received a warning for coaching from the stands. But ultimately, Justine had lain to rest the ghost of Doha and re-established the pecking order.

Now only an injured Anastasia Myskina stood between Henin-Hardenne and another big final, with few neutrals daring to believe the tournament favourite would be denied. This particular Russian, suffering from a troublesome shoulder, was dispatched far more quietly than the first. The 6–1, 6–1 score line helped conserve Justine's energies for the forthcoming battle against the formidable American, Lindsay Davenport.

* * *

The temperature inside the Indian Wells Tennis Garden for this Pacific Life Open Final was an intimidating 104 degrees fahrenheit (40 degrees centigrade). If the searing heat alone wasn't enough to contend with, Justine knew that Lindsay was the local favourite, led their head-to-heads 5–2, and had shocked pundits by crushing Henin-Hardenne in the opening games of their Australian Open showdown in Melbourne earlier that same year. Despite this, Justine had every reason to feel confident. Somehow she had recovered to win in Melbourne, notching successive victories against Davenport in the process. She didn't intend to start slowly again, nor would she allow local support from a 15,000 sell-out crowd to become a factor. The burning skies above the Californian desert were already hostile enough.

The one-sided nature of the first set still stunned most onlookers, who had expected the in-form Lindsay to put up a more spectacular show. With bruising forehands and deep-lashed backhands, Justine broke immediately and soon surged into a commanding lead. Even though just 30 per cent of her first serves had found their target, she still romped away with the first set 6–1, the crosscourt bullet she fired to take the seventh game already her fifteenth winner of the match.

Davenport played better in the second set and took a 3-1 lead, but she never quite seemed to believe in herself, unlike Henin-Hardenne. No one was surprised when the number one seed battled back to 5–4 with her fourth ace of the match. But it was the manner in which she set up a winning platform in the final game that left some of us gasping with admiration. Justine conjured two audacious backhand lobs on her way to championship point, and even at that late stage, she still seemed to be developing new weapons in her armoury.

Perhaps the biggest turn-up, given Justine's uncompromising mood on the day, was the fact that she needed five match points to take the title, the eighteenth of her career. But a magical forehand winner, quite unanswerable, had journalists reaching for the record books yet again. This time, Henin-Hardenne surpassed all others with her ranking points total. She began the match on 7,262 points, only eleven short of the all-time WTA record set by Serena Williams in February 2003. Now, Justine had amassed an amazing 7,626 points, with Clijsters stranded back on 6,389 and the other players nowhere to be seen.

Though the WTA Tour Rankings only began in 1975, the statistics now available suggested that Justine Henin-Hardenne, the little girl from Han-sur-Lesse, was simply the greatest player of the modern age. But such a claim couldn't be true in terms of Grand Slams won, or even held simultaneously, though at the time she reigned as queen of the French, US and Australian Open tournaments. If the argument is restricted to Grand Slams, then Serena Williams had done even better on her way to her own impressive points total the previous year. But Justine's new record suggested that not even Serena had achieved quite such a consistent level of excellence in the lesser tournaments on the WTA calendar.

That consistency is the true story of Justine's record-breaking ranking points total. And the figures proclaimed that there had never been anyone quite like her. Henin-Hardenne had satisfied the demands of the modern game unflinchingly. Perhaps she had paid a personal price, but she had emerged even stronger. Now she appeared to be edging ever closer to sporting perfection. 'I know that nothing is impossible for me now,' Justine commented after the Indian Wells final. And considering what she had already achieved, it was hard to disagree.

Content with her latest triumph, Justine retreated to Saddle Brook, Florida, to brace herself for more physical punishment at the hands of her fitness coach and guru, Pat Etcheberry. But, as she revealed to reporters after her semi-final at Indian Wells, there were other, more personal joys to look forward to by the Florida beaches. For a start, she was to be reunited with her husband, Pierre-Yves, who had taken some time away from the grind of the circuit. And her coach, Carlos Rodriguez, too, also intended to fly in his family to sample the rich atmosphere at the resort, as he savoured the latest chapter in his player's success story. Henin-Hardenne revealed: 'First, I just want to take some rest and be with my family. That's very important, because I see Carlos' family as my family, and the kids are going to be there. So I will enjoy that . . .'

There was no public mention of Sarah, though that didn't mean Justine had forgotten her promise to her kid sister. Even if she was about to embrace her coach's family as her own, one sensed that for at least one member of Justine's biological family, there would be another window of opportunity when the world number one returned to Europe later that spring. In any case, the demands of a school year back in Belgium wouldn't have allowed Sarah to dash off to Florida in March or April 2004.

Anyone with a heart hopes for a positive conclusion for the two surviving Henin sisters. And despite the difficult backdrop of the feud between Justine and her father, there seems to be a reassuring inevitability about the sisters' proposed meeting. Their chances of forging a new understanding, after all they have been through, still look bright. After all, it was Justine who had taken the important step to try to include Sarah in her life again, even though tennis initially caused a frustrating delay in their hopes of making up for lost time.

If the sisters are to start doing it for themselves and hooking up again whenever they feel like it, what will such a development mean for other family members? Will Sarah and Justine gradually build a bridge between the estranged elements of the Henin clan, or is that too much to expect? Only time will tell. But whatever her decision with regard to her surviving family, it seems from the outside that Justine has taken a step in the right direction. Sporting success and a tragic past have combined to give her certain opportunities. To her credit, she already has a good understanding of her own potential as a positive force. Her work in establishing her own cancer charity has shown us that with her independence also firmly established, Justine appeared to want to extend that warmth to Sarah as well.

* * *

From a distance, it is easy to hope that Justine's generosity of spirit will one day embrace all of her family, so that those to whom she was once so close may share Sarah's optimism. But in the end, you sense that the choice has to be Justine's. It has never been the intention of this book to judge or condemn, only to paint a picture for Justine and others to consider. All sides of the argument have been considered and respected wherever possible. So many tragedies have struck Justine's family on both sides and survivors of such tragedies can be very complex. Most of us recognise and appreciate that there is no perfect way to handle one's family anyway.

There is no such thing as a perfect tennis player either. But as March 2004 drifted into April, Justine was still on top of the world. Even so, her long-term position above the rest appeared to be threatened by Serena Williams' triumphant comeback in the Nasdaq 100 tournament in Miami. Justine's climb to the top had been a tough one, and the battle to stay at the summit is rarely easy. How long she would remain the best, and how far she might go towards developing the perfect all-round game, no one could say.

José Henin, Justine's father, saw the very concept of perfection as a dangerous one, especially if the boundaries between sport and everyday life become blurred. He insisted: 'Life is about love, not perfection. Love is good, perfection is bad, since nobody and nothing is perfect.' To different degrees, we all probably come to realise that in time. And for all the remarkable sporting heights she has hit, perhaps it is Justine Henin-Hardenne's unusual response to human imperfection that makes her such an absorbing personality. Sometimes you can only marvel at the extraordinary course she continues to plot through her action-packed life. It hasn't always been easy to understand the choices she has made, but in most aspects of life, elements of mystery usually remain. When all is said and done, the choices Justine Henin-Hardenne has made appear to have brought her a considerable amount of happiness, both personally and professionally. Like the other survivors in her traumatic story, I wish her well for the rest of her journey.